Here's what the critics say about Frommer's:

"Amazingly easy to use. Very portable, very complete."

—*Booklist*

♦

"The only mainstream guide to list specific prices. The Walter Cronkite of guidebooks—with all that implies."

—*Travel & Leisure*

♦

"Complete, concise, and filled with useful information."

—*New York Daily News*

♦

"Hotel information is close to encyclopedic."
—*Des Moines Sunday Register*

♦

"Detailed, accurate and easy-to-read information for all price ranges."

—*Glamour Magazine*

Frommer's®

P O R T A B L E

Washington, D.C.
3rd Edition

by Elise Hartman Ford

IDG Books Worldwide, Inc.
An International Data Group Company
Foster City, CA • Chicago, IL • Indianapolis, IN • New York, NY

ABOUT THE AUTHOR

Elise Hartman Ford, the author of *Frommer's Washington, D.C.,* and *Frommer's Washington, D.C., from $60 a Day,* has been a freelance writer in the Washington, D.C., area since 1985. She contributes regularly to such newspapers as the *Washington Post,* and to *Washingtonian* and other magazines. In addition to this guide, she is the author of two books about places to rent for special events and meetings: *Unique Meeting, Wedding and Party Places in Greater Washington,* now in its fourth edition, and *Unique Meeting Places in Greater Baltimore.*

IDG BOOKS WORLDWIDE, INC.

An International Data Group Company
909 Third Avenue
New York, NY 10022

Find us online at **www.frommers.com**

ISBN: 0-7645-6155-3
ISSN: 1092-3918

Editor: John Rosenthal/Dog-Eared Pages
Production Editor: Tammy Ahrens
Photo Editor: Richard Fox
Design by Michele Laseau
Cartographer: John Decamillis
Production by IDG Books Indianapolis Production Department

SPECIAL SALES

For general information on IDG Books Worldwide's books in the U.S., please call our Consumer Customer Service department at 1-800-762-2974. For reseller information, including discounts, bulk sales, customized editions, and premium sales, please call our Reseller Customer Service department at 1-800-434-3422.

Manufactured in the United States of America

5 4 3 2 1

Contents

List of Maps

*For my husband, Jim, my most reliable source, who not only keeps me informed of
the latest hot spots around town, but is ready to stay out all night trying them.*

AN INVITATION TO THE READER

In researching this book, we discovered many wonderful places—hotels,
restaurants, shops, and more. We're sure you'll find others. Please tell us about
them, so we can share the information with your fellow travelers in upcoming
editions. If you were disappointed with a recommendation, we'd love to know
that, too. Please write to:

Frommer's Portable Washington, D.C., 3rd Edition
IDG Books Worldwide, Inc.
909 Third Avenue
New York, NY 10022

AN ADDITIONAL NOTE

Please be advised that travel information is subject to change at any time—and
this is especially true of prices. We therefore suggest that you write or call ahead
for confirmation when making your travel plans. The authors, editors, and pub-
lisher cannot be held responsible for the experiences of readers while traveling.
Your safety is important to us, however, so we encourage you to stay alert and be
aware of your surroundings. Keep a close eye on cameras, purses, and wallets, all
favorite targets of thieves and pickpockets.

WHAT THE SYMBOLS MEAN
✪ Frommer's Favorites

Our favorite places and experiences—outstanding for quality, value, or both.

The following abbreviations are used for credit cards:

AE	American Express	EC	Eurocard
CB	Carte Blanche	JCB	Japan Credit Bank
DC	Diners Club	MC	MasterCard
DISC	Discover	V	Visa
ER	EnRoute		

FIND FROMMER'S ONLINE

www.frommers.com offers up-to-the-minute listings on almost 200 cities
around the globe—including the latest bargains and candid, personal articles
updated daily by Arthur Frommer himself. No other Web site offers such comprehensive and timely coverage of the world of travel.

Planning a Trip to Washington, D.C.

*T*here's never a bad time of year to visit the nation's capital. Well, okay, maybe August, when it's sweltering. But no matter when you go, you can minimize the hassles by doing some advance planning. A number of sightseeing attractions sell tickets as far as 6 months in advance. If you have your heart set on seeing a popular destination, you can avoid long lines and possible disappointment by reserving advance tickets.

1 Visitor Information

Before you leave, contact the **Washington, D.C. Convention and Visitors Association,** 1212 New York Ave. NW, Washington, DC 20005 (☎ **202/789-7000;** www.washington.org), and ask them to send you a free copy of the *Washington, D.C. Visitors Guide.* Also call the **D.C. Committee to Promote Washington** (☎ **800/422-8644**) and request free brochures listing additional information about Washington.

The *Washington Post* Web site, **www.washingtonpost.com**, gives you up-to-the-minute news, weather, visitor information, restaurant reviews, and nightlife insights.

2 When to Go

Washington is one of the country's top tourist destinations, and there's seldom a lull in visitors. The city's peak seasons generally coincide with two activities: the sessions of Congress and springtime, starting with the appearance of the cherry blossoms along the Potomac. Specifically, when Congress is "in," from about the second week in September until Thanksgiving, and again from about mid-January through June, hotels are quite full with guests whose business takes them to Capitol Hill or to conferences. April through June traditionally is the most frenzied season, when families and school groups descend upon the city to see the cherry blossoms and enjoy Washington's sensational spring. Hotel rooms are at a premium and airfares tend to be higher.

If crowds turn you off, consider visiting Washington in early September, when Congress is still "out," and families return home to get their children back to school, or between Thanksgiving and mid-January, when Congress leaves again and many people are ensconced in their own holiday-at-home celebrations. Hotel rates are cheapest at this time, too.

You might also consider visiting in July and August, but be forewarned: The weather is very hot and humid. Also, if you're a theater buff, many of Washington's stages go dark in summer. Of course, Independence Day (July 4th) in the capital is a spectacular celebration.

WASHINGTON CALENDAR OF EVENTS

Washington's most popular annual events are the Cherry Blossom Festival in spring, the Fourth of July celebration in summer, the Taste of D.C. food fair in the fall, and the lighting of the National Christmas Tree in winter. You can also check the Washington, D.C. Convention and Visitors Association Web site, **www. washington.org**, to keep up with the schedule.

Information phone numbers for these events seem to change constantly; if the number you try doesn't get you the details you need, call the **Washington, D.C. Convention and Visitors Association** at ☎ **202/789-7000.**

January

• **Martin Luther King, Jr.'s Birthday.** Events include speeches by prominent civil rights leaders and politicians; readings; dance, theater, and choral performances; prayer vigils; a wreath-laying ceremony at the Lincoln Memorial (call ☎ **202/ 619-7222**); and concerts. Many events take place at the Martin Luther King Memorial Library, 901 G St. NW (☎ **202/ 727-0321**). Third Monday in January.

February

• **Chinese New Year Celebration.** A friendship archway, topped by 300 painted dragons and lighted at night, marks China-town's entrance at 7th and H streets NW. The celebration begins the day of the Chinese New Year and continues for 10 or more days, with traditional firecrackers, dragon dancers, and colorful street parades. Some area restaurants offer special menus. For details, call ☎ **202/638-1041.** Early February.

- **Abraham Lincoln's Birthday.** Lincoln Memorial. Marked by the laying of a wreath and a reading of the Gettysburg Address at noon. Call ☎ **202/619-7222.** February 12.
- **George Washington's Birthday.** Washington Monument. Similar celebratory events to Lincoln's birthday. Call ☎ **202/ 619-7222** for details. Both presidents' birthdays also bring annual citywide sales. February 22.

March

- **Smithsonian Kite Festival.** Throngs of kite enthusiasts fly their unique creations on the Washington Monument grounds and compete for ribbons and prizes. To compete, just show up with your kite and register between 10am and noon. Call ☎ **202/357-2700** or 202/357-3030 for details. A Saturday in mid- or late March, or early April.

April

✪ **Cherry Blossom Events.** Washington's best-known annual event: the blossoming of the 3,700 famous Japanese cherry trees by the Tidal Basin in Potomac Park. Festivities include a major parade (marking the end of the festival) with floats, concerts, celebrity guests, and more. For information, call ☎ **202/ 547-1500.** See the section in chapter 5 on Potomac Park for more information about the cherry blossoms. Early April (national news programs monitor the budding).

✪ **White House Easter Egg Roll.** The biggie for little kids. In past years, entertainment on the White House South Lawn and the Ellipse has included clog dancers, clowns, puppet and magic shows, military drill teams, an egg-rolling contest, and a hunt for 1,000 or so wooden eggs, many of them signed by celebrities, astronauts, or the president. *Note:* Attendance is limited to children ages 3 to 6, who must be accompanied by an adult. Hourly timed tickets are issued at the National Parks Service Ellipse Visitors Pavilion just behind the White House at 15th and E streets NW beginning at 7am. Call ☎ **202/456-2200** for details. Easter Monday between 10am and 2pm; enter at the southeast gate on East Executive Avenue, and arrive early.

- **White House Spring Garden Tours.** These beautifully landscaped creations are open to the public for free afternoon tours. Call ☎ **202/456-2200** for details. Two days only, in mid-April.

- **Filmfest DC.** This annual international film festival presents as many as 75 works by filmmakers from around the world. Screenings are staged throughout the festival at movie theaters, embassies, and other venues. Tickets are usually $7.50 per movie and go fast (you can purchase them online); some events are free. Call ☎ **202/628-FILM;** www.capaccess.org/filmfestdc. Two weeks in early to mid-April.

- **Taste of the Nation.** An organization called Share Our Strength (SOS) sponsors this fund-raiser for which 70 to 90 major restaurants and many wineries set up tasting booths at Union Station and offer some of their finest fare. For the price of admission, you can do the circuit, sampling everything from barbecue to bouillabaisse; wine flows freely, and there are dozens of great desserts. Tickets are $65 if purchased in advance, $75 at the door, and 100% of the profits go to feed the hungry. To obtain tickets and information, call ☎ **800/955-8278;** also check out the Web site, www.strength.org. Late April.

- **Smithsonian Craft Show.** National Building Museum, 401 F St. NW. Features one-of-a-kind limited-edition crafts by more than 100 noted artists (it's a juried show) from all over the country. There's an entrance fee of about $10 per adult, $7 per child, each day. For details, call ☎ **202/357-2700** (TDD 202/357-1729) or 202/357-4000. Four days in late April.

May

- **Georgetown Garden Tour.** View the remarkable private gardens of one of the city's loveliest neighborhoods. Admission (about $25) includes light refreshments. Call ☎ **202/338-1796** for details. Early to mid-May.

- **Washington National Cathedral Annual Flower Mart.** The cathedral grounds feature displays of flowering plants and herbs, decorating demonstrations, ethnic food booths, children's rides and activities (including an antique carousel), costumed characters, puppet shows, and other entertainment. Admission is free. Call ☎ **202/537-6200** for details. First Friday and Saturday in May.

- ✪ **Memorial Day.** At 11am, a wreath-laying ceremony takes place at the Tomb of the Unknowns in Arlington National Cemetery, followed by military band music, a service, and an address by a high-ranking government official (sometimes the president); call ☎ **202/685-2851** for details. There's also a ceremony at 1pm at the Vietnam Veterans Memorial, including a wreath-laying, speakers, and the playing of taps (call ☎ **202/ 619-7222** for details), and activities at the U.S. Navy Memorial (☎ **202/737-2300**). On the Sunday before Memorial Day, the National Symphony Orchestra performs a free concert at 8pm on the West Lawn of the Capitol to officially welcome summer to Washington; call ☎ **202/619-7222** for details.

June

- **Shakespeare Theatre Free For All.** This free theater festival presents a different Shakespeare play each year for a 2-week run at the Carter Barron Amphitheatre in upper northwest Washington. Tickets are required but they're free. Evenings in mid-June. Call ☎ **202/547-3230.**

- **Smithsonian Festival of American Folklife.** A major event with traditional American music, crafts, foods, games, concerts, and exhibits. Folklife Festival 2001 highlights activities on the National Mall and throughout the city, as well as a program on children's toys and play. All events are free; most events take place outdoors. Call ☎ **202/357-2700,** or check the listings in the *Washington Post* for details. For 5 to 10 days, always including July 4.

July

✪ **Independence Day.** The festivities include a massive National Independence Day Parade down Constitution Avenue, complete with lavish floats, princesses, marching groups, and military bands. There are also celebrity entertainers and concerts. (Most events take place on the Washington Monument grounds.) A morning program in front of the National Archives includes military demonstrations and a reading of the Declaration of Independence. In the evening the National Symphony Orchestra plays on the west steps of the Capitol with guest artists. And big-name entertainment also precedes the fabulous fireworks display behind the Washington Monument. You can attend an 11am free organ recital at Washington's National Cathedral. Consult the *Washington Post* or call ☎ **202/789-7000** for details. July 4, all day.

September

- **Labor Day Concert.** West Lawn of the Capitol. The National Symphony Orchestra closes its summer season with a free performance at 8pm; call ☎ **202/619-7222** for details. Labor Day. (Rain date: same day and time at Constitution Hall.)

✪ **Kennedy Center Open House Arts Festival.** A day-long festival of the performing arts, featuring local and national artists on the front plaza and river terrace (which overlooks the Potomac), and throughout the stage halls of the Kennedy Center. Kids' activities usually include a National Symphony Orchestra "petting zoo," where children get to bow, blow, drum, or strum a favorite instrument. Admission is free, although you may have to stand in a long line for the inside performances. Check the *Washington Post* or call ☎ **800/444-1324** or 202/467-4600 for details. A Sunday, in early to mid-September, noon to 6pm.

• **Black Family Reunion.** National Mall. Performances, food, and fun are part of this celebration of the African-American family and culture. Free. Call ☎ **202/737-0120.** Mid-September.

• **Washington National Cathedral's Open House.** Events include demonstrations of stone carving and other crafts utilized in building the cathedral; carillon and organ demonstrations; and performances by dancers, choirs, strolling musicians, jugglers, and puppeteers. This is the only time visitors are allowed to ascend to the top of the central tower to see the bells; it's a tremendous climb, but you'll be rewarded with a spectacular view. For details, call ☎ **202/537-6200.** A Saturday in late September or early October.

October

• **Taste of D.C. Festival.** Pennsylvania Avenue, between 9th and 14th streets NW. Dozens of Washington's restaurants offer food tastings, along with live entertainment, dancing, storytellers, and games. Admission is free; purchase tickets for tastings. Call ☎ **202/724-5347** for details. Three days, including Columbus Day weekend.

• **White House Fall Garden Tours.** For 2 days, visitors have an opportunity to see the famed Rose Garden and South Lawn. Admission is free. A military band provides music. For details, call ☎ **202/456-2200.** Mid-October.

November

• **Veterans Day.** The nation's war dead are honored with a wreath-laying ceremony at 11am at the Tomb of the Unknowns in Arlington National Cemetery followed by a memorial service. Call ☎ **202/685-2951** for information. At the Vietnam Veterans Memorial (☎ **202/619-7222**), observances include speakers, wreath placement, a color guard, and the playing of taps. November 11.

December

- **Christmas Pageant of Peace/National Tree Lighting.** Northern end of the Ellipse. The president lights the national Christmas tree to the accompaniment of orchestral and choral music. The lighting inaugurates the 3-week Pageant of Peace, a tremendous holiday celebration with seasonal music, caroling, a Nativity scene, 50 state trees, and a burning Yule log. Call ☎ **202/ 619-7222** for details. A select Wednesday or Thursday in early December at 5pm.

- **White House Candlelight Tours.** On 3 evenings after Christmas from 5 to 7pm, visitors can see the president's Christmas holiday decorations by candlelight. Lines are long; arrive early. Call ☎ **202/456-2200** for dates and details.

3 Tips for Travelers with Special Needs

FOR TRAVELERS WITH DISABILITIES

Washington, D.C., is one of the most accessible cities in the world for travelers with disabilities. **The Washington, D.C. Convention and Visitors Association** publishes a fact sheet detailing general accessibility of Washington hotels, restaurants, shopping malls, and attractions. For a free copy, call ☎ **202/ 789-7093** or write to WCVA, 1212 New York Ave. NW, Suite 600, Washington, DC 20005.

The **Washington Metropolitan Transit Authority** also publishes a free guide on Metro's bus and rail system accessibility for the elderly and physically disabled. Call ☎ **202/637-1328** to order the guide, or visit www.wmata.com. Each Metro station is equipped with an elevator (complete with Braille number plates) to train platforms, and rail cars are fully accessible. Metro has installed 24-inch sections of punctuated rubber tiles leading up to the granite-lined platform edge to warn visually impaired Metro riders that they are nearing the tracks. Most of the District's Metrobuses have wheelchair lifts and kneel at the curb. The TDD number for Metro information is ☎ **202/727-8062.** For other questions about Metro services, call ☎ **202/962-6464.**

All **Smithsonian** museum buildings are accessible to wheelchair visitors. A comprehensive free publication called "Smithsonian Access" lists all services available to visitors with

Your Tax Dollars at Work

Based on ticket availability, your senators or representative can provide you with advance tickets for tours of the Capitol, the White House, the FBI, the Bureau of Engraving and Printing, the Supreme Court, and the Kennedy Center. (See chapter 5 for detailed touring information about each site.) This is no secret. Thousands of people know about it and do write, so make your request as far in advance as possible—even 6 months ahead is not too early. The allotment of tickets for each site is limited, so there's no guarantee you'll secure them, but it's worth a try. (Advance tickets are not necessary to tour an attraction; they just preclude a long wait.)

Address requests to representatives as follows: name of your congressperson, U.S. House of Representatives, Washington, DC 20515; or name of your senator, U.S. Senate, Washington, DC 20510. Don't forget to include the exact dates of your Washington trip. When you write, also request tourist information and literature. You can also correspond by e-mail; check out the Web sites www.senate.gov and www.house.gov for e-mail addresses, individual member information, legislative calendars, and much more. You also might try calling a senator or representative's local office; in some states you can obtain passes by phone. The switchboard for the Senate is ☎ **202/ 224-3121;** for the House switchboard, call ☎ **202/225-3121.**

disabilities, including parking, building access, sign-language interpreters, and more. To obtain a copy, call ☎ **202/357-2700** or TTY 202/357-1729. You can also use the TTY number to get information on all Smithsonian museums and events.

White House visitors in wheelchairs do not need tickets. Go directly to the East Visitors' Gate (along East Executive Avenue) between 10:30am and noon. For details, call ☎ **202/456-2322.**

The **Lincoln, Jefferson, and Vietnam memorials** and the **Washington Monument** are also equipped to accommodate visitors with disabilities and keep wheelchairs on the premises. There's limited parking for visitors with disabilities on the south side of the Lincoln Memorial. Call ahead to other sightseeing attractions for accessibility information and special services: ☎ **202/619-7222** or TDD 202/619-7083.

Call your senator or representative to arrange wheelchair-accessible tours of the **Capitol;** they can also arrange special tours for the blind or deaf. If you need further information on these tours, call ☎ **202/224-4048.**

Union Station, the **Shops at National Place,** the **Pavilion at the Old Post Office,** and **Georgetown Park Mall** are well-equipped shopping spots for visitors with disabilities.

FOR SENIORS

Always mention the fact that you're a senior citizen when making your travel arrangements and carry identification that shows your date of birth. Discounts abound for seniors, beginning with the 10%-off-your-airfare deal that most **airlines** offer to anyone 62 or older. **Amtrak** (☎ **800/USA-RAIL;** www.amtrak.com) also offers senior discounts.

And many hotels offer seniors discounts; in Washington, the Clarion Hampshire Hotel is a **Choice Hotels** property, which means that if you're over 50 you may be entitled to 30% off the hotel's published rates if you book your room through the nation-wide toll-free reservations number, rather than directly through the hotel or through a travel agent. Many theaters, museums, stores, and even the Metro offer discounts to seniors.

Members of the **American Association of Retired Persons (AARP),** 601 E St. NW, Washington, DC 20049 (☎ **800/ 424-3410** or 202/434-2277; www.aarp.org), get discounts not only on hotels but on airfares and car rentals, too. Available to anyone who calls is a copy of the free brochure, "Purchase Privilege," listing hotels, car rentals, and airlines that offer discounts.

FOR GAY & LESBIAN TRAVELERS

Washington, D.C., has a strong gay and lesbian community, the complete source for which is the *Washington Blade,* a compre-hensive weekly newspaper distributed free at about 700 locations in the District. Every issue provides an extensive events calendar and a list of hundreds of resources. Gay restaurants and clubs are, of course, also listed and advertised. You can subscribe to the Blade for $30 a year, check out its online site at **www. washingtonblade.com**, or pick up a free copy at Olsson's Books/Records, 1307 19th St. NW; Borders, 18th and L streets; and Kramerbooks, 1517 Connecticut Ave. NW, at Dupont Circle. Call the Blade office at ☎ **202/797-7000** for other locations.

Washington's gay bookstore, **Lambda Rising,** 1625 Connecticut Ave. NW (☎ **202/462-6969**), also informally serves as an information center for the gay community, which centers in the Dupont Circle neighborhood.

4 Getting There

BY PLANE
D.C.'s Area Airports

Ronald Reagan Washington National Airport (everyone except flag-waving Republicans still calls it National) lies across the Potomac River in Virginia, about 20 minutes from downtown in non-rush-hour traffic. It's the easiest and closest airport to the capital, accessible by the Metro. **Washington Dulles International Airport** (Dulles) lies 26 miles outside the capital, in Chantilly, Virginia, a 35- to 45-minute ride to downtown in non-rush-hour traffic. **Baltimore–Washington International Airport (BWI)** is located about 45 minutes from downtown, a few miles outside of Baltimore. Often overlooked by Washingtonians, BWI's bargain fares make it worth considering. Call ☎ **410/859-7111** for airport information; the Web site is www.bwiairport.com.

Shuttle Service from New York, Boston & Chicago

Delta, US Airways, and United are competing to dominate the lucrative shuttle service. All three airlines operate hourly shuttle service daily between Boston's Logan Airport and Washington, and New York's La Guardia Airport and Washington. Both the Delta Shuttle (☎ **800/221-1212**) and the US Airways Shuttle (☎ **800/428-4322**) fly into and out of National. United Airlines and United Express together offer hourly service daily between La Guardia and Dulles, and United alone travels hourly between Boston's Logan and Dulles.

Getting Downtown from the Airports

The best way to get into the city from National Airport is by **Metro** (☎ **202/637-7000**), whose Yellow and Blue lines stop at the airport. The 20-minute, nonrush hour ride to downtown is safe, convenient, and cheap: $1.10 nonrush hour, $1.40 during rush hour.

SuperShuttle buses (☎ **800/258-3826;** www.supershuttle. com) offer shared-ride, door-to-door service from all three airports to destinations in the District and the suburbs. Fares are based on ZIP code; expect to pay $9 to reach downtown and about $25 for Maryland and Virginia suburbs.

The **Washington Flyer Express Bus** (☎ 888-927-4359 or 703/685-1400) runs between Dulles and the Washington Convention Center at New York Ave NW and 11th St. NW downtown, and between Dulles and National Airports. From the Convention Center, a courtesy shuttle will take you to Union Station, the Washington Marriott Wardman Park, Omni Shoreham, Washington Hilton, Renaissance Mayflower, Washington Renaissance, Grand Hyatt, J. W. Marriott, or Hotel Harrington. Fares to either destination are $16 one way, $26 round-trip. Children 6 and under ride free. Service between Dulles and downtown runs in each direction about every 30 minutes weekdays, less frequently weekends. Service between the airports runs hourly weekdays, less frequently weekends.

Amtrak (☎ 800/872-7245) and the **Maryland Rural Commuter** service (☎ 800/325-7245) travel between the BWI Railway Station and Washington's Union Station, about a 30-minute ride. Amtrak's service is daily ($19 per person, one-way), while MARC's is weekdays only ($5 per person, one-way). A courtesy shuttle runs every 10 minutes or so between the airport and the train station; stop at the desk near the baggage claim area to check for the next departure time of both the shuttle bus and the train. Trains depart **Taxi** service is available at the exits of Terminal A from the upper level roadway, and along the lower level roadway to Terminals B and C (just look for the signs).

Taxi fares are about $9 between National Airport and downtown; from BWI or Dulles, the fare is approximately $45.

BY TRAIN

Amtrak offers daily service to Washington from New York, Boston, Chicago, and Los Angeles (you change trains in Chicago). In 2000, Amtrak announced increased service between Washington and several cities in Florida, and a new service to Dallas, via New Orleans. Amtrak trains arrive at historic Union Station, 50 Massachusetts Ave. NE, a turn-of-the-century beaux arts masterpiece that was magnificently restored in the late 1980s. This stunning depot is conveniently located and connects with Metro service. There are always taxis available there. For rail reservations, contact Amtrak (☎ 800/USA-RAIL; www.amtrak.com).

Metroliner service—which costs a little more but provides faster transit and roomier, more comfortable seating—is available between New York and Washington, D.C., and points in between. *Note:* Metroliner fares are substantially reduced on weekends.

BY CAR

Major highways approach Washington, D.C., from all parts of the country. Specifically, these are I-270, I-95, and I-295 from the north; I-95 and I-395, Route 1, and Route 301 from the south; Route 50/301 and Route 450 from the east; and Route 7, Route 50, I-66, and Route 29/211 from the west. No matter what road you take, there's a good chance you will have to navigate some portion of the Capital Beltway (I-495 and I-95) to gain entry to D.C. The Beltway girds the city, 66 miles around, with 56 interchanges or exits, and is nearly always congested, but especially weekdays, during the morning and evening rush hours, roughly between 7 to 9am and 3 to 7pm.

Note: If you're coming to Washington from the south and plan to drive into the city via I-95 to I-395, find an alternate route; an enormous highway construction project along this route, at the point where I-395 and I-495 meet, near Springfield, is closing lanes and diverting traffic, and will continue to do so for the next 8 years. This juncture is called "the mixing bowl" and is an accident magnet. The alternate route I would recommend is Route 1: From I-95, take exit 161, Route 1 North, marked "Fort Belvoir/Mt. Vernon." Continue north about 6 miles along a traffic light–controlled drive until you reach Route 235 North, where you turn right. This route, which now becomes quite picturesque, puts you on the George Washington Memorial Parkway and takes you past Mount Vernon, alongside the Potomac River, through Old Town Alexandria (where the parkway is called Washington Street), and past Ronald Reagan Washington National Airport.

The District is 240 miles from New York City, 40 miles from Baltimore, 700 miles from Chicago, nearly 500 miles from Boston, and about 630 miles from Atlanta.

2

Getting to Know
Washington, D.C.

*R*eally want to get hip to Washington? Hop on the Metro. Spend an afternoon at a sidewalk cafe near the White House in springtime, eavesdropping and watching the passersby. Eat lunch in the Library of Congress cafeteria. Flirt with a fellow browser in Kramerbooks at Dupont Circle. Stay out until 2am carousing the clubs along Connecticut Avenue, south of Dupont Circle. Visit your senator or representative, then hang out in a bar on Capitol Hill, listening to staffers talk Capitol Hill–ese. You get the idea: Don't dangle your toes, jump right in.

1 Orientation

VISITOR INFORMATION

INFORMATION CENTERS If you haven't already called ahead for information from the **Washington, D.C. Convention and Visitors Association** (☎ 202/789-7038), stop in at their headquarters at 1212 New York Ave. NW, Suite 600; they're open Monday through Friday from 9am to 5pm.

Far more convenient and accessible is the new **DC Chamber of Commerce Visitor Information Center** (☎ 202/328-4748; www.dcvisit.com), inside the Ronald Reagan Building and International Trade Center; they're open Monday through Saturday from 8am to 6pm and sometimes on Sunday depending on the season. This very large and just-completed office at 1300 Pennsylvania Ave. NW is on the ground floor of the building, off the Wilson Plaza entrance, near the Federal Triangle Metro.

The **White House Visitor Center,** on the first floor of the Herbert Hoover Building, Department of Commerce, 1450 Pennsylvania Ave. NW (between 14th and 15th streets), is open daily from 7:30am to 4pm (call ☎ **202/208-1631,** or 202/456-7041 for recorded information).

The **Smithsonian Information Center,** in the "Castle,"
1000 Jefferson Dr. SW (☎ 202/357-2700 or TTY 202/
357-1729; www.si.edu), is open every day but Christmas from
9am to 5:30pm. Stop in for a free copy of the Smithsonian's
"Planning Your Smithsonian Visit," which is full of valuable tips.
A calendar of Smithsonian exhibits and activities for the coming
month appears the third Friday of each month in the *Washington
Post*'s "Weekend" section.

The **American Automobile Association (AAA)** has a large
central office near the White House, at 701 15th St. NW,
Washington, DC 20005-2111 (☎ 202/331-3000). Hours are
8:30am to 6pm, Monday through Friday.

NEWSPAPERS   Washington has two daily newspapers: the
Washington Post and the *Washington Times.* The *Post*'s Friday
"Weekend" section is essential for finding out what's going
on, recreation-wise. *City Paper,* published every Thursday and
available free at downtown shops and restaurants, covers some of
the same material but is a better guide to the club and art gallery
scene. If you're staying in the suburbs, the Friday *Journal* papers
(one for each area county) provide comprehensive coverage of
activities beyond downtown. At the airport, pick up a free copy
of the *Washington Flyer* (www.washingtonflyermag.com), which
carries news about coming events, from transportation to restaurant
openings, in Washington.

CITY LAYOUT

The U.S. Capitol marks the center of the city, which is divided
into quadrants: **northwest (NW), northeast (NE), southwest
(SW),** and **southeast (SE).** Almost all the areas of interest to
tourists are in the northwest. If you look at your map, you'll see
that some addresses—for instance, the corner of G and 7th
streets—appear in all quadrants. Hence, you must observe the
quadrant designation (NW, NE, SW, or SE) when looking for an
address.

MAIN ARTERIES & STREETS   The primary artery of Washington is **Pennsylvania Avenue,** scene of parades, inaugurations,
and other splashy events. Pennsylvania runs northwest in a direct
line between the Capitol and the White House before continuing
on to Georgetown.

Since May 1995, Pennsylvania Avenue between 15th and 17th
streets NW has been closed to cars.

Helpful Telephone Numbers & Web Sites

- **National Park Service** (☎ 202/619-7222; www.nps.gov/ nacc). You reach a real person and not a recording when you call the phone number with questions about the monuments, the National Mall, national park lands, and activities taking place at these locations. National Park Service information kiosks are located near the Jefferson, Lincoln, Vietnam Veterans, and Korean War memorials, and at several other locations in the city.
- **Dial-A-Park** (☎ 202/619-7275). This is a recording of information regarding park service events and attractions.
- **Dial-A-Museum** (☎ 202/357-2020; www.si.edu). This recording informs you about the locations of the 14 Washington Smithsonian museums and of their daily activities.
- **Recreation and Parks** (☎ 202/673-7660; www. dcparksandrecreation.org). This is the number for the D.C. Department of Recreation and Parks, which maintains city parks and recreation areas not under federal jurisdiction.

Constitution Avenue and **Independence Avenue** both run east-west, flanking both the Capitol and the Mall. If you hear Washingtonians talk about the "House" side of the Hill, they're referring to the southern half of the Capitol, home to Congressional House offices and the House Chamber. The Senate side is the northern half of the Capitol, where Senate offices and the Senate Chamber are found, closer to Constitution Avenue.

Washington's longest avenue, **Massachusetts Avenue,** runs parallel to Pennsylvania (a few avenues north). Along the way, you'll find Union Station and then Dupont Circle, which is central to the area known as Embassy Row.

Connecticut Avenue starts at Lafayette Square, intersects Dupont Circle, and eventually takes you to the National Zoo, on to the charming residential neighborhood known as Cleveland Park, and into Chevy Chase, Maryland, where you can pick up the Beltway to head out of town. Downtown Connecticut Avenue, with its posh shops and clusters of restaurants, is a good street to stroll.

Wisconsin Avenue originates in Georgetown; its intersection with M Street forms Georgetown's hub. Antiques shops, trendy boutiques, discos, restaurants, and pubs all vie for attention. Wisconsin Avenue basically parallels Connecticut Avenue

FINDING AN ADDRESS　Once you understand the city's layout, it's easy to find your way around.

Each of the four corners of the District of Columbia is exactly the same distance from the Capitol dome. Numbered streets run north–south, beginning on either side of the Capitol with First Street. Lettered streets run east–west and are named alphabetically, beginning with A Street. (Don't look for a B, a J, an X, Y, or Z Street, however.) After W Street, street names of two syllables continue in alphabetical order, followed by street names of three syllables; the more syllables in a name, the farther the street is from the Capitol.

Avenues, named for U.S. states, run at angles across the grid pattern and often intersect at traffic circles. For example, New Hampshire, Connecticut, and Massachusetts avenues intersect at Dupont Circle.

With this in mind, you can easily find an address. On lettered streets, the address tells you exactly where to go. For instance, 1776 K St. NW is between 17th and 18th streets (the first two digits of 1776 tell you that) in the northwest quadrant (NW). *Note:* I Street is often written Eye Street to prevent confusion with 1st Street.

To find an address on numbered streets, you'll probably have to use your fingers. For instance, 623 8th St. SE is between F and G streets (the sixth and seventh letters of the alphabet; the first digit of 623 tells you that) in the southeast quadrant (SE). One thing to remember: You count B as the second letter of the alphabet (even though there's no B Street) but, since there's no J Street, K becomes the 10th letter, L the 11th, and so on.

THE NEIGHBORHOODS IN BRIEF

Adams–Morgan　This ever-trendy, multiethnic neighborhood is about the size of a postage stamp, though crammed with boutiques, clubs, and restaurants. Everything is located on either 18th Street NW or Columbia Road NW. Parking during the day is okay, but forget it at night. But you can easily walk (be alert— the neighborhood is edgy) from the Dupont Circle or Woodley Park Metro stops, or taxi here for a taste of Malaysian, Ethiopian, Spanish, or some other international cuisine. Friday and Saturday nights, the hot nightlife here rivals Georgetown and Dupont Circle.

Capitol Hill   Everyone's heard of "the Hill," the area crowned by the Capitol. When people speak of Capitol Hill, they refer to a large section of town, extending from the western side of the Capitol to the D.C. Armory going east, bounded by H Street to the north and the Southwest Freeway to the south. It contains not only the Capitol building, but also the Supreme Court building, the Library of Congress, the Folger Shakespeare Library, Union Station, and the U.S. Botanic Garden. Much of it is a quiet residential neighborhood of tree-lined streets and Victorian homes. There are many restaurants in the vicinity and a smattering of hotels, mostly near Union Station.

Downtown   The area roughly between 7th and 22nd streets NW going east to west, and P Street and Pennsylvania Avenue going north to south, is a mix of the Federal Triangle's government office buildings, K Street ("Lawyer's Row"), Connecticut Avenue restaurants and shopping, historic hotels, the city's poshest small hotels, and the White House. You'll also find the Historic Penn Quarter, a part of downtown that is taking on new life with the opening of the MCI Center, trendy new restaurants, and art galleries. The total downtown area takes in so many blocks and attractions that I've divided discussions of accommodations (chapter 3) and dining (chapter 4) into two sections: "Downtown, 16th Street NW and west," and "Downtown, east of 16th Street NW." 16th Street and the White House form a natural point of separation.

Dupont Circle   My favorite part of town, Dupont Circle is fun day or night. It takes its name from the traffic circle minipark, where Massachusetts, New Hampshire, and Connecticut avenues collide. The streets extending out from the circle are lively with all-night bookstores, really good restaurants, wonderful art galleries and art museums, nightspots, movie theaters, and Washingtonians at their loosest. It is also the hub of D.C.'s gay community.

Foggy Bottom   The area west of the White House and south-east of Georgetown, Foggy Bottom was Washington's early industrial center. Its name comes from the foul fumes emitted in those days by a coal depot and gasworks, but its original name, Funkstown (for owner Jacob Funk), is perhaps even worse. There's nothing foul (and not much funky) about the area today.

This is a low-key part of town, enlivened by the presence of the Kennedy Center and George Washington University.

Georgetown   This historic community dates from colonial times. It was a thriving tobacco port long before the District of Columbia was formed, and one of its attractions, the Old Stone House, dates from pre-Revolutionary days. Georgetown action centers on M Street and Wisconsin Avenue NW, where you'll find numerous boutiques, chic restaurants, and popular pubs (the student body of Georgetown University ensures that there is lots of nightlife here). But get off the main drags and see the quiet tree-lined streets of restored colonial row houses, stroll through the beautiful gardens of Dumbarton Oaks, and check out the C&O Canal.

Glover Park   Mostly a residential neighborhood, this section of town, just above Georgetown and just south of the Washington National Cathedral, is worth mentioning because of the increasing number of good restaurants opening along its main stretch, Wisconsin Avenue NW, Glover Park sits between the campuses of Georgetown and American universities, so there's a large student presence here.

The Mall   This lovely tree-lined stretch of open space between Constitution and Independence avenues, extending for 2½ miles from the Capitol to the Lincoln Memorial, is the hub of tourist attractions. It includes most of the Smithsonian Institution museums and many other visitor attractions. The 300-foot-wide Mall is used by natives as well as tourists—joggers, food vendors, kite-flyers, and picnickers among them.

U Street Corridor   D.C.'s newest nightlife neighborhood between 12th and 15th streets NW is rising from the ashes of nightclubs and theaters frequented decades ago by African-Americans. At the renovated Lincoln Theater, where Duke Ellington, Louis Armstrong, and Cab Calloway once performed, patrons today can enjoy performances by popular black artists. The corridor offers at least six alternative rock and contemporary music nightclubs and several restaurants.

Woodley Park   Home to Washington's largest hotel (the Washington Marriott Wardman Park) and the Omni Shoreham, Woodley Park boasts the National Zoo, many good restaurants, and some antique stores. Washingtonians are used to seeing conventioneers wandering the neighborhood's pretty residential streets with their name tags still on.

2   Getting Around

Washington is one of the easiest U.S. cities to navigate. Only New York rivals its comprehensive transportation system, but Washington's clean, efficient subways put the Big Apple's underground nightmare to shame. A complex bus system covers all major D.C. arteries, as well, and it's easy to hail a taxi anywhere at any time. But because Washington is of manageable size and marvelous beauty, you may find yourself shunning transportation and getting around on foot.

BY METRORAIL

Metrorail's 78 stations and 96 miles of track include locations at or near almost every sightseeing attraction and extend to suburban Maryland and northern Virginia.

Metrorail stations are cool, clean, and attractive. Cars are air-conditioned and comfortable, fitted with upholstered seats; rides are quiet. Service has deteriorated a little after 24 years, but then, Washingtonians are spoiled. You can still expect service so frequent that you'll usually get a seat during off-peak hours (basically weekdays from 10am to 3pm, weeknights after 7pm, and all day weekends).

Passengers traveling at rush hour, on the other hand, should expect delays and crowded trains. Eating, drinking, and smoking are strictly prohibited on the Metro and in the station.

There are five lines in operation—Red, Blue, Orange, Yellow, and Green—with extensions planned for the future. The lines connect at several points, making transfers easy. All but Yellow and Green Line trains stop at Metro Center; all except Red Line trains stop at L'Enfant Plaza; all but Blue and Orange Line trains stop at Gallery Place/Chinatown.

Metro stations are indicated by discreet brown columns bearing the station's name and topped by the letter M. Below the M is a colored stripe or stripes indicating the line or lines that stop there. When entering a Metro station for the first time, go to the kiosk and ask the station manager for a free "Metro System Pocket Guide" (available in English, German, Spanish, Korean, Japanese, and French). It contains a map of the system, explains how it works, and lists the closest Metro stops to points of interest. The station manager can also answer questions about routing or purchase of farecards.

To enter or exit a Metro station, you need a computerized farecard, available at vending machines near the entrance. The

Major Metro Stops

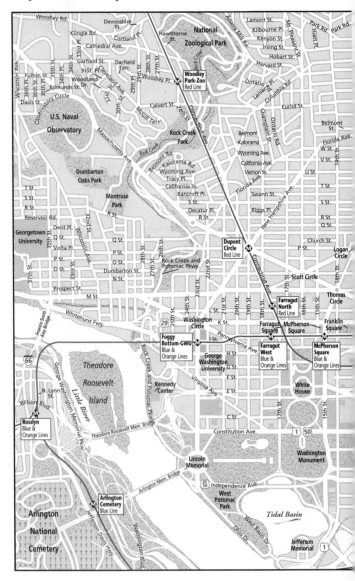

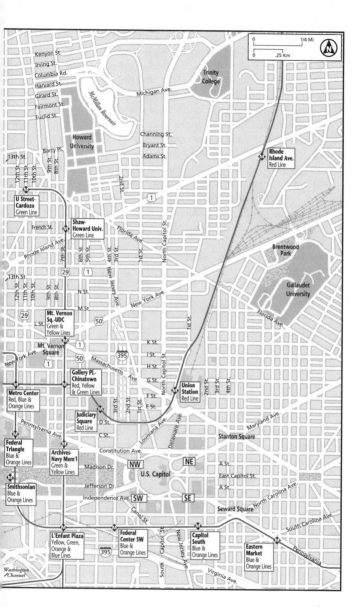

Kenyon St.
Irving St.
Columbia Rd.
Harvard St.
Girard St.
Fairmont St.
Euclid St.

Michigan Ave.

Trinity College

McMillan Reservoir

13th St.
12th St.
10th St.
9th St.
8th St.

Barry Pl.

Howard University

Channing St.
Bryant St.
Adams St.

Rhode Island Ave.
Red Line

U Street-Cardozo
Green Line

French St.

Shaw-Howard Univ.
Green Line

Florida Ave.

Brentwood Park

Rhode Island Ave.

7th St.
6th St.
5th St.
4th St.
3rd St.

2nd St.

North Capitol St.

1st St.

Gallaudet University

13th St.
12th St.
11th St.
10th St.
9th St.
8th St.

29

29

N St.

New Jersey Ave.

New York Ave.

Florida Ave.

Mt. Vernon Sq.-UDC
Green & Yellow Lines

M St.

L St.

Mt. Vernon Square

New York Ave.

50

50

Massachusetts Ave.

395

K St.

I St.

H St.

G St.

1st St.

North Capitol St.

2nd St.
3rd St.
4th St.

Union Station
Red Line

Metro Center
Red, Blue & Orange Lines

Gallery Pl.-Chinatown
Red, Yellow & Green Lines

F St.

E St.

Maryland Ave.

Pennsylvania Ave.

Judiciary Square
Red Line

3rd St.
2nd St.
1st St.

D St.

Louisiana Ave.

Delaware Ave.

Stanton Square

Federal Triangle
Blue & Orange Lines

Archives-Navy Mem'l
Green & Yellow Lines

C St.

Constitution Ave.

Smithsonian
Blue & Orange Lines

Madison Dr.

NW

NE

A St.

East Capitol St.

A St.

U.S. Capitol

Jefferson Dr.

SW

SE

North Carolina Ave.

Independence Ave.

Seward Square

L'Enfant Plaza
Yellow, Green, Orange & Blue Lines

Canal St.

395

Federal Center SW
Blue & Orange Lines

South Capitol St.

New Jersey Ave.

Capitol South
Blue & Orange Lines

Eastern Market
Blue & Orange Lines

South Carolina Ave.

Washington Channel

South

Virginia Ave.

Pennsylvania Ave.

0   1/4 Mi
0   .25 Km

minimum fare to enter the system is $1.10, which pays for rides to and from any point within 7 miles of boarding during non-peak hours; during peak hours (Monday through Friday from 5:30 to 9:30am and 3 to 7pm), $1.10 takes you only 3 miles. The machines take nickels, dimes, quarters, and bills from $1 to $20; they can return up to $4.95 in change (coins only). If you plan to take several Metrorail trips during your stay, put more value on the farecard to avoid having to purchase a new card each time you ride. There's a 10% bonus on all farecards of $20 or more. Up to two children under 5 can ride free with a paying passenger. Senior citizens (65 and older) and people with disabilities (with valid proof) ride Metrorail and Metrobus for a reduced fare.

Discount passes, called **One-Day Rail passes,** cost $5 per person and allow you unlimited passage for the day, after 9:30am weekdays, and all day on Saturday, Sunday, or holidays. You can buy them at most stations; at Washington Metropolitan Area Transit Authority, 600 5th St. NW (☎ **202/637-7000;** www.wmata.com); at Metro Center, 12th and G streets NW; or at a Giant or Safeway grocery store. Other passes are available—check out the Web site or call the main number for further information.

When you insert your card in the entrance gate, the time and location are recorded on its magnetic tape, and your card is returned. Don't forget to snatch it up and keep it handy; you have to reinsert it in the exit gate at your destination, where the fare will automatically be deducted. The card will be returned if there's any value left on it. If you arrive at a destination and your farecard doesn't have enough value, add what's necessary at the Exitfare machines near the exit gate.

Metrorail opens at 5:30am weekdays and 8am Saturday and Sunday, operating until midnight Sunday through Thursday, and until 1am Friday and Saturday (it's likely that Metro will be running until 2am Friday and Saturday, by the time you read this).

BY BUS

While a 10-year-old can understand the Metrorail system, the **Metrobus** system is considerably more complex. The 12,490 stops on the 1,489-square-mile route (it operates on all major D.C. arteries as well as in the Virginia and Maryland suburbs) are indicated by red, white, and blue signs. However, the signs tell you only what buses pull into a given stop, not where they go. For routing information, call ☎ **202/637-7000.** Calls are taken

Monday through Friday from 6am to 10:30pm, weekends and holidays from 8am to 10:30pm. This is the same number you call to request a free map and time schedule, information about parking in Metrobus fringe lots, and for locations and hours of those places where you can purchase bus tokens.

Base fare in the District is $1.10; bus transfers cost 25¢. There are additional charges for travel into the Maryland and Virginia suburbs. Bus drivers are not equipped to make change, so be sure to carry exact change or tokens. If you'll be in Washington for a while and plan to use the buses a lot, consider buying a 2-week pass ($20), also available at the Metro Center station and other outlets.

Most buses operate daily almost around the clock. Service is quite frequent on weekdays, especially during peak hours. On weekends and late at night, service is less frequent.

Up to two children under 5 ride free with a paying passenger on Metrobus, and there are reduced fares for senior citizens (☎ **202/962-7000**) and people with disabilities (☎ **202/ 962-1245** or 202/962-1100; see also "Tips for Travelers with Special Needs" in chapter 1).

BY CAR

Don't drive in D.C. Traffic is always thick during the week, parking spaces often hard to find, and parking lots ruinously expensive. Park your car at your hotel and take Metrorail or taxis.

You will, however, want to drive to most attractions in Virginia and Maryland. If you don't have a car, you can rent one from any of the major car-rental companies. They have locations at all three major airports, as well as the following downtown outposts: **Avis,** 1722 M St. NW (☎ 800/331-1212 or 202/467-6585) and 4215 Connecticut Ave. NW (☎ 202/686-5149); **Budget,** Union Station (☎ 800/527-0700 or 703/920-3360); **Enterprise,** 1015 Wisconsin Ave. NW (☎ 202/338-0015); **Hertz,** 901 11th St. NW (☎ 800/654-3131 or 202/628-6174); **National,** Union Station (☎ 800/227-7368 or 202/842-7454); and **Thrifty,** 12th and K streets NW (☎ 800/367-2277 or 202/783-0400) and 1310 Wisconsin Ave. NW (☎ 202/338-9500).

BY TAXI

District cabs operate on a zone system instead of meters. By law, basic rates are posted in each cab. If you take a trip from one point to another within the same zone, you pay just $4, regardless of the distance traveled. So it would cost you $4 to travel a few blocks from the U.S. Capitol to the National Museum of American History, but the same $4 could take you from the Capitol all the way to Dupont Circle. They're both in Zone 1, as are most other tourist attractions: the White House, most of the Smithsonian, the Washington Monument, the FBI, the National Archives, the Supreme Court, the Library of Congress, the Bureau of Engraving and Printing, the Old Post Office, and Ford's Theatre. If your trip takes you into a second zone, the price is $5.50, $6.90 for a third zone, $8.25 for a fourth, and so on.

So far, the fares seem modest. But here's how they could add up: There's a $1.50 charge for each additional passenger after the first, so a $4 Zone 1 fare can become $8.50 for a family of four (though one child under 5 can ride free). There's also a rush-hour surcharge of $1 per trip between 7 and 9:30am and 4 and 6:30pm weekdays. Surcharges are also added for large pieces of luggage and for arranging a pickup by telephone ($1.50). Try **Diamond Cab Company** (☎ **202/387-6200**), **Yellow Cab** (☎ **202/544-1212**), or **Capitol Cab** (☎ **202/546-2400**).

The zone system is not used when your destination is an out-of-District address (such as an airport); in that case, the fare is based on mileage—$2 for the first half-mile or part thereof and 70¢ for each additional half-mile or part. You can call ☎ **202/331-1671** to find out the rate between any point in D.C. and an address in Virginia or Maryland. Call ☎ **202/645-6018** to inquire about fares within the District.

It's generally easy to hail a taxi (a lot easier, in fact, than phoning for one, since you're often put on hold forever), although even taxis driven by black cabbies often ignore African-Americans to pick up white passengers. Unique to the city is the practice of allowing drivers to pick up as many passengers as they can comfortably fit, so expect to share (unrelated parties pay the same as they would if they were not sharing). To register a complaint, note the cab driver's name and cab number and call (☎ **202/ 645-6010**).

BY TOURMOBILE

If you're looking for an easy-on/easy-off tour of major sites, consider ✪ **Tourmobile Sightseeing** (☎ **202/554-5100** or 888/868-7707; www.tourmobile.com), the only narrated sightseeing shuttle tour authorized by the National Park Service. These comfortable red, white, and blue sightseeing trams travel to as many as 25 sites, as far out as Arlington National Cemetery and even Mount Vernon.

Board a Tourmobile at any of the following locations:

- Arlington National Cemetery (three different locations)
- Arts and Industries Building/Hirshhorn Museum
- Bureau of Engraving and Printing/U.S. Holocaust Memorial Museum
- East Face of the Capitol/Library of Congress/Supreme Court
- Ford's Theater/FBI Building
- Franklin D. Roosevelt Memorial
- Jefferson Memorial
- Kennedy Center
- Lincoln/Vietnam Veterans/Korean War Veterans Memorials
- National Air and Space Museum
- National Gallery of Art
- National Law Enforcement Memorial Visitor's Center
- National Museum of American History
- National Museum of Natural History
- National Portrait Gallery/National Museum of American Art/MCI Center
- Old Post Office Pavilion
- U.S. Navy Memorial/National Archives
- Union Station/National Postal Museum
- Washington Monument
- West Face of the Capitol
- White House
- White House Visitor Center

Pay the driver when you board. Along the route, you may get off at any stop to visit monuments or buildings. When you finish exploring each area, just show your ticket and climb aboard the next Tourmobile that comes along. The buses serve each stop about every 15 to 30 minutes. The charge for the Washington/Arlington Cemetery tour is $16 for anyone 12 and older, $7 for children 3 to 11. Well-trained narrators give commentaries about sights along the route and answer questions.

Tourmobiles operate daily year-round, except Christmas. From June 15 to Labor Day, they ply the Mall between 9am and 6:30pm. After Labor Day, the hours are 9:30am to 4:30pm. In Arlington Cemetery, between October and March, they start at 9:30am and end at 4:30pm; April through September, the hours are 8:30am to 6:30pm.

A service similar to Tourmobile's is **Old Town Trolley Tours** of Washington (☎ **202/832-9800**). These buses operate daily from 9am to 4pm all year round. The cost is $24 for adults, $12 for children 4 to 12, free for children under 4. The full tour, which is narrated, takes 2 hours, and trolleys come by every 30 minutes or so.

FAST FACTS: Washington, D.C.

Airports   See "Getting There" in chapter 1.

American Express   There's an American Express Travel Service office at 1150 Connecticut Ave. NW (☎ **202/457-1300**) and another in upper northwest Washington at 5300 Wisconsin Ave. NW, in the Mazza Gallerie (☎ **202/362-4000**). Each office functions as a full travel agency and currency exchange.

Baby-sitters   If your hotel does not offer a baby-sitting service, you can contact White House Nannies (☎ **301/652-8088**). Each caregiver has first-aid training. Rates are $10 to $12 per hour (4-hour minimum), plus a one-time referral fee of $25.

Congresspersons   To locate a senator or congressional representative, call the Capitol switchboard (☎ **202/224-3121**). Or access the Web sites, www.senate.gov and www.house.gov, to contact individual senators and congressional representatives by e-mail, find out what bills are being worked on and the calendar for the day, and more.

Doctors/Dentists   Prologue (☎ **800/DOCTORS**) can refer you to any type of doctor or dentist you need. Hours are Monday through Friday from 8:30am to 6pm and Saturday from 9am to 4pm. The **Washington Hospital Center** (☎ **202/ 877-DOCS**) referral service operates weekdays from 8am to 6pm, and will point you to a nearby doctor.

Drugstores   CVS, Washington's major drugstore chain (with more than 40 stores), has two convenient 24-hour locations: 14th Street and Thomas Circle NW, at Vermont Avenue (☎ **202/628-0720**), and at Dupont Circle (☎ **202/ 785-1466**), both with round-the-clock pharmacies. Check your phone book for other convenient locations.

Emergencies/Hotlines   To reach a 24-hour **poison-control hotline,** call ☎ **202/625-3333;** to reach a 24-hour **crisis line,** call ☎ **202/561-7000;** and to reach the 24-hour **drug and alcohol abuse hotline,** call ☎ **888/294-3572.**

Hospitals   In case of a life-threatening emergency, call ☎ **911.** If you don't require immediate ambulance transportation but still need emergency-room treatment, call one of the following hospitals, and be sure to get directions: **Children's Hospital National Medical Center,** 111 Michigan Ave. NW (☎ **202/884-5000** for general information and 202/884-5203 for the emergency room); **George Washington University Hospital,** 901 23rd St. NW (entrance on Washington Circle; ☎ **202/715-4911** for emergency room or 202/994-1000 for general information); **Georgetown University Hospital,** 3800 Reservoir Rd. NW (☎ **202/784-3111** for emergency room or 202/687-2000 for general information); **Howard University Hospital,** 2041 Georgia Ave. NW (☎ **202/865-1141** for emergency room or 202/865-6100 for general information).

Liquor Laws   The minimum drinking age is 21. Establishments can serve alcohol Monday through Friday from 8am to 2am, Saturday until 3am, and Sunday from 10am to 3am. Liquor stores are closed on Sunday. District gourmet grocery stores, mom-and-pop grocery stores, and 7-Eleven convenience stores often sell beer and wine, even on Sunday.

Police   In an emergency, dial ☎ **911.** For a nonemergency, call ☎ **202/727-1010.**

Safety   In Washington, you're quite safe throughout the day in all the major tourist areas, and you can also safely visit the Lincoln Memorial after dark. Riding the Metro is safe. U Street Corridor, Adams–Morgan, and Capitol Hill are the least safe neighborhoods, but only at nighttime. In fact, you should be alert at nighttime regardless of where you go in Washington.

Taxes   Sales tax in the district is 5.75% on merchandise but 10% on restaurant meals. In Maryland, it's 5% for either, and it's 4.5% in Virginia. Hotel tax is 13% plus $1.50 per night occupancy tax in the district. In Virginia, it's 9.75% and in Maryland it's 10% (expect an additional 5% to 7% in city and local taxes).

Taxis   See "Getting Around," earlier in this chapter.

Time   Washington is in the eastern time zone. Clocks are advanced 1 hour April through October. To find out what time it is, call ☎ **202/844-2525.**

Transit Information   See "Getting There" in chapter 1 and "Getting Around," earlier in this chapter.

Weather   Call ☎ **202/936-1212.**

3

Accommodations

*T*he Washington metropolitan area has about 92,000 hotel and motel rooms, more than one-quarter in the city itself, and that number is increasing all the time, due to the immense amount of hotel construction underway. At last count, 7 new hotels were in various stages of completion, including a Ritz-Carlton in George-town, a Residence Inn by Marriott at Dupont Circle, and an elegant European-style Hotel Monaco, which will open in the renovated landmark Tariff Building, downtown. An enormous new convention center slated to open in 2003 would seem to herald even more hotel construction in the center of the city.

Increased competition is not bringing the room rate down, however. In spring 2000, the average room rate for a D.C. hotel logged in at $142.23, as opposed to about $109 for the entire metropolitan area. And then, there are taxes: In the District, in addition to your hotel rate, you pay a 14.5% hotel tax. Rates quoted in this chapter for each hotel do not include this tax. Other costs, like parking, can be hefty (the Grand Hyatt's nightly valet parking charge is a whopping $26!). But, with a little planning, there are a multitude of ways to get yourself a rate you can live with, in a hotel of your own choosing.

HOW TO GET THE BEST RATE

As you peruse this chapter, keep these thoughts in mind:

- **Consider all the hotels regardless of the rate category.** Even the best and most expensive hotels may be ready to negotiate and often offer bargain rates at certain times, especially weekends.
- **Try booking during Washington's less busy periods:** on weekends, in July, August, and early September, and between Thanksgiving and early January.
- As a rule, when you call a hotel, you should **ask whether there are special promotions or discounts available.** Most hotels offer discounts of at least 10% to members of the American Automobile Association (AAA) and the American Association

of Retired Persons (AARP). The magnificent Willard Hotel, for instance, offers 50% off its published rates for guests older than 65—on a space-available basis. Many hotels in Washington, like the Hotel Lombardy and the Clarion Hampshire Hotel, discount rates for government, military, or embassy-associated guests.

* **Ask about family rates:** Families often receive special rates, as much as 50% off on a room adjoining the parents' room.
* **Dial direct.** When booking a room in a chain hotel, call the hotel's local line, as well as the toll-free number, and see where you get the best deal. A hotel makes nothing on a room that stays empty. The clerk who runs the place is more likely to know about vacancies and will often grant deep discounts in order to fill up.

1 Capitol Hill/The Mall

VERY EXPENSIVE

✪ **Hotel George.** 15 E St. NW, Washington, DC 20001. ☎ **800/576-8331** or 202/347-4200. Fax 202/347-4213. www.hotelgeorge.com. 147 units. A/C MINIBAR TV TEL. Weekdays $245–$285 double, weekends $149 double; $375–$500 suite. Ask about seasonal and corporate rates. Extra person $20. Children under 16 stay free in parents' room. AE, CB, DC, DISC, MC, V. Parking $20. Metro: Union Station.

Posters throughout this hotel, housed in a 1928 building, depict a modern-day George Washington, sans wig, thereby setting the tone. Rather than stick to old-style traditions, this place brings a hip attitude to Washington à la 2000. The sleek white lobby contains colorful splashes of red, blue, and black furnishings. The large guest rooms are bright and white, with fluffy white comforters on the beds. All rooms have robes, umbrellas, hair dryers, coffeemakers, interactive cable TV with on-demand movies, irons and ironing boards, two-line telephones with data port and voice mail, and granite-topped executive desks. As of spring 2000, all rooms also have two-line cordless phones and stereo CD/clock radios that play nature sounds, like those of the ocean, forest, and wind. A speaker in the spacious, mirrored, marble bathrooms broadcasts TV sound from the other room. Eighth-floor rooms feature extras: high-speed Internet access and fax machines. The hotel attracts groups, policy wonks waiting to make their mark on Capitol Hill, and stars like Alanis Morissette.

Washington, D.C., Accommodations

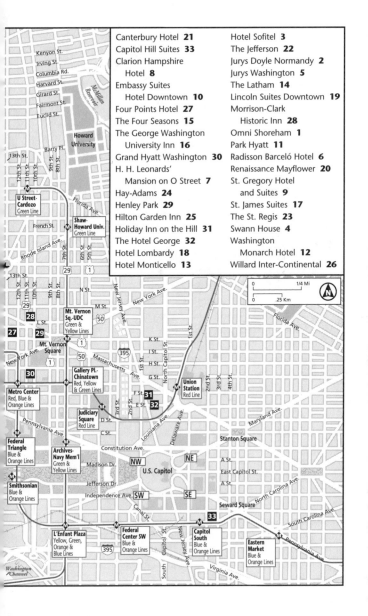

Canterbury Hotel **21**
Capitol Hill Suites **33**
Clarion Hampshire
    Hotel **8**
Embassy Suites
    Hotel Downtown **10**
Four Points Hotel **27**
The Four Seasons **15**
The George Washington
    University Inn **16**
Grand Hyatt Washington **30**
H. H. Leonards'
    Mansion on O Street **7**
Hay-Adams **24**
Henley Park **29**
Hilton Garden Inn **25**
Holiday Inn on the Hill **31**
The Hotel George **32**
Hotel Lombardy **18**
Hotel Monticello **13**

Hotel Sofitel **3**
The Jefferson **22**
Jurys Doyle Normandy **2**
Jurys Washington **5**
The Latham **14**
Lincoln Suites Downtown **19**
Morrison-Clark
    Historic Inn **28**
Omni Shoreham **1**
Park Hyatt **11**
Radisson Barceló Hotel **6**
Renaissance Mayflower **20**
St. Gregory Hotel
    and Suites **9**
St. James Suites **17**
The St. Regis **23**
Swann House **4**
Washington
    Monarch Hotel **12**
Willard Inter-Continental **26**

Dining/Diversions: The hotel's immensely popular restaurant, **Bistro Bis,** serves French bistro food. Chef Jeff Buben co-owns Bis and the acclaimed **Vidalia** with his wife, Sallie.

Amenities: 24-hour concierge, overnight shoe shine, weekday delivery of *Washington Post,* laundry and valet, room service from 7am to 11pm, express checkout, VCR and CD player rentals, cigar-friendly billiards room, business/secretarial services, 1,600 square feet of meeting/banquet space, 24-hour fitness center with men's and women's steam rooms.

EXPENSIVE

Capitol Hill Suites. 200 C St. SE, Washington, DC 20003. ☎ **800/ 424-9165** or 202/543-6000. Fax 202/547-2608. 152 units. A/C TV TEL. $119–$219 double. Extra person $20. Rates include continental breakfast. Children under 18 stay free in parents' room. AE, CB, DC, DISC, MC, V. Valet parking $20. Metro: Capitol South.

This well-run, all-suite property (on the House side of the Capitol) comprises two converted apartment houses on a residential street near the Library of Congress, the Capitol, and Mall attractions. Photographs of the numerous representatives who stay here are displayed in the pleasant lobby. A recent $3 million renovation has made the hotel a lot more attractive, by adding lamps and mirrors from Pottery Barn, putting new comforters on the beds, and changing the overall decor. Every suite has a kitchenette with coffeemaker, toaster oven, and microwave, and every suite comes with a hair dryer, iron, and ironing board. Bathrooms are small, some even tiny. Most units are efficiencies, with the kitchenette, bed, and sofa all in the same room. The best are the one-bedroom units that have the kitchenette and a living room separate from the bedroom. A third option is the "studio double," with two queen beds, a sofa, and a kitchenette, but no living room area. Some rooms in each category have pull-out sofas.

A food market and more than 20 nearby restaurants (many of which deliver to the hotel) compensate for the lack of on-premises dining facilities. Guests have privileges to dine at the Capitol Hill Club, the members-only Republican headquarters 1 block away, and can charge their meals and drinks to their hotel bill. Complimentary continental breakfast is offered daily in the first-floor breakfast room.

MODERATE

♦ **Holiday Inn on the Hill.** 415 New Jersey Ave. NW. ☎ **800/638-1116** or 202/638-1616. Fax 202/638-0707. www.basshotels.com/holiday-inn.

343 units. A/C TV TEL. $89–$189 double (Mon and Tues are most expensive days). Extra person $20. Children under 19 stay free in parents' room. Children 12 and under eat free. AE, CB, DC, DISC, JCB, MC, V. Parking $15. Metro: Union Station.

Refurbished in 1999 and a great choice for families, this hotel has added new bedspreads, drapes, shower curtains, TVs with Nintendo, individually controlled thermostats, and other items in every room. It has also expanded its 24-hour fitness center and upgraded the overall look and feel of the place. The staff aims to make you feel at home. Rooms are standard size, though bathrooms are larger than expected, with a small vanity ledge just outside the bathroom for overflow counter space. Each room has a coffeemaker, hair dryer, iron, and ironing board.

Clientele are mostly people with business on the Hill, especially "labor" folks—that is, people who have business with one of the several labor union headquarters located nearby. Some rooms offer high-speed Internet access for an extra $9.95 a day. Best of all is the Discovery Zone—available from 4 to 10pm daily in summer for $5 per kid per day—an adult-supervised program offering fun but educational activities for children ages 4 to 14. To get the best deals and perks, ask about summer promotions, the "Great Rates" package, and the hotel's "Priority Club" frequent guest membership. The hotel restaurant, **Senators Grille,** serves American food; room service is available from 6am to 11pm daily. The hotel has eight meeting rooms, each equipped for high-speed Internet access; the second largest ballroom on Capitol Hill; a gift shop and an ATM in the lobby; and eight rooms for the disabled, including four with a roll-in shower.

2 Downtown, East of 16th Street NW

VERY EXPENSIVE

Grand Hyatt Washington. 1000 H St. NW, Washington, DC 20001. ☎ **800/233-1234** or 202/582-1234. Fax 202/637-4781. www.washington. grand.hyatt.com. 900 units, including 60 suites. A/C MINIBAR TV TEL. Weekdays $305 double, weekends $119–$139 double; $300–$1,700 suite. Extra person $25. Children under 18 stay free in parents' room. AE, CB, DC, DISC, JCB, MC, V. Valet parking $26; self parking $20. Metro: Metro Center.

Hotel as circus—that's the Grand Hyatt. There's always something going on in the vast lobby, whose atrium is 12 stories high and enclosed by a glass, mansard-style roof. The hotel's waterfalls, baby grand piano floating on its own island in the 7,000-square-foot "lagoon," catwalks, 22-foot-high trees, and an array of bars and restaurants on the periphery will keep you permanently entertained. Should you get bored, head to the nearby nightspots and restaurants, or hop on the Metro, to which the Hyatt has direct access. The hotel is across from the Convention Center, between Capitol Hill and the White House, and 2 blocks from the MCI Center.

Guest rooms seem tame by comparison, which is probably a good thing. They are attractive and comfortable but don't have much personality. Each room has cable TV with free HBO, a hair dryer, an iron, and ironing board. Suites were renovated in 2000 to individualize designs along certain themes, such as "The Orient." Among the potpourri of special plans and packages available is one for business travelers: Pay an extra $20 and you stay in an 8th- or 9th-floor room equipped with a large desk, fax machine, computer hookup, and coffeemaker; have access to printers and other office supplies on the floor; and are entitled to complimentary continental breakfast. Tourists should ask about a variety of package deals. Also look on the Web site for these and other special deals.

Dining/Diversions: On site are three restaurants: the **Zephyr Deli,** the informal **Grand Cafe,** and the smaller **Via Pacifica,** which features Italian and Asian cuisine. There are three bars: the lobby **Via Bar,** the large **Grand Slam** sports bar, and **Butlers— The Cigar Bar.**

Amenities: Concierge, room service, dry cleaning/laundry service, twice-daily maid service, express checkout, courtesy car available on a first come, first served basis to nearby destinations; two-story health club with whirlpool, lap pool, exercise room, steam and sauna room, and aerobics program (hotel guests pay $9 for club use); two large ballrooms, a 102-seat theater, and 40,000 square feet of meeting space.

✪ Willard Inter-Continental. 1401 Pennsylvania Ave. NW, Washington, DC 20004. ☎ **800/327-0200** or 202/628-9100. Fax 202/637-7326. www.washington.interconti.com. 341 units. A/C MINIBAR TV TEL. Weekdays $395–$480 double; weekends $209–$319 double; $1,000–$3,300 suite. Extra person $30. Children under 18 stay free in parents' room. AE, DC, DISC, JCB, MC, V. Parking $20. Metro: Metro Center.

If you're lucky enough to stay here, you'll be a stone's throw from the White House and the Smithsonian museums, in the heart of downtown near plenty of excellent restaurants, down the block from the National Theater, and down the avenue from the Capitol. Rooms are sumptuous, spacious, and furnished with Edwardian and Federal-period reproductions. Half of the Willard's 12 floors are no-smoking. And, because of the many heads of state (more than 100 in the last decade) who bunk here, the hotel offers one floor as "Secret Service–cleared." Eight rooms are outfitted to accommodate guests with disabilities. Twenty-one suites have kitchenettes. The rooms with the best views are the oval suites overlooking Pennsylvania Avenue to the Capitol and the rooms fronting Pennsylvania Avenue. If it's quiet you're after, opt for a room facing the courtyard. The best room is the "Jenny Lind" suite perched in the curve of the 12th floor's southeast corner— a round bull's-eye window captures glimpses of the Capitol. If you're here on a weekend, you may choose from one of five complimentary options, including an upgrade to a suite, valet parking, or a second room at half price. Rooms have phones with dual lines, voice mail, and data-port plugs, and cable TVs with pay-movie channels, video message, and retrieval/checkout. Each room has an in-room safe, an iron, and an ironing board. In the oversize marble bathrooms are a hair dryer, scale, phone, and TV speaker.

The Willard's designation as a National Historic Landmark in 1974 and magnificent restoration in the 1980s helped revitalize Pennsylvania Avenue and this part of town. Stop in at the Round Robin Bar to hear bartender and manager Jim Hewes spin tales about the history of the 1901 Willard and its predecessor, the City Hotel, built on this site in 1815. The Willard's spectacular lobby and restaurant makes it a favorite location for movie and TV show shoots. Most guests are corporate travelers.

Dining/Diversions: The **Willard Room** (the term *power lunch* originated here) is stunning. The circular **Round Robin Bar** is where Henry Clay mixed the first mint julep in Washington (see "Behind Bars" in this chapter). The **Café Espresso** (open until 3pm) offers croissant sandwiches, pastas, pastries, and vintage wines by the glass.

Amenities: Twice-daily maid service, 24-hour room service, currency exchange, airline/train ticketing, express checkout, newspaper delivery, fax and cellular phone rental, full business center, meeting rooms, complete fitness center, upscale boutiques.

EXPENSIVE

✪ **Henley Park.** 926 Massachusetts Ave. NW (at 10th St.), Washington, DC 20001. ☎ **800/222-8474** or 202/638-5200. Fax 202/638-6740. www. henleypark.com. 95 units. A/C MINIBAR TV TEL. Weekdays $145–$225 double, summer and weekends $99 double; $315–$725 suite. Senior discounts. Extra

---

Behind Bars:
The Willard's Round Robin Bartender Tells All

A good hotel bar is a haven. Whether you are a woman alone, a couple in love, old friends catching up with each other, colleagues talking business, or a journalist interviewing a subject, a hotel bar can offer a comfortable, relaxing place for quiet conversation and a well-mixed drink or glass of wine. In Washington, exceptional bars include those at the **Jefferson, St. Regis, Hay–Adams, Mayflower, Canterbury,** and **Tabard.**

The **Willard Hotel's Round Robin Bar** is in a class of its own, largely because of its legendary bartender. Jim Hewes, who has bartended at the Round Robin since the renovated Willard reopened in 1986, is steeped in nearly 2 centuries' worth of knowledge of presidential drink preferences and Washington political and social life. A cast of characters from Hewes's stories are depicted in the black-and-white portraits that line the green felt-covered walls of the bar: Charles Dickens, Samuel Clemens, Warren Harding, and Abraham Lincoln are just some of the many famous people who have stopped in or stayed at the Willard. If you care for an easy and amiable history lesson, along with that classic gin and tonic, grab a stool at the round mahogany bar and let the ponytailed Hewes regale you.

"In the old days, everything took place within 10 blocks of the White House. The center of activity was supposed to be the Capitol, but it was really around here, and the Willard, starting in the 1840s and 1850s, gained a reputation as a meeting place. Presidents Zachary Taylor, Millard Fillmore, James Buchanan, Calvin Coolidge, Warren Harding, and Abraham Lincoln each lived or stayed for a time at the Willard. Washington Irving brought Charles Dickens (a port, brandy, and wine drinker) here for a drink. Samuel Clemens (better

---

person $20. Children under 14 stay free in parents' room. AE, CB, DC, DISC, MC, V. Parking $16. Metro: Metro Center, Gallery Place, or Mt. Vernon Square.

This is an intimate English-style hotel housed in a converted 1918 Tudor-style apartment house with 119 gargoyles on its facade. The lobby, with its exquisite Tudor ceiling, archways, and leaded windows, is particularly evocative of the period. Luxurious

known as Mark Twain) palled around with Senator Stewart from Nevada, imbibing bourbon at the bar. Walt Whitman wrote a poem about the Willard bar. Nathaniel Hawthorne, in the capital to cover the Civil War for *The Atlantic* magazine, wrote 'You adopt the universal habit of the place, and call for a mint-julep, a whiskey-skin, a gin cocktail, a brandy smash, or a glass of pure old Rye, for the conviviality of Washington sets in at an early hour and, so far as I have had the opportunity to observe, never terminates at any hour.'"

"Throughout the 19th century, and up until World War I, people drank constantly throughout the day," says Hewes. "Popular in the 1840s was the Mamie Taylor, a potent mix of Scotch whiskey, lime juice, and ginger soda that was invented in Washington to honor Old Rough and Ready's sweetie, a hard-drinking, corn-cob-smoking first lady," notes Hewes. The mint julep, introduced at the Round Robin by statesman Henry Clay in 1850, quickly caught on and has been associated with the Round Robin ever since. (For the past few Kentucky Derby Days, Hewes has discussed the history of the mint julep for National Public Radio's *All Things Considered*.) Ulysses S. Grant was among the presidents to enjoy the julep.

"Bill Clinton is a Tanqueray and tonic man, and he likes his beer, though usually he'll have what the others in his party are having. Bush liked martinis. Reagan, and Nixon, too, introduced the city to California wines and Schramsburg sparkling wine," says Hewes. He adds that "George W. Bush is a teetotaler and Al Gore doesn't go in much for drinking.")

And Hewes's favorite drink? "A good Irish whiskey, or a beer," he says. If you're intent on hitting the Round Robin when Hewes is tending bar, better call ahead (☎ **202/ 637-7348**) since he's not there every day.

rooms make this a good choice for upscale romantic weekends, although these lodgings fill up with corporate travelers weekdays. Rooms are decorated in the English country house mode, with Hepplewhite-, Chippendale-, and Queen Anne–style furnishings, including lovely period beds. Bathrooms have phones and luxury toiletries, and in-room amenities include terry-cloth robes, and, in some rooms, fax machines. All the suites have wet bars (small refrigerator and sink). The hotel has one room equipped for disabled travelers. Guests headed off to the airport can order room service to go: "The Red Eye," a choice of sandwich, fruit, and beverage, for $10.

Dining/Diversions: The hotel's restaurant, **Coeur de Lion,** serves classic continental cuisine; the menu highlights seafood and the wine list is excellent. The **Blue Bar,** a delightful cocktail lounge, is the setting for piano bar entertainment weeknights, live jazz and dancing Friday and Saturday nights. Afternoon tea (reservations required) is served daily between 4 and 6pm in the octagonal **Wilkes Room,** a charming parlor with a working fireplace.

Amenities: 24-hour concierge and room service, *Washington Post* delivery each weekday morning, complimentary shoe shine, complimentary weekday sedan service from 7:30 to 10am to downtown and Capitol Hill locations, access to a fitness room in the Morrison-Clark Historic Inn (see listing below) across the street.

MODERATE

✪ **Morrison–Clark Historic Inn.** 1015 L St. NW (at 11th St. and Massachusetts Ave. NW), Washington, DC 20001. ☎ **800/332-7898** or 202/898-1200. Fax 202/289-8576. www.morrisonclark.com. 54 units. A/C MINIBAR TV TEL. Weekdays $155–$225 double, weekends $99–$225 double; $175–$325 suite. Extra person $20. Children under 16 stay free in parents' room. AE, CB, DC, DISC, MC, V. Parking $15. Metro: Metro Center or Mt. Vernon Square.

This magnificent inn, occupying twin 1865 Victorian brick town houses—with a newer wing in converted stables across an interior courtyard—is listed in the National Register of Historic Places. Guests enter via a turn-of-the-20th-century parlor, with velvet- and lace-upholstered Victorian furnishings and lace-curtained bay windows. A delicious continental breakfast ($9.50) or full breakfast is served in the adjoining Club, which boasts an original white marble fireplace and 13-foot windows flanking gilded mirrors. In warm weather, you can breakfast in the lovely brick-paved courtyard.

High-ceilinged guest rooms are individually decorated with original artworks, sumptuous fabrics, and antique or reproduction 19th-century furnishings. Most popular are the grand Victorian-style rooms, with new chandeliers and bedspreads added in the past year. Four Victorian rooms have private porches; many other rooms have plant-filled balconies. All rooms have robes, hair dryer, iron and ironing board, and two phones equipped with computer jacks.

Room service is available from the inn's highly acclaimed **restaurant.** Other amenities include twice-daily maid service, complimentary *Washington Post* weekdays, business services, and fresh flowers in every room. A tiny fitness center is on the premises.

INEXPENSIVE

✪ **Four Points Hotel, by Sheraton, Washington, D.C., Downtown.** 1201 K St. NW, Washington, DC 20005. ☎ **800/481-7191** or 202/ 289-7600. Fax 202/289-3310. www.fourpointswashingtondc.com. 265 units. A/C TV TEL. Weekdays $99–$189 double, weekends $99–$135 double. Extra person $20. Children under 18 stay free in parents' room. AE, CB, DC, DISC, MC, V. Parking $18.50. Metro: McPherson Square or Metro Center.

This former Days Inn has totally metamorphosed into a contemporary property that offers all the latest gizmos, from high-speed Internet access in all the rooms to a 2,000-square-foot fitness center. A massive renovation undertaken by Starwood Hotels essentially gutted the old building, but the location is still as terrific as ever. It's close to the Convention Center, MCI Center, and downtown, making it the perfect choice for both business and leisure visitors.

Five types of rooms are available: those with the standard two double beds, one queen bed, one king bed, a junior suite, or a one-bedroom suite. In addition to the Internet access, all guest rooms feature minibars, oversized work desks, two-line phones with voice mail, data ports, iron and ironing board, hair dryer, and coffeemaker.

Best of all, the rates are reasonable, and spectacular hotel amenities make this an even better value: a heated indoor pool; a restaurant and bar; room service from 7am to 1am; free shuttle service daily from 7am to 11pm to attractions within 5 miles and to National Airport; an on-site gift shop, a business center, and meeting space; underground parking; and complimentary *USA Today* and *Washington Post.*

Hilton Garden Inn, Washington, DC, Franklin Square. 815 14th St. NW, Washington, DC 20005. ☎ **800/HILTONS** or 202/783-7800. Fax 202/ 783-7801. www.washingtondcfranklinsquare.gardeninn.com. 320 units. AC TV TEL. $99–$189 double. Extra person $20. Children under 18 stay free in parents' room. AE, CB, DC, DISC, MC, V. Parking $17.50. Metro: McPherson Square.

Located downtown between H and I streets, the Hilton Garden Inn is across the street from Metro's Blue Line McPherson Square station (and three stops from the Smithsonian museums station) and within walking distance of the White House, the convention center, and the MCI Center. It's a great deal for the price. Each room has a refrigerator, microwave, coffeemaker, hair dryer, iron and ironing board, large desk, adjustable lighting with ergonomic chairs, and two multiline phones with voice mail and data ports. Rooms are spacious, with either king-size or double beds, and are designed for relaxing—a comfortable chair with ottoman is in each. About five rooms are available for disabled guests. Available 24 hours a day are a business center (use is complimentary to guests) and the Pavilion Pantry, which is a small sundries shop that also carries microwaveable foods. The **American Grill** restaurant serves all meals and provides room service from 6am to 11pm. Use of the indoor pool and fitness center are free. Complimentary *USA Today* is delivered to your door weekdays.

3 Downtown, 16th Street NW & West

VERY EXPENSIVE

✪ **The Hay–Adams.** 16th and H sts. NW, Washington, DC 20006. ☎ **800/ 424-5054** or 202/638-6600. Fax 202/638-2716. www.hayadams.com. 143 units. A/C MINIBAR TV TEL. Weekdays $310–$540 double, weekends $219–$360 double. Extra person $30. Children under 16 stay free in parents' room. AE, DC, DISC, JCB, MC, V. Parking $22. Metro: Farragut West or McPherson Square.

One block from the president's abode, the Hay–Adams offers the best vantage point in town. Reserve a room on the 6th through 8th floors on the H Street side of the hotel (or as low as the 2nd floor in winter, when the trees are bare), pull back the curtains from the windows, and enjoy a full frontal view of Lafayette Square, the White House, and the Washington Monument in the background. (You'll pay more for rooms with these views). The view from rooms facing 16th Street isn't bad, either: Windows overlook the yellow-painted exterior of St. John's Episcopal Church, built in 1815, and known as the "church of the presidents."

The Hay–Adams is one in the triumvirate of exclusive hotels built by Harry Wardman in the 1920s (the Jefferson and the St. Regis are the other two). Its architecture is Italian Renaissance, and the building's interior has walnut wainscoting, arched alcoves, and intricate Tudor and Elizabethan ceiling motifs. The hotel is working to improve other less charming features: rattling pipes and thin windows and walls. Among the hotel's first guests were Amelia Earhart, Sinclair Lewis, Ethel Barrymore, and

Charles Lindbergh. More recent guests have included everyone from Denzel Washington to Prince Bandar of Saudi Arabia.

The high-ceilinged guest rooms are individually furnished with antiques and superior appointments that might include 18th-century–style furnishings, silk-covered walls hung with botanical prints, a molded plaster ceiling, and French silk floral-print bedspreads and upholstery. Many rooms have ornamental fireplaces. All rooms have plush bathrobes, hair dryers, and three two-line phones with data ports and voice mail. Check out special packages on the hotel's Web site, like the $219 deal, which offers a choice of full American breakfast for two, afternoon tea for two, or valet parking.

Dining/Diversions: The sunny **Lafayette Restaurant** (overlooking the White House) is an exquisite dining room that serves contemporary American/continental fare. Washingtonians love the daily afternoon tea ($19.95 per person) and Sunday brunch ($37.50 per person). A pianist performs nightly during dinner and each afternoon during tea. Off the Record is the hotel's bar and serves complimentary hors d'oeuvres and a light-fare menu.

Amenities: 24-hour room and concierge service, daily delivery of *Washington Post,* complimentary shoe shine, access to a local health club, secretarial and business services, in-room fax on request, meeting rooms, complimentary morning car service.

✪ **The Jefferson.** 1200 16th St. NW (at M St.), Washington, DC 20036. ☎ **800/368-5966** or 202/347-2200. Fax 202/331-7982. www.camberleyhotels. com. 100 units. A/C MINIBAR TV TEL. Weekdays $319–$339 double, $350–$1,200 suite; weekends $189 double, from $289 suite. Extra person $25. Children under 12 stay free in parents' room. AE, CB, DC, JCB, MC, V. Parking $20. Metro: Farragut North.

Opened in 1923 just 4 blocks from the White House, the Jefferson is one of the city's three most exclusive venues (along with the Hay–Adams and the St. Regis), proffering discreet hospitality to pols, royalty, literati, and other notables. With a very high staff-to-guest ratio, the Jefferson puts utmost emphasis on service; if you like, a butler will unpack your luggage and press clothes wrinkled in transit.

Set foot in the lobby and you won't want to leave. An inviting sitting room with a fireplace at the rear of an extended vestibule draws you past green velvet loveseats placed back-to-back down the middle and enclosed terraces opening off each side. A fine art collection, including original documents signed by Thomas Jefferson, graces the public area as well as the guest rooms.

Each antique-filled guest room evokes a European feel. Yours might have a four-poster bed (many topped by canopies) with plump eyelet-trimmed comforter and pillow shams, or a cherry-wood bookstand from the Napoleonic period filled with rare books. In-room amenities include two-line speakerphones; fax machines (you get your own fax number when you check in); VCRs; CD players; and, in the bathrooms, terry robes, hair dryers, and phones.

Dining/Diversions: Off the lobby is the **Restaurant at the Jefferson,** one of the city's premier dining rooms and a cozy bar/lounge. In the paneled lounge, you can sink into a red leather chair and enjoy a marvelous high tea daily from 3 to 5pm, or cocktails anytime—the bar stocks a robust selection of single-malt scotches and a fine choice of Davidoff cigars.

Amenities: 24-hour butler service, overnight shoe shine, morning newspaper delivery, 24-hour room and multilingual concierge service, video and CD rentals, express checkout, business/secretarial services, meeting rooms, and for a fee of $20, guests have access to full health club facilities (including pool) at the University Club across the street.

✪ **Renaissance Mayflower.** 1127 Connecticut Ave. NW (between L and M sts.), Washington, DC 20036. ☎ **800/228-7697** or 202/347-3000. Fax 202/466-9082. www.renaissancehotels.com. 660 units. A/C MINIBAR TV TEL. Weekdays $265–$340 double, weekends $149–$209 double. Extra person $25. Children under 12 stay free in parents' room. AE, CB, DC, DISC, JCB, MC, V. Parking $26. Metro: Farragut North.

Superbly located in the heart of downtown, the Mayflower is the hotel of choice for guests as varied as Monica Lewinsky and Wynton Marsalis. The lobby, which extends an entire block from Connecticut Avenue to 17th Street, is always active, since Washingtonians tend to use it as a shortcut in their travels.

The Mayflower is imbued with history: It was the site of Calvin Coolidge's inaugural ball in 1925, the year it opened. (Coolidge didn't attend—he was mourning his son's death from blood poisoning.) President-elect FDR and family lived in rooms 776 and 781 while waiting to move into the White House; this is where he penned the words, "The only thing we have to fear is fear itself." A major restoration in the 1980s uncovered large skylights and renewed the lobby's pink marble bas-relief frieze and spectacular promenade.

Graciously appointed guest rooms have high ceilings, cream moiré wall coverings, and mahogany reproduction furnishings

(Queen Anne, Sheraton, Chippendale, Hepplewhite). Amenities include ironing board and iron, three phones, terry robe, hair dryer, and a small color TV in the bathroom. Inquire about summer value rates.

Dining/Diversions: Washington lawyers and lobbyists gather for power breakfasts in the **Café Promenade.** Under a beautiful domed skylight, the restaurant is adorned with Edward Laning's murals, crystal chandeliers, marble columns, and lovely flower arrangements. A full English tea is served here Monday through Saturday in the afternoon. The clubby, mahogany-paneled **Town and Country** is the setting for light buffet lunches and complimentary hors d'oeuvres during cocktail hour. Bartender Sambonn Lek has quite a following as much for his conversation as for his magic tricks. **The Lobby Court,** a Starbucks espresso bar just opposite the front desk, serves coffee and fresh-baked pastries each morning and becomes a piano/cocktail bar later in the day.

Amenities: Coffee, tea, or hot chocolate and *USA Today* with wake-up call, 24-hour room service, twice-daily maid service, complimentary overnight shoe shine, concierge, express checkout, valet parking, business center, full on-premises fitness center, florist, gift shop.

The St. Regis. 923 16th St. NW, Washington, DC 20006. ☎ **800/562-5661** or 202/638-2626. Fax 202/638-4231. www.stregis.com. 192 units. A/C MINIBAR TV TEL. Weekdays $220–$460 double, weekends $189–$405 double; $600–$2,500 suite. Children under 16 stay free in parents' room. AE, CB, DC, DISC, JCB, MC, V. Parking $22. Metro: Farragut West or McPherson Square.

Ah, luxury! Guest rooms are quietly opulent and decorated in tastefully coordinated colors, with duvets on the beds, desks set in alcoves, a mirror-covered armoire, and creamy silk moiré wall coverings. The marble bathrooms have hair dryers, lighted makeup mirrors, and Crabtree & Evelyn toiletries. Other amenities include three direct-dial telephones with voice mail and modem capabilities, personal safes, and fax machines. Eight rooms are specially designed for wheelchair access. Guests have included everyone from Queen Elizabeth to the Rolling Stones.

You may just want to hang out in the lobby, designed to resemble a Milan palazzo, with Palladian windows hung with rich damask draperies, elaborately gilded ceilings, Louis XVI chandeliers, plush green oversized sofas, and cozy chairs.

Dining/Diversions: Timothy Dean is the name of both the restaurant and the chef. The restaurant is quite elegant, though not as expensive as its predecessor, Lespinasse. The **Library**

Lounge, which might be the best hotel bar in Washington, has a working fireplace and paneled walls lined with bookcases. High tea is offered Friday, Saturday, and Sunday in the posh lobby.

Amenities: 24-hour concierge and room service, pressing service, complimentary coffee or tea in the lobby from 6 to 9:30am, free morning newspaper, complimentary shoe shine, complimentary one-way transportation within 10 blocks of hotel from 7 to 9:30am weekdays, 24-hour state-of-the-art fitness room and access to a complete health club (at the University Club, hotel guests pay $20 for access), 10,000 square feet of meeting space, ballroom.

MODERATE

✪ **Lincoln Suites Downtown.** 1823 L St. NW, Washington, DC 20036. ☎ **800/424-2970** or 202/223-4320. Fax 202/223-8546. www.lincolnhotels. com. 99 suites. A/C TV TEL. Weekdays $139–$179 suite, weekends $99–$139 suite. Children under 16 stay free in parents' room. AE, DC, DISC, MC, V. Parking $16 (in adjoining garage). Metro: Farragut North or Farragut West.

Lots of long-term guests stay at this all-suite, 10-story hotel in the heart of downtown, just 5 blocks from the White House, and the congenial staff must have something to do with it. But the hotel is also quite nice, in an unfancy sort of way. Suites are large and comfortable, with about 27 of them offering full kitchens; others have minirefrigerators, wet bars, coffeemakers, and microwaves. Rooms are fairly spacious, well kept, attractive, and equipped with hair dryers and irons and ironing boards. The property also has a coin-operated washer and dryer and a small meeting room.

The hotel is connected to **Mackey's,** an Irish pub featuring reasonably priced Irish food. **Luigi's,** an Italian restaurant around the corner, provides room service for lunch and dinner. Complimentary copies of the *Washington Post* are delivered to your door Monday through Saturday (and are for sale in the lobby on Sunday). The hotel serves complimentary milk and homemade cookies each evening and complimentary continental breakfast weekend mornings in the lobby. Guests enjoy free use of the well-equipped Bally's Holiday Spa nearby.

4 Adams–Morgan

EXPENSIVE

Hotel Sofitel. 1914 Connecticut Ave. NW, Washington, DC 20009. ☎ **800/424-2464** or 202/797-2000. Fax 202/462-0944. www.sofitel.com. 144 units. A/C MINIBAR TV TEL. Weekdays $199–$259 double, weekends $139–$159 double. Extra person $20. Children under 12 stay free in parents' room. AE, CB, DC, MC, V. Valet parking $17 ($9 for just the day). Metro: Dupont Circle.

The front desk greets you with "Bonjour," your room amenities include a bottle of Evian and Roger Gallet toiletries, the hotel's Trocadero restaurant serves French bistro food, and you get a fresh baguette at checkout. Guess what—the Sofitel is part of a French hotel chain. The 1906 building, a registered historic property, sits on a hill a short walk from lively Dupont Circle; its elevated position allows for great city views from upper-floor rooms. You're also just a short walk from trendy Adams–Morgan: cross Connecticut and walk up Columbia Road. Rooms, in muted shades of champagnes and peach, are spacious, each with a breakfast/study alcove and many with sitting areas. Thirty-six suites have kitchenettes. A multilingual staff sees to the needs of an international clientele of diplomats, foreign delegations, and corporate travelers. If you're looking for a romantic getaway at a reasonable rate, ask about the hotel's "Romantic Rendezvous" and "Weekend Superbe" packages. The former gets you a suite, champagne, flutes, roses, and breakfast in bed for $199. The latter upgrades your room and provides continental breakfast in bed, for $125.

Dining/Diversions: The Trocadero is open for breakfast, lunch, and dinner; the Pullman Lounge bar adjoins the restaurant.

Amenities: Full-service concierge, 24-hour room service, dry cleaning and laundry, major national and European newspapers available in lobby or delivered to your door upon request, twice-daily maid service, baby-sitting, secretarial services including faxing and copying, express checkout, fitness center with Nautilus and other equipment, conference rooms.

INEXPENSIVE

✪ **Jurys Normandy.** 2118 Wyoming Ave. NW (at Connecticut Ave.), Washington, DC 20008. ☎ **800/424-3729** or 202/483-1350. Fax 202/387-8241. www.doylehotels.com. 75 units. A/C TV TEL. $79–$155 double. Extra person $10. Children under 18 stay free in parents' room. AE, DC, DISC, MC, V. Parking $10. Metro: Dupont Circle.

This gracious small hotel is a gem. Situated in a neighborhood of architecturally impressive embassies, the hotel receives many embassy-bound guests (the French Embassy is the Normandy's largest customer). You may discover this for yourself on a Tuesday evening, when guests gather in the charming Tea Room to enjoy complimentary wine and cheese served from the antique oak sideboard. This is also where you'll find the daily continental breakfast (for $7), complimentary coffee and tea throughout the day, and cookies after 3pm. You can lounge or watch TV in the conservatory, or, in nice weather, you can move outside to the garden patio.

The six-floor Normandy has small but pretty twin and queen guest rooms (all remodeled in 1998), with tapestry-upholstered mahogany and cherry-wood furnishings in 18th-century styles, and pretty floral-print bedspreads covering firm beds. Amenities include minifridges, coffeemakers, irons and ironing boards, in-room safes, hair dryers, access to the neighboring Washington Courtyard's pool and exercise room, and a complimentary *Washington Post* weekdays. The Normandy is an easy walk from both Adams–Morgan and Dupont Circle.

5 Dupont Circle

EXPENSIVE

Canterbury Hotel. 1733 N St. NW, Washington, DC 20036. ☎ **800/ 424-2950** or 202/393-3000. Fax 202/785-9581. www.canterburydc.com. 99 units. A/C MINIBAR TV TEL. Weekdays $160–$400 double (most are under $200), weekends and off-season weekdays $119–$140 double. Extra person $20. Rates include continental breakfast. Children under 12 stay free in parents' room. AE, CB, DC, DISC, JCB, MC, V. Parking $15. Metro: Dupont Circle.

Located on a lovely residential street, this small European-style hotel is close to many tourist attractions. Each individually decorated room is actually a junior suite, whose layout includes a sofa/sitting area, separate dressing room, and separate kitchenette. Attractively decorated, these spacious accommodations sport 18th-century mahogany English reproduction furnishings (a few have four-poster beds). Among the amenities are cable TVs with CNN and pay-movie stations, irons and ironing boards, coffeemakers, electronic locks, and phones with voice mail. Bathrooms have makeup mirrors, hair dryers, phones, and baskets of fine toiletries.

Dining/Diversions: The hotel's wonderful restaurant, **Brighton,** serves American regional fare at all meals. And the Tudor-beamed **Union Jack Pub,** complete with dartboard and a menu featuring fish-and-chips, is the perfect place to relax after a busy day on the town. English beers on tap are served in pint mugs.

Amenities: Room service during restaurant hours, daily delivery of the *Washington Post,* complimentary *Wall Street Journal* available

Adams–Morgan & Dupont Circle
Accommodations

Canterbury Hotel **9**
Clarion Hampshire Hotel **8**
Embassy Suites Hotel Downtown **11**
The George Washington University Inn **13**
H. H. Leonards' Mansion on O Street **7**
Hay-Adams **20**
Hilton Garden Inn **21**
Hotel Lombardy **15**
Hotel Sofitel **3**
The Jefferson **18**
Jurys Doyle Hotel Washington **5**

Jurys Doyle Normandy **2**
Lincoln Suites Downtown **16**
Omni Shoreham **1**
Radisson Barceló Hotel **6**
Renaissance Mayflower **17**
St. Gregory Hotel and Suites **10**
St. James Suites **14**
The St. Regis **19**
Swann House **4**
Washington Monarch Hotel **12**

in lobby and restaurant, express checkout, secretarial services, meeting space for up to 75 people. Guests enjoy free use of the nearby YMCA/National Capital Health Center's extensive workout facilities, including an indoor lap pool.

✪ **Embassy Suites Hotel Downtown.** 1250 22nd St. NW, Washington, DC 20037. ☎ **800/EMBASSY** or 202/857-3388. Fax 202/293-3173. www. embassysuitesdcmetro.com. 318 suites. AC TV TEL. Weekdays $169–$289. Ask for AAA discounts or check the Web site for best rates. Extra person $20. Children 18 under stay free in parents' room. AE, CB, DC, DISC, JCB, MC, V. Parking $16. Metro: Foggy Bottom.

This hotel offers unbelievable value for its reasonable price and convenient location, within walking distance of Foggy Bottom, Georgetown, and Dupont Circle. You enter into a green and glassy eight-story atrium with two waterfalls constantly running. This is where you enjoy an ample complimentary breakfast— not your standard croissant and coffee but stations from which you can choose omelets made to order, waffles, bacon, fresh fruit, juices, bagels, and pastries. Tables are scattered in alcoves throughout the atrium to allow for privacy.

The accommodations are nicer than your average hotel room, with better amenities. Every room is a suite, with a living room that closes off completely from the rest of the suite and contains a queen-size sofa bed, TV, phone, easy chair, and large table with four comfortable chairs around it. The bedroom lies at the back of the suite, overlooking a quiet courtyard of brick walkways or the street. A king-size bed or two double beds, TV, sink, easy chair, and chest of drawers furnish this space. Between the living room and the bedroom are the bathroom, small closet, iron and ironing board, a sink, and microwave, refrigerator, and coffee-maker. In all: three sinks, two TVs, two phones with voice mail and data ports.

Dining/Diversions: The hotel's northern Italian restaurant, **Panevino's,** is popular among local business folks for the lunchtime antipasto buffet, available weekdays for $13.95. Also popular is the cocktail reception offered from 5:30 to 7:30pm nightly in the atrium: All beverages (including mixed drinks) and light cold snacks are complimentary.

Amenities: *USA Today* delivered daily to your door; state-of-the-art fitness facility includes indoor pool, whirlpool, sauna, game room; atrium can be reserved for banquet lunches.

Radisson Barceló Hotel. 2121 P St. NW, Washington, DC 20037. ☎ **800/333-3333** or 202/293-3100. Fax 202/857-0134. www.radisson.com. 301 units.

A/C TV TEL. Weekdays $199–$265 double, weekends $99–$169 double; in-season weekdays $265–$750 suite, weekends and off-season weekdays $205–500 suite. Extra person $20. Children under 16 stay free in parents' room. AE, DC, DISC, MC, V. Parking $16. Metro: Dupont Circle.

The first American venture for this Mallorca-based firm, the 10-story Barceló offers friendly European-style service, an unbeatable location midway between Dupont Circle and Georgetown, and a superb restaurant. The Barceló's art deco–style, marble-floored lobby is inviting, and its accommodations (formerly apartments) are larger than most (the standard room is 500 square feet). All offer workspaces with desks and living room areas containing sofas and armchairs. In-room amenities include cable TVs with HBO and more than 200 pay-movie options; three phones with voice mail and modem jacks; marble bathrooms with hair dryers and shaving mirrors; irons and ironing boards; coffee and coffeemakers. Each room also has a sofa bed. *Note:* Ask about weekend bed-and-breakfast packages on Friday and Saturday nights in summer—they can go as low as $109 per night for a double, including breakfast for two.

Dining/Diversions: Gabriel features first-rate Latin American/ Mediterranean cuisine; its pleasant bar/lounge (featuring tapas and sherry) is popular with the after-work crowd.

Amenities: Concierge, room service (during breakfast and dinner hours), complimentary *Washington Post* in the morning at the front desk, faxing and other secretarial services, express checkout, rooftop sundeck and swimming pool, small fitness room, gift shop.

✪ St. Gregory Hotel and Suites. 2033 M St. NW, Washington, DC 20036. ☎ **800/829-5034** or 202/223-0200. Fax 202/223-0580. www. stgregoryhotelwdc.com. 154 units, including 100 suites. A/C TV TEL. Weekdays $189–$209 double, $229–$269 suite; weekends $129–$209 double or suite. Extra person $20. Children under 16 stay free in parents' room. AE, DC, MC, V. Parking $18. Metro: Dupont Circle or Farragut North.

The same company that owns the St. James Suites Hotel opened the St. Gregory (can we look forward to a saints hotel chain, a St. Lucy perhaps, a St. Augustine?) in June 2000, distinguishing this one as a luxury property, with marble floors and chandeliers. The hotel is well situated at the corner of 21st and M streets, not far from Georgetown, Dupont Circle, Foggy Bottom, and the White House, and with many good restaurants within a literal stone's throw. The best Italian restaurant in the city, Galileo, is just down the street.

The best rooms are the "sky" suites on the 9th floor, each with terrace and city views. Most of the 100 suites have fully appointed kitchens, including microwaves, cooking ranges, sinks, ovens, and full-size refrigerators. All of the suites have sitting rooms with pull-out sofas, TVs, stereos, CD players, workstations, and high-speed Internet access. Decor throughout the hotel is an attractive mélange of olive green and gold, with un-hotel-like lamps, mirror frames, and fabrics. Every room includes a coffeemaker, two-line phones with modem access and voice mail, iron and ironing board, electronic lock, and marble bathroom with hair dryer and Gilchrist & Soames toiletries. Like the St. James, the St. Gregory offers special rates to long-term and government guests, and to those from the diplomatic community.

Dining: Donna's Cafe and Coffee Bar, an American eatery, is open daily for breakfast, lunch, dinner, and Sunday brunch. There's sidewalk seating seasonally.

Amenities: Room service (7am–7pm), state-of-the-art fitness center, coin-operated laundry room, complimentary weekday *Washington Post* delivery, meeting space and equipment, six guest rooms available for disabled guests.

MODERATE

Clarion Hampshire Hotel. 1310 New Hampshire Ave. NW (at N St.), Washington, DC 20036. ☎ **800/368-5691** or 202/296-7600. Fax 202/293-2476. 87 suites. A/C MINIBAR TV TEL. Weekdays $129–$209 suite, weekends and off-season weekdays $99–$129 suite. Extra person $20. Children under 12 stay free in parents' room. AE, CB, DC, DISC, JCB, MC, V. Parking $12. Metro: Dupont Circle.

The Clarion Hampshire is within easy walking distance of Georgetown and 2 blocks from Dupont Circle, convenient to numerous restaurants, nightspots, and offices. The hotel serves a mostly business clientele, so you should inquire about low summer rates.

Spacious junior suite accommodations are furnished with 18th-century reproductions and offer lots of closet space, big dressing rooms, couches, coffee tables, and desks. Most rooms have kitchenettes, which come with microwaves and coffeemakers; some have cooking ranges. Balconies at the front of the hotel (the New Hampshire Avenue side) offer city views. Amenities include hair dryers, chocolates on arrival, data port–equipped phones, in-room safety deposit boxes, and daily delivery of the *Washington Post.* Guests also receive free passes to the large YMCA health club with indoor pool, 10 minutes away.

The hotel's new restaurant, **L'Etoile,** is a French bistro.

H. H. Leonards' Mansion on O Street. 2020 O St. NW, Washington, DC 20036. ☎ **202/496-2000.** Fax 202/659-0547. www.erols.com/mansion. 6 suites and a 5-bedroom guest house. A/C TV TEL. $125 double with shared bathroom, $150 double with private bathroom; $500 log cabin suite; $1,000 for 5-bedroom guest house. Government and nonprofit rates available. Except for the guest house, rates include breakfast. AE, MC, V. Parking $15 by reservation. Metro: Dupont Circle.

A legend in her own time, H. H. Leonards operates this Victorian property, made up of three five-story town houses, as a museum with rotating exhibits, an event space, an art gallery, an antiques emporium, and—oh, yeah—a B&B. If you stay here, you may find yourself buying a sweater, a painting, or (who knows?) an antique bed. Everything's for sale. Guest rooms are so creative they'll blow you away. Most breathtaking is a log cabin loft suite, with a bed whose headboard encases an aquarium. The art deco–style penthouse takes up an entire floor and has its own elevator, 10 phones, and 7 televisions. The International Room has a non-working fireplace and four TVs. All rooms have king-size beds and computer-activated telephones that can hook you up to the Internet; most have a whirlpool and some have kitchens. Elsewhere on the property are an outdoor pool, 8 office/conference spaces, 28 far-out bathrooms, art and antiques everywhere, an exercise room, and thousands and thousands of books. Full business services are available, including multiline phones, fax machines, IBM and Mac computers, LCD projectors, and satellite feeds. The Light House (guest house) has a separate entrance and five bedrooms—all with white walls with light streaming in from windows and skylights; rates include maid service.

♻ **Jurys Washington Hotel.** 1500 New Hampshire Ave. NW, Washington, DC 20036. ☎ **800/42-DOYLE** or 202/483-6000. Fax 202/232-1130. www. doylehotels.com. 314 units. A/C MINIBAR TV TEL. Low season $135 double, high season $185 double. Extra person $15. Children 17 and under stay free in parents' room. AE, DC, DISC, MC, V. Parking $15. Metro: Dupont Circle.

This hotel gets high marks for convenience (it's located right on Dupont Circle), service, and comfort. A friend of mine arrived at 10am on a busy high-season weekday and was shown to her room immediately, though check-in is set at 3pm. The large rooms are furnished with two double beds with firm mattresses, an armoire with TV, a desk, a wet bar alcove, and a small but attractive bathroom. Decor is art decoish, with lots of light wood furniture, a circular mirror, and purple plaid and stripe fabrics. Despite its prime location in a sometimes raucous neighborhood, the hotel's rooms are insulated from the noise. In-room amenities include

Bath & Body Works toiletries, coffeemakers, hair dryers, irons and ironing boards, safes, and on-demand movies. *USA Today* arrives free at your door weekdays. The comfortable and attractive hotel pub, **Biddy Mulligan's,** proudly features a bar imported from Ireland. **Claddaghs** serves a full Irish breakfast every morning and American fare with an Irish flair at other meals; room service is available daily from 6:30am to midnight. Also on-site is an exercise room with treadmills, stationary bikes, and Stairmasters.

✪ **Swann House.** 1808 New Hampshire Ave. NW, Washington, DC 20009. ☎ **202/265-4414.** Fax 202/265-6755. www.swannhouse.com. 9 units. A/C TV TEL. $110–$250 depending on unit and season. Extended stay and government rates available. Extra person $20. Rates include expanded continental breakfast. Limited off-street parking $12. AE, MC, V. Metro: Dupont Circle.

This stunning 1883 mansion, standing prominently on a corner 4 blocks north of Dupont Circle, has nine exquisite guest rooms, two with private entrances. The coolest is the Blue Sky Suite, which has the original rose-tiled (working) fireplace, a queen-size bed and sofa bed, a gabled ceiling, and its own roof deck. The most romantic room is probably the Il Duomo, with Gothic windows, a cathedral ceiling, a working fireplace, and a turreted bathroom with angel murals. The Jennifer Green Room has a queen-size bed, working fireplace, oversize marble steam shower, and private deck overlooking the pool area and garden. The Regent Room has a king-size bed in front of a carved working fireplace, whirlpool, double shower, outdoor hot tub, TV, VCR, and stereo. There are three suites, each with a kitchen. The beautiful window treatments and bed coverings throughout are the handiwork of innkeeper Mary Ross. You'll want to spend some time on the main floor of the mansion, which has 12-foot ceilings, fluted woodwork, inlaid wood floors, a turreted living room, a columned sitting room, and a sunroom (where breakfast is served) leading through three sets of French doors to the garden and pool. Laundry facilities, meeting space, and business services are available.

6 Foggy Bottom/West End

VERY EXPENSIVE

Park Hyatt. 1201 24th St. NW, Washington, DC 20037. ☎ **202/789-1234.** Fax 202/457-8823. www.hyatt.com. 223 units. A/C MINIBAR TV TEL. Weekdays

① Family-Friendly Hotels

Embassy Suites Hotel Downtown *(see p. 48)*   You're close to both a Red line and a Blue line Metro station (Zoo on the Red line, Smithsonian museums on the Blue line) and within walking distance of Georgetown. Your kids can sleep on the pull-out sofa in the separate living room. You've got some kitchen facilities, but you might not use them—complimentary breakfast in the atrium is unbelievable. And there's an indoor pool and a free game room.

Holiday Inn on the Hill *(see p. 32)*   Children receive a free toy and a book on arrival during summer promotions. Kids 12 and under eat free in the restaurant with an adult dining. The hotel is near Union Station, Capitol Hill, and the Mall and Smithsonian museums, and the kitchen will pack a picnic for you to enjoy on the Mall. Connecting rooms are available. Kids ages 4 to 14 can participate in the hotel's Discovery Zone program of activities 4 to 10pm daily in summer. The hotel has a rooftop outdoor pool.

Omni Shoreham *(see p. 60)*   Adjacent to Rock Creek Park, the Omni is also within walking distance of the zoo and Metro and is equipped with a large outdoor pool and kiddie pool.

$340 double, weekends $199 double; weekdays $380 suite, weekends $224 suite. Extra person $25. Children under 17 stay free in parents' room. AE, CB, DC, DISC, JCB, MC, V. Valet parking $20, $8 as part of group. Metro: Foggy Bottom or Dupont Circle.

This luxury hotel across the street from the Washington Monarch also underwent a comprehensive renovation in 1999. The large guest rooms now have goose-down duvets on the beds, and new furniture, wall coverings, and fabrics. Specially commissioned artwork hangs throughout the hotel. The 131 suites now have dressing rooms with full vanities. Every room has an iron and ironing board, and each bathroom has a TV and radio, telephone, hair dryer, and makeup mirror. The 13-year-old 10-story hotel prides itself on going the extra mile to please a customer, even if it means taking out a wall to enlarge a suite, as the Park Hyatt did for Lily Tomlin, right after the hotel opened. Guests include big names, royal families (who use the Presidential Suite, with its fireplace and grand piano), lobbyists, and tour bus travelers.

Executive suites have separate living and dining areas, fax machines, and a second TV. Rooms are handsome and service is superb. Use of the fitness center is free.

Dining/Diversions: The bright and lovely **Melrose** dining room offers four-star cuisine with an emphasis on seafood; look for the amiable chef, Brian McBride, who's been known to pop into the dining room from time to time to make sure all is well. Adjoining Melrose is a bar; outdoors is lovely cafe.

Amenities: 24-hour concierge, room service, business center, valet/laundry service, currency exchange, shoe shine, twice-daily maid service, daily delivery of *Washington Post,* express checkout, gift shop. Hair and skin salon, health club including indoor pool, heated whirlpool, sauna and steam rooms, and extensive exercise room.

Washington Monarch Hotel. 2401 M St. NW, Washington, DC 20037. ☎ **877/222-2266** or 202/429-2400. Fax 202/457-5010. www. washingtonmonarch.com. 415 units. A/C MINIBAR TV TEL. Weekdays $309 double, weekends $269 double; $700–$1,700 suite. Extra person $30. Children under 18 stay free in parents' room. AE, CB, DC, DISC, JCB, MC, V. Valet parking $19. Metro: Foggy Bottom.

A $12 million renovation completed in 1999 has given the guest rooms new bed linens, carpets, and curtains, and has replaced the tile in the bathrooms with Italian marble. Also spruced up are the function rooms and the interior courtyard, known as the Colonnade. Best rooms in the house are the 146 that overlook the Colonnade, which, by the way, is a popular local spot for wedding receptions.

Amenities in guest rooms include large desks, terry robes, irons and ironing boards, three phones (one in the bathroom) with voice mail, safes, and Molton Brown toiletries. The 9th floor is a secured executive club level, popular with many of the business travelers who stay here (guests on this level pay no health club fee). The hotel has nine ADA-approved rooms to help disabled guests. Ask about summer weekend packages for best values.

Dining/Diversions: Sunday brunch in the **Colonnade** is among the best in Washington. **The Bistro** serves fresh regional American cuisine; cocktails, coffee, and pastries are available in the Lobby Lounge.

Amenities: 24-hour room service, concierge, dry cleaning and laundry service, twice-daily maid service, express checkout, valet parking, complimentary shoe shine, business center, 5,500-square-foot ballroom, an ergonomically designed 90-seat auditorium with workstations, more than 29,000 square feet of meeting space. The 17,500-square-foot **Fitness Company West End** includes an indoor pool and spa facilities, squash and racquetball courts, and every kind of exercise equipment. When in town, Arnold Schwarzenegger stays at the Monarch and uses this fitness center, working out next to visiting and local celebrities, like D.C. Mayor Anthony Williams, who comes here nearly every day. Guests pay $10 a day to use exercise equipment or to take aerobics classes but may use the pool, sauna, steam room, and whirlpool for free.

EXPENSIVE

Hotel Lombardy. 2019 Pennsylvania Ave. NW, Washington, DC 20006. ☎ **800/424-5486** or 202/828-2600. Fax 202/872-0503. www.hotellombardy. com. 125 units. A/C MINIBAR TV TEL. Weekdays $140–$219 double, weekends and some off-season weekdays $99–$219 double; weekdays $179–$359 suite for 2, weekends $119–$359 suite for 2. Extra person $20. Children under 16 stay free in parents' room. AE, CB, DC, DISC, MC, V. Self-parking $17. Metro: Farragut West or Foggy Bottom.

From its handsome walnut-paneled lobby with carved Tudor-style ceilings to its old-fashioned manual elevator (fasten your seat belts, it's going to be a bumpy ride), the 11-story Lombardy offers a lot of character and comfort for the price and location (about 5 blocks west of the White House). George Washington University's campus is just across Pennsylvania Avenue, which means this part of town remains vibrant long after other downtown neighborhoods have shut down for the night. Peace Corps, World Bank, and corporate guests make up a large part of the clientele, but other visitors will also appreciate the Lombardy's warm, welcoming ambience and the attentive service of the multilingual staff.

Spacious rooms, entered via pedimented louver doors, differ slightly in decor from one another, but all share a 1930s northern Italian motif. Large desks, precious dressing rooms, roomy walk-in closets, refrigerators, coffeemakers, irons and ironing boards, terry-cloth robes, data ports, and hair dryers enhance. Some suites have full kitchens.

Dining/Diversions: Moderately priced and open for all meals, the **Café Lombardy,** a sunny, glass-enclosed restaurant, serves simple American fare. You can also dine in the **Venetian Room,** an exquisitely decorated haven with velvet upholstery, antique lanterns, mother-of-pearl inlaid Moorish cocktail tables, and a custom-made cherry-wood bar. The Venetian Room shares a menu with the cafe, or you may choose from a special menu of appetizers.

Amenities: Free overnight shoe shine, daily delivery of the *Washington Post*, access to health club 1 block away ($5 per visit), two small meeting rooms.

MODERATE

✪ George Washington University Inn. 824 New Hampshire Ave. NW, Washington, DC 20037. ☎ **800/426-4455** or 202/337-6620. Fax 202/298-7499. www.gwuinn.com. 95 units. A/C TV TEL. Weekdays $130–$165 double, weekends $99–$135 double; weekdays $140–$185 efficiency, weekends $110–$155 efficiency; weekdays $155–$220 1-bedroom suite, weekends $125–$170 1-bedroom suite. Children under 12 stay free in parents' room. AE, DC, MC, V. Limited parking $14. Metro: Foggy Bottom.

It is rumored that this whitewashed brick inn, another former apartment building, was a favorite spot for clandestine trysts for high-society types. These days you're more likely to see Kennedy Center performers and visiting professors. The university purchased the hotel (formerly known as the Inn at Foggy Bottom) in 1994 and renovated it.

Rooms are a little larger and corridors are a tad narrower than those in a typical hotel, and each room includes a roomy dressing chamber. One-bedroom suites are especially spacious, with living rooms that hold a sleeper sofa and a TV hidden in an armoire (there's another in the bedroom). Guest rooms are equipped with a minifridge, a microwave, and a coffeemaker; efficiencies and suites have kitchens. The roominess and the kitchen facilities make this a popular choice for families and for long-term guests, and if it's not full, the inn may be willing to offer reduced rates. Mention prices quoted in the inn's *New York Times* ad, if you've seen it, or your affiliation with George Washington University, if you can. This is a fairly safe and lovely neighborhood, within easy walking distance to Georgetown, the Kennedy Center, and downtown. But keep an eye peeled—you must pass through wrought-iron gates into a kind of cul-de-sac to find the inn.

Off the lobby is the well-received restaurant Zuki Moon, a Japanese "noodle house" designed like a tea garden. Amenities include a complimentary *Washington Post* delivered Monday through Saturday, 24-hour message service, room service from 7am to 11pm, and same-day laundry/valet service. There's a coin-operated laundry on the premises, five rooms designed for guests with disabilities, and a meeting room for 50.

St. James Suites. 950 24th St. NW (off Washington Circle), Washington, DC 20037. ☎ **800/852-8512** or 202/457-0500. Fax 202/466-6484. www.stjamesuiteswdc.com. 195 suites. A/C MINIBAR TV TEL. Weekdays $165–$185 suite, weekends $109–$120 suite. Extra person $20. Rates include breakfast. Children under 17 stay free in parents' room. AE, DC, DISC, MC, V. Parking $18. Metro: Foggy Bottom.

The St. James is a home away from home for many of its guests, a number of whom book these luxury suites for more than a month at a time. Most of the suites are one-bedroom, with separate living and sleeping areas, marble bathrooms, two-line telephones with modem capability, and kitchens equipped with everything from china and flatware to cooking utensils. (About 13 suites are studios and 2 suites have two bedrooms.) Each living room includes a pull-out sofa. Unlike other hotels in this residential neighborhood of old town houses, the St. James was built in the 1980s, with an eye to accommodating people with disabilities. A ramp in the lobby leads to the reception area, and 10 suites are available for travelers with disabilities, one with roll-in shower. The St. James is near Georgetown, George Washington University, and the Kennedy Center. Corporate club members (pay an extra $20 to become one) receive extra perks, such as evening cocktails and hors d'oeuvres served in the club's pleasant second-floor quarters. *Tip:* For best rates, check the hotel's Web site or look for the hotel's ad in the *New York Times.*

Amenities include room service from 11am to 11pm, dry cleaning, laundry service, the *Washington Post* and *New York Times* available in the breakfast room or delivered to your room on request, concierge assistance, business services, and overnight shoe shine. There is also an outdoor pool, a 24-hour state-of-the-art fitness center, nearby tennis courts and jogging/biking paths, and conference rooms.

7 Georgetown

VERY EXPENSIVE

✪ **Four Seasons.** 2800 Pennsylvania Ave. NW, Washington, DC 20007. ☎ **800/332-3442** or 202/342-0444. Fax 202/944-2076. www.fourseasons.com. 260 units. A/C MINIBAR TV TEL. Weekdays $370–$570 double, weekends $285 double; weekdays $800–$5,050 suite, weekends from $550 suite. Extra person $40. Children under 16 stay free in parents' room. AE, DC, JCB, MC, V. Parking $24. Metro: Foggy Bottom.

Set just at the mouth of Georgetown, this hotel is where the rich and famous stay. And the reason is the service. Staff are trained to know the names, preferences, even allergies of guests, and repeat clientele rely on this discreet attention.

Accommodations, many of them overlooking Rock Creek Park or the C&O Canal, have a residential atmosphere: walls hung with gilt-framed antique prints; beds outfitted with down-filled bedding, dust ruffles, and scalloped spreads; and large desks and plump cushioned armchairs with hassocks. In-room amenities include bathrobes, hair dryers, lighted cosmetic mirrors, and upscale toiletries. In the suites you will also find VCRs and CD players. In 1999, an adjoining building was renovated to add 25 rooms and 35 suites for clients who want state-of-the-art business amenities (each is soundproof and has an office equipped with fax machine, at least three telephones with two-line speakers, portable telephones, and headsets for private TV listening). These rooms are also larger than those in the main hotel. Three of the suites have kitchenettes. The renovation expanded the space and facilities of the health club, too (see below).

Dining/Diversions: The elegant and highly acclaimed **Seasons** is reviewed in chapter 4. The delightful **Garden Terrace** is bordered by tropical plants, ficus trees, and flower beds and has a wall of windows overlooking the canal. It's open for lunch, a lavish Sunday jazz brunch, and classic English-style afternoon teas.

Amenities: Twice-daily maid service, 24-hour room service and concierge, complimentary sedan service weekdays within the District, gratis newspaper of your choice, car windows washed when you park overnight, complimentary shoe shine, beauty salon, gift shop, jogging trail, business facilities, children's programs, extensive state-of-the-art fitness club and spa that includes personal trainers, a Vichy shower, hydrotherapy, and synchronized massage (two people work on you at the same time).

The Latham. 3000 M St. NW, Washington, DC 20007. ☎ **800/528-4261** or 202/726-5000. Fax 202/337-4250. www.staywashingtondc.com. 143 units. A/C TV TEL. Weekdays $215–$445 double, weekends $179–$329 double. Extra person $20. Children under 12 stay free in parents' room. AE, CB, DC, DISC, MC, V. Valet parking $20. Metro: Foggy Bottom, with a 20-min. walk, or take a cab.

The Latham is at the hub of Georgetown's trendy nightlife/ restaurant/shopping scene, but since its accommodations are set back from the street, none of the noise of nighttime revelers will reach your room. Charming earth-tone rooms are decorated in

French-country motif, with pine furnishings and multipaned windows; cable TVs are housed in forest-green armoires. All rooms are equipped with large desks, hair dryers, and irons and ironing boards. Some 7th- through 10th-floor rooms offer gorgeous canal views; 3rd-floor accommodations, all two-room suites, have windows facing a hallway designed to replicate a quaint Georgetown street. Most luxurious are the two-story carriage suites with cathedral ceilings and full living rooms. Fax machines are in a third of the rooms; CD players with headphones are in 3rd-floor and carriage suites.

Dining/Diversions: Michel Richard's highly acclaimed **Citronelle,** one of D.C.'s hottest restaurants, is on the premises. And fronting the hotel is the country-French **La Madeleine.**

Amenities: Room service during restaurant hours, concierge, valet parking, free delivery of *Washington Post,* business services, express checkout, small (unheated) outdoor pool and bilevel sundeck, jogging and bike path along the C&O Canal, meeting rooms, audiovisual services.

EXPENSIVE

Hotel Monticello. 1075 Thomas Jefferson St. NW (just below M St.), Washington, DC 20007. ☎ **800/388-2410** or 202/337-0900. Fax 202/ 333-6526. www.hotelmonticello.com. 47 suites. A/C TV TEL. Weekdays $195–$250 1-bedroom suite for 2, weekends $195–$220 1-bedroom suite for 2; $250–$350 2-bedroom duplex penthouse (sleeps 6); $220 penthouse suite. Extra person $20. Rates include continental breakfast. Children under 14 stay free in parents' room. AE, CB, DC, DISC, MC, V. Parking $20. Metro: Foggy Bottom, with a 20-min. walk. Bus: 32, 34, and 36 go to all major Washington tourist attractions.

Many European and South American guests, usually embassy folks, stay at this inn. It's also a favorite for families to celebrate weddings or graduations; they book several suites, or maybe a whole floor. Personalized service is a hallmark of the hotel, whose staff greet you by name and protect your privacy.

Accommodations are moderately sized one- and two-bedroom apartmentlike suites, nine of them duplex penthouses with one and a half bathrooms; all have wet bars with a microwave and refrigerator. A major renovation in 2000 renamed the property (used to be called the Georgetown Dutch Inn) and created a more upscale venue. Bathrooms are wall-to-wall marble and have built-in magnified makeup mirrors, hair dryers, telephones, bathrobes, and Hermès toiletries. Other amenities include irons and ironing boards, coffeemakers, and four-line phones. You'll see the top sheet on the bed is monogrammed, the sofa in the living room folds out, the phones offer voice mail and modem access, and there's a good-size workstation.

Complimentary continental breakfast is served in the lobby each morning. Guests also enjoy free use of nearby state-of-the-art health clubs, one with an indoor pool. The C&O Canal towpath, just down the block, is ideal for jogging and cycling, though be wary at night.

8 Woodley Park

EXPENSIVE

Omni Shoreham. 2500 Calvert St. NW (near Connecticut Ave.), Washington, DC 20008. ☎ **800/843-6664** or 202/234-0700. Fax 202/265-7972. www. omnihotels.com. 836 units. A/C TV TEL. $149–$309 double. Extra person $30. Children under 18 stay free in parents' room. AE, CB, DC, DISC, JCB, MC, V. Valet parking $17; self-parking $14. Metro: Woodley Park–Zoo.

A massive $80 million renovation of all guest rooms and the lobby was recently completed. The spacious guest rooms remain twice the size of normal hotel rooms, but their new decor restores a traditional, elegant look through the use of chintz fabrics, mahogany furnishings, and porcelain fixtures. Fifty-two suites have kitchenettes. The hotel sits on 11 acres overlooking Rock Creek Park; many of the rooms offer spectacular views. A new air-conditioning system has been installed throughout the hotel, the pool is restructured, and the already excellent health club now includes a spa with a dry sauna and whirlpool.

The hotel is popular as a meeting and convention venue, whose business travelers appreciate the two-line telephones with voice mail and the ability to program their own wake-up call. Leisure travelers should consider the Shoreham for its large outdoor swimming pool, its proximity to the National Zoo and excellent restaurants, and the immediate access to biking, hiking, and jogging paths through Rock Creek Park. The hotel is just down the street from the Woodley Park–Zoo Metro station. You can also walk to the hipper neighborhoods of Adams–Morgan and Dupont Circle from the hotel; the stroll to Dupont Circle, taking you over the bridge that spans Rock Creek Park, is especially nice (and safe at night too). Built in 1930, the Shoreham has been the scene of inaugural balls for every president since FDR.

Dining/Diversions: The main restaurant is **Robert's,** which has a terrace overlooking Rock Creek Park and serves continental cuisine—a little bit of everything. The Little Something serves gourmet food to go. The **Marque Lounge** is the bar where you can also get a bite of something light.

Amenities: 24-hour room service; concierge; dry cleaning and laundry service; express checkout; shops; travel/sightseeing desk; business center and conference rooms; 10 miles of jogging, hiking, and bicycle trails; health and fitness center; 1½-mile Perrier par course; 22 meeting rooms; 7 ballrooms.

4

Dining

*B*ring your appetite. The capital has hundreds of fine restaurants: longtime favorites like La Colline and Galileo, promising new ones, like Etrusco, and branches of successful restaurants from around the country such as New York's Maloney & Porcelli.

With so many choices, you'd think it would be easy to book a reservation. You'd be wrong. Saturday nights book up especially fast. Best to call ahead, if you're really counting on a table at a certain restaurant. A number of restaurants are affiliated with an online reservation service called www.opentable.com, so if you've got Internet access, you might reserve your table on the Web.

You still might be successful calling the same day or the day before for a reservation, if you don't mind dining really early, say 5:30 or 6pm, or really late (by Washington standards, 9 or 9:30pm qualifies as late; this is not a late-night town). Finally, you can choose a restaurant that doesn't take reservations and take your chances. This practice seems to be on the upswing and works for places like Pesce, where the atmosphere is casual, the wait becomes part of the experience, and the food is worth standing in line for.

Few places require men to wear a jacket and tie, but those that do are so noted. If you're driving, check whether my listing indicates valet parking, complimentary or otherwise—on Washington's crowded streets, this service can be a true bonus.

1 Capitol Hill

For information on eating at the Capitol and other government buildings, see "Dining at Sightseeing Attractions," later in this chapter. There's a branch of **Il Radicchio** (see Dupont Circle for write-up) at 223 Pennsylvania Ave. SE (☎ **202/547-5114**).

EXPENSIVE
B. Smith's. Union Station, 50 Massachusetts Ave. NE. ☎ **202/289-6188.** www.bsmithsrestaurant.com. Reservations recommended. Main courses mostly

$10.95–$24. AE, CB, DC, DISC, MC, V. Mon–Sat 11:30am–4pm; Mon–Thurs 5–10pm, Fri–Sat 5–11pm; Sun 11:30am–9pm. Free validated parking for 2 hours. Metro: Union Station. TRADITIONAL SOUTHERN.

Union Station's most upscale restaurant is the creation of former model Barbara Smith; it occupies the room where presidents once greeted visiting monarchs and dignitaries. The dining room has 29-foot ceilings, imposing mahogany doors, white marble floors, gold-leafed moldings, and towering Ionic columns. Background music is mellow (Nat King Cole, Ray Charles, Sarah Vaughan). The restaurant features live jazz on Friday and Saturday evenings and at Sunday brunch. Chef James Oakley's menu offers such appetizers as jambalaya or red beans and rice studded with andouille sausage and tasso (spicy smoked pork). Among the main dishes are sautéed Virginia trout piled high with crabmeat/vegetable "stuffing" and served over mesclun with rice and a medley of roasted vegetables. A basket of minibiscuits, corn and citrus-poppyseed muffins, and sourdough rolls accompanies all dishes. Desserts include pecan sweet potato pie. An almost all-American wine list features many by-the-glass selections.

✪ **Barolo.** 223 Pennsylvania Ave. NW. ☎ **202/547-5011.** www.robertodonna.com. Reservations recommended. Lunch main courses $12.50–$15.50; dinner main courses $13.50–$24. AE, DC, MC, V. Mon–Fri 11:30am–2:30pm; Mon–Thurs 5:30–10pm, Fri–Sat 5:30–10:30pm. Free valet parking at dinner. Metro: Capitol South. ITALIAN.

This excellent upscale Italian restaurant is a much-needed addition to Capitol Hill dining. Another jewel in Roberto Donna's restaurant crown, Barolo is situated above another Donna creation, the inexpensive Il Radicchio (see write-up for Dupont Circle location). The intimate main room is paneled and has wooden floors, a working fireplace, and well-spaced tables; encircling the upper reaches of the room is a charming, narrow balcony set with tables for two; look out the window and you'll just be able to see the Capitol.

Though the menu changes daily, you can expect Piedmontese-style cuisine that may include a white asparagus salad with fresh fava beans and slices of Parma prosciutto; saffron pappardelle with sautéed lobster, asparagus, roasted garlic, and fresh basil; or roasted fillet of red snapper over sweet potato, rosemary, black olives, and fresh basil. You can also expect to see Washington notables dining here; among those we've spotted are California representatives Mary Bono and Jerry Lewis (not the comedian),

Downtown Washington, D.C., Dining

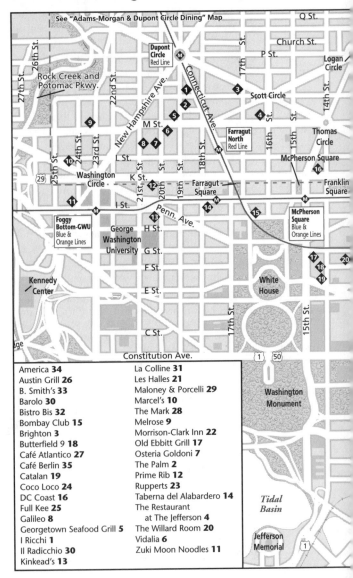

See "Adams-Morgan & Dupont Circle Dining" Map

Q St.

Church St.

Dupont Circle
Red Line

P St.

Logan Circle

Scott Circle

Farragut North
Red Line

Thomas Circle

Rock Creek and Potomac Pkwy.

M St.

McPherson Square

L St.

Washington Circle

K St.

Farragut Square

Franklin Square

I St.

McPherson Square
Blue & Orange Lines

Foggy Bottom-GWU
Blue & Orange Lines

Penn. Ave.

H St.

George Washington University

G St.

Kennedy Center

F St.

E St.

White House

C St.

Constitution Ave.

1   50

Washington Monument

Tidal Basin

Jefferson Memorial

1

Rhode Island Ave.

13th St.

12th St.
11th St.
10th St.
9th St.
8th St.
7th St.
6th St.
5th St.
4th St.
3rd St.

Florida Ave.

(29)
(1)

New York Ave.

1st St.

N St.

M St.

New Jersey Ave.

N. Capitol St.

1st St.

(29)

22

Mt. Vernon
Sq.-UDC
Green &
Yellow Lines

23

L St.

(50)

K St.

Mt. Vernon
Square

I St.

New York Ave.

(1)

24

25

(1)

(50)

Massachusetts Ave.

H St.

(395)

Union
Station
Red Line

33

2nd St.

G St.

Metro Center
Red, Blue &
Orange Lines

7th St.

3rd St.

2nd St.

1st St.

F St.

34

E St.

26

Judiciary
Square
Red Line

E St.

32

21

27

28

D St.

31

35

Pennsylvania Ave.

Indiana
29 Ave.

C St.

Louisiana Ave.

Delaware Ave.

Federal
Triangle
Blue &
Orange Lines

Constitution Ave.

30

Archives-
Navy Mem'l
Green &
Yellow Lines

NW

NE

Madison Dr.

Smithsonian
Blue &
Orange Lines

Jefferson Dr.

U.S. Capitol

Independence Ave.

SW

SE

Canal St.

Washington
/ Channel

L'Enfant Plaza
Yellow, Green,
Orange &
Blue Lines

(395)

Federal
Center SW
Blue &
Orange Lines

South Capitol St.

New Jersey Ave.

Capitol
South
Blue &
Orange Lines

0   1/8 Mi
0   .125 Km

as well as the owner himself. The wine list is entirely Italian, focusing on Piedmont wines, with emphasis on those produced from the Barolo grape.

Bistro Bis. 15 E St. NW. ☎ **202/661-2700.** www.bistrobis.com. Reservations recommended. Breakfast $6.75–$12; lunch main courses $8–$22; dinner main courses $7–$28. AE, DC, DISC, MC, V. Daily 7–10am, 11:30am–2:30pm, and 5:30–10:30pm. Valet parking at dinner. Metro: Union Station. FRENCH BISTRO.

Hotel George is the home for this excellent French restaurant, whose owner-chef, Jeff Buben, and his wife Sallie, also run Vidalia (see listing under "Downtown, 16th Street NW & West"). You can sit at tables in the bar area (though even without a crowd it's loud), on the balcony overlooking the bar, or at leather banquettes in the main dining room, where you can watch Buben and staff at work in the glass-fronted kitchen. (In warm weather, there's a sidewalk cafe.) The menu covers French classics like bouillabaisse, pistou, steak frites, as well as Buben's own take on grilled tuna au poivre, pan-seared red snapper, and seared scallops with tomatoes, garlic, olives, and an eggplant custard. The restaurant has been popular from the day it opened, with hungry movers and shakers intermingling with ordinary folk who just love good food. The wine list is mostly French. There's always a traditional plat du jour, for example, Dover sole on Wednesday, or bouillabaisse every Friday.

✪ **La Colline.** 400 N. Capitol St. NW. ☎ **202/737-0400.** Reservations recommended. Breakfast $5–$8.75; lunch main courses $8.75–$16.25; dinner main courses $18.75–$21. AE, CB, DC, MC, V. Mon–Fri 7–10am and 11:30am–3pm; Mon–Sat 6–10pm. Free garage parking after 5pm—enter on E St. Metro: Union Station. FRENCH.

This is the perfect spot for the breakfast fund-raiser. Hill people like La Colline for its convenience to the Senate side of the Capitol, the great bar, the four private rooms, the high-backed leather booths that allow for discreet conversations, and, last but not least, the food. You'll always get a good meal here. The regular menu offers an extensive list of French standards, including salade Niçoise, terrine of foie gras, and fish—poached, grilled, or sautéed. Almost as long is the list of daily specials—the soft-shell crab is superb here in season. The wine list concentrates on French and California wines; wine-by-the-glass choices change with the season to complement the menu. Don't let the dessert cart roll past you; the apple pie is a winner, as is the restaurant, which has been in business for 19 years.

MODERATE

America. Union Station, 50 Massachusetts Ave. NE. ☎ **202/682-9555.**
www.arkrestaurants.com. Reservations recommended. Main courses $6.95–
$17.95; sandwiches, burgers, and salads $3.50–$13.95; brunch $7.25–$13.50.
AE, DC, DISC, MC, V. Sun–Thurs 11:30am–midnight, Fri–Sat 11:30am–1am. Free
validated parking for 2 hours. Metro: Union Station. AMERICAN REGIONAL.

Our helpful waiter gave us the lowdown: Candice Bergen,
Clarence Thomas, Newt Gingrich, and Alec Baldwin are among
those who have eaten here at one time or another (not together,
though what an interesting lunch that would be). People-
watching is one reason to come to this vast four-level restaurant,
but sightseeing is another. Ask for a seat in the uppermost Capital
Wine Room. You'll see the Capitol dome, and, in the other
direction (between the Roman legionnaire statues), there's a
grand view of Union Station. This area seats parties no larger than
four. Walls are decorated with WPA-style murals, a large painting
of the American West, and a whimsical frieze depicting surfers,
athletes, astronauts, and superheroes in outer space.

A vast American classic menu comprises about 150 items, each
with the name of the city, state, or region in which the dish
supposedly originated: spaghetti and meatballs (Cleveland?), chili
dogs (Fort Lee, New Jersey?). The BLT (Newport) is a safe bet,
the nachos (Eagle Pass, Texas) too greasy, and you'll definitely
find better crab cakes (Ocean City, Maryland) elsewhere in the city.

✪ **Café Berlin.** 322 Massachusetts Ave. NE. ☎ **202/543-7656.** Reservations recommended. Main courses $11.95–$16.95; soups, sandwiches, and
salads $7.95–$11.95 at lunch. AE, DC, DISC, MC, V. Mon–Thurs 11am–10pm,
Fri–Sat 11am–11pm, Sun 4–10pm. Metro: Union Station. GERMAN.

You have to walk past the dessert display on your way to your
table at Café Berlin, so forget your diet. These delicious homemade confections are the best reason to come here. The vast
spread might include a dense pear cheesecake, raspberry linzer
torte, sour cherry crumb cake, or vanilla custard cake. Entrees
feature things like the *rahm schnitzel,* which is a center-cut of veal
topped with a light cream and mushroom sauce, or a *wurstplatte*
of mixed sausages. Seasonal items highlight asparagus in spring,
game in the fall, and so on. Lunch is a great deal: a simple chicken
salad sandwich (laced with tasty bits of mandarin orange), the
soup of the day, and German potato salad, all for $7.95. The
owners and chef are German; co-owner Peggy Reed emphasizes
that their dishes are "on the light side—except for the beer and

desserts." The 14-year-old restaurant occupies two prettily decorated dining rooms on the bottom level of a Capitol Hill town house, whose front terrace serves as an outdoor cafe in warm weather.

2 Downtown, East of 16th Street NW

VERY EXPENSIVE

Maloney & Porcelli. Indiana Ave. NW, between 6th and 7th sts. NW. ☎ **202/478-8300.** Reservations recommended. Lunch main courses $9.25–$26.75; dinner main courses $17–$29.75. AE, DC, DISC, MC, V. Mon–Fri 11:30am–11:30pm, Sat 5–11:30pm, Sun 5–11pm. Free valet parking at dinner. Metro: Archives–Navy Memorial. AMERICAN.

First, a word about the location: The street address is 601 Pennsylvania Ave. NW, because the restaurant is in an office building, across from the National Gallery of Art, that fronts Pennsylvania Avenue. But the entrance is on Indiana Avenue and it can be difficult to find the first time around. The menu is a lot easier to negotiate, since it is short and to the point. I chose the lemon Dover sole over the crackling pork shank because the shank looked hard to eat—it's massive. But the restaurant is famous for that crackling pork, and a number of diners around us were ordering it and happily eating it. The sole, however, proved heavenly, with its tastes of ginger, julienned carrots, and snow peas. The bread basket is plentiful and delicious: Try the salt-topped rolls. For dessert, I ordered The Boardwalk, an amusing plate of tiny samples of cotton candy, eclair, napoleon, fruit tart, and lollipop. Maloney & Porcelli's, part of a chain, seems to have taken off immediately in D.C. (it opened in 2000). Nice touch: Table centerpieces include a narrow pad of paper for note-taking lawyers and lobbyists (and restaurant reviewers). Service was excellent, but we worried about the waiters, who seemed under a lot of stress.

✪ **Ruppersts.** 1017 7th St. NW. ☎ **202/783-0699.** Reservations required. Main courses $25. AE, DC, MC, V. Thurs 11:30am–2:30pm; Wed–Thurs 6–10pm, Fri–Sat 6–11pm. Metro: Mount Vernon Square–UDC or Gallery Place–Chinatown. AMERICAN.

Within spitting distance of both the current and coming D.C. Convention Centers, Ruppersts lies in a marginal neighborhood; thankfully, a boom in downtown development is rapidly bringing other restaurants and nightlife a little closer.

The restaurant's success is a tribute to the chef's simple but excellent preparations using seasonal produce. The menu changes daily, sometimes three times a day, to incorporate the freshest ingredients. You may see a foie gras and figs dish on the menu in late fall or soft-shell crabs and grilled rhubarb in spring. The food is not heavy or laden with sauces. With dinner come four different freshly baked breads. The wine list is eclectic, everything from a $225 bottle of Batard/Montrachet to a $15 Verdejo. Desserts, like truffle ice cream, are too hip for me.

This is a one-room understated restaurant with a casual atmosphere. Patrons don't seem to fall into any identifiable group—most people are in business dress at lunch, less formal attire in the evening.

✪ **Willard Room.** In the Willard Inter-Continental Hotel, 1401 Pennsylvania Ave. NW. ☎ **202/637-7440.** www.washington.interconti.com. Reservations recommended. Jacket and tie preferred. Breakfast $5.50–$12.50; American buffet $17.50; lunch main courses $22–$38; dinner main courses $32–$42; pretheater dinner $28 fall–spring Mon–Sat 6–7pm. AE, DC, DISC, JCB, MC, V. Mon–Fri 7:30–10am and 11:30am–2pm; Mon–Sat 6–10pm. Free valet parking at dinner. Metro: Metro Center. AMERICAN REGIONAL/CLASSIC EUROPEAN.

Like the rest of the hotel, the Willard dining room has been restored to its original turn-of-the-20th-century splendor, with gorgeous carved oak paneling, towering scagliola columns, brass and bronze torchères and chandeliers, and a faux-bois beamed ceiling. Scattered among the statesmen and diplomats dining here are local couples seeking romance; the Willard has been the setting for more than one betrothal. The room has also been used in many movies.

Chef de cuisine Gerard Madani changes the lunch menu daily, the dinner menu seasonally, and emphasizes lightness in cooking at all times. Some examples: steamed Dover sole with a sorrel-flavored vermouth cream sauce, veal kidney with celery root mustard seed sauce, beef tenderloin with bordelaise sauce, and grilled whole Maine lobster. Two of the most popular desserts are the double-vanilla crème brûlée and the chocolate tears, which combines dark chocolate and white chocolate in a tear-shaped mousselike confection. The wine list offers more than 250 fine selections.

EXPENSIVE

✪ **Café Atlantico.** 405 8th St. NW. ☎ **202/393-0812.** Reservations required. Lunch main courses $8–$15; dinner main courses $17–$24; Latino dim sum $19.95 all you can eat (Sat 11:30am–1:30pm). AE, DC, MC, V. Mon–Fri 11:30am–2:30pm; Sun–Thurs 5–10pm, Fri–Sat 5–11pm. The bar stays open late on weekends. Metro: Archives–Navy Memorial. LATIN AMERICAN/ CARIBBEAN.

This place rocks on weekend nights, a favorite hot spot in Washington's burgeoning downtown. The colorful three-tiered restaurant throbs with Latin, calypso, and reggae music, and everyone is having a good time—including, it seems, the waiters. If the place is packed, see if you can snag a seat at the second-level bar, where you can watch the genial bartender mix the potent drinks for which Café Atlantico is famous: the *caipirinha,* made of limes, sugar, and *cachacha* (sugar cane liqueur); the *mojito,* a rum and crushed mint cocktail; or the passion fruit cocktail, a concoction of passion fruit juice, ginger, and jalapeño mixed with mandarin orange–flavored vodka.

Seated at the bar or table, you get to watch the waiter make fresh guacamole right in front of you. As for the main dishes, you can't get a more elaborate meal for the price. The ceviche, Ecuadorean seared scallops, and Argentine rib eye are standouts, and tropical side dishes and pungent sauces produce a burst of color on the plate. The menu changes every week, so feel free to ask your waiter for guidance.

DC Coast. 1401 K St. NW. ☎ **202/216-5988.** www.dccoast.com. Reservations recommended. Lunch main courses $12–$18; dinner main courses $16–$23; light fare $6–$8. AE, DC, DISC, MC, V. Mon–Thurs 11:30am–2:30pm and 5:30–10:30pm, Fri 11:30am–11pm (light fare weekdays 2:30–5:30pm), Sat 5:30–11pm. Valet parking after 5:30pm $4. Metro: McPherson Square. AMERICAN.

The dining room is sensational: two stories high, glass-walled balcony, immense oval mirrors hanging over the bar, and a full-bodied stone mermaid poised to greet you at the entrance. Gather at the bar first to feel a part of the loud and trendy scene. This is one of the city's hottest restaurants, so call way ahead to book a reservation. The food is sometimes sensational. Chef Jeff Tunks has returned from stints in Texas, California, and New Orleans, and some of the dishes Washingtonians remember from his years at the River Club have returned with him: Chinese-style smoked lobster with fried spinach is the most famous. And it's still tasty. Other entrees to recommend: the "tower of crab" (a crab cake upon a fried soft-shell crab) and the fish fillet encrusted with portobello paste. Seafood is a big part of the menu, but there are plenty of meat dishes, too.

✪ **Les Halles.** 1201 Pennsylvania Ave. NW. ☎ **202/347-6848.** www. leshalles.com. Reservations recommended. Lunch main courses $11.75–$20;

dinner main courses $13.25–$22.50. AE, CB, DC, DISC, MC, V. Daily 11:30am–midnight. Free valet parking after 6:30pm. Metro: Metro Center or Federal Triangle. FRENCH/STEAK HOUSE.

Anyone who believes that red meat is passé hasn't eaten here. At lunch and dinner, people are devouring the *onglet* (a boneless French cut hangar steak hard to find outside France), steak au poivre, steak tartare, New York sirloin, and other cuts. Every steak is always accompanied by frites (fries), which are a must. The menu isn't all beef, but it is classic French: cassoulet, confit de canard, escargots, onion soup, and such. I can never resist the frisée aux lardons, a savory salad of chicory studded with hunks of bacon and toasts smeared thickly with Roquefort.

Les Halles is big and charmingly French, with French-speaking waiters providing breezy, flirtatious service. The banquettes, pressed tin ceiling, mirrors, wooden floor, and side bar capture the feel of a brasserie. A vast windowfront overlooks Pennsylvania Avenue and the awning-covered sidewalk cafe, which is a superb spot to dine in warm weather. Every July 14, this is the place to be for the annual Bastille Day race, which Les Halles hosts. (See chapter 2, "Calendar of Events," for details.) Les Halles is a favorite hangout for cigar smokers, but the smoking area is well ventilated. Need a pick-me-up? Served all day at the bar and through the afternoon in the dining room are "les bouchies des Halles" (little mouthfuls), hors d'oeuvres that include a cheese plate, salmon tartare, canapés, and so on, each for under $4.

The Mark. 401 Seventh St. NW. ☎ **202/783-3133.** www.mark-restaurant. com. Reservations recommended. Lunch main courses $5–$14; dinner main courses $13–$28; $4–$13 bar fare ("foreplates menu") daily 4:30pm–closing at the bar. AE, CB, DC, DISC, MC, V. Mon–Sat 11:30am–3pm; Mon 5–9pm, Tues–Thurs 5–10pm, Fri–Sat 5–11pm; Mon–Fri Happy Hour 4:30–7:30pm. Valet parking at dinner. Metro: Gallery Place or Archives/Navy Memorial. AMERICAN REGIONAL.

I didn't like this place the first time around—I was shown to the windowless back room, where my companion and I shared unremarkable lunch fare. The second time around went much better: We sat in the storefront window at rush hour counting the number of people walking by with a cellular phone to the ear (The Mark is in the middle of downtown, right near the MCI Center), as we munched on fried calamari, slurped up corn chowder with andouille sausage, and savored the Copper River salmon with fiddlehead ferns. Chef Allison Swope favors Southern and Southwestern cuisine, which you'll notice particularly in sauces like red chile butter sauce on salmon, and side dishes, which include garlic grits. Don't miss dessert; try the mocha pot de crème or chocolate hazelnut tart. Great deal: Every Monday after 5pm, you can order a bottle of wine or champagne for half price with an entree.

MODERATE

✪ **Coco Loco.** 810 7th St. NW (between H and I sts.). ☎ **202/289-2626.** Reservations recommended. Tapas mostly $6–$12; churrascaria with antipasti bar $23 (dinner only); antipasti bar $6.95 lunch, $9.95 dinner. AE, MC, V. Tues–Fri 11:30am–2:30pm; Tues–Thurs 5:30–10pm, Fri–Sat 5:30–11pm (These are the hours food is served; the restaurant turns into a nightclub about 10pm and stays open until 2 or 3am) Call to make sure the restaurant is open; it sometimes closes for lunch. Metro: Gallery Place. BRAZILIAN/MEXICAN.

At 9pm on a Thursday night, the floor is filled with young, well-dressed couples learning the salsa—lessons are free and first come, first served. Weekends, you can't even get in the joint. Besides the music and dancing, much of the action emanates from the open kitchen and the U-shaped bar. If you want a quieter setting, head for the window-walled front room or the garden patio. The exuberantly tropical interior space centers on a daily changing buffet table where cheeses, fresh fruits, salads (ranging from roasted tomatoes with mozzarella to garbanzos with figs), cold cuts, and other antipasti are temptingly arranged on palm fronds and banana leaves.

An extensive selection of Mexican tapas includes interesting quesadillas and pan-roasted shrimp on chewy black (squid-infused) Chinese jasmine rice. Coco Loco's most popular dish is *churrascaria,* the Brazilian mixed grill. Waiters serve you chunks of sausage, chicken, beef, and pork from skewers. It comes with salsa, fried potatoes, and coconut-flavored rice, plus antipasti bar offerings. All this and Mexican chocolate rice pudding for dessert, too. The small wine list is well chosen.

✪ **Old Ebbitt Grill.** 675 15th St. NW (between F and G sts.). ☎ **202/347-4801.** www.clydes.com. Reservations recommended. Breakfast $4.50–$9.95; brunch $5.95–$24.95; lunch main courses $8.95–$24.95; dinner main courses $10.95–$24.95; burgers and sandwiches $6.25–$10.95; raw bar $8.95–$18.50. AE, DC, DISC, MC, V. Mon–Wed 7:30am–1am, Thurs–Fri 7:30am–2am, Sat 8:30am–1am, Sun 9:30am–1am. Bar Sun–Thurs to 2am, Fri–Sat to 2:30am. Raw bar open until midnight daily. Free valet parking from 6pm Mon–Sat, from noon Sun. Metro: McPherson Square or Metro Center. AMERICAN.

Located 2 blocks from the White House, this is the city's oldest saloon, founded in 1856. Among its artifacts are animal trophies bagged by Teddy Roosevelt and Alexander Hamilton's wooden bears—one with a secret compartment in which it's said he hid whiskey bottles from his wife. The Old Ebbitt is an attractive place, with Persian rugs strewn on beautiful oak and marble floors, beveled mirrors, flickering gaslights, etched-glass panels, and paintings of Washington scenes. The long, dark mahogany Old Bar area gives it the feeling of a men's saloon.

You may see preferential treatment given to movers and shakers, and you'll always have to wait for a table if you don't reserve ahead. The waiters are friendly and professional in a programmed sort of way; service could be faster. Menus change daily but always include certain favorites: burgers, trout Parmesan (Virginia trout dipped in egg batter and Parmesan cheese, deep-fried), crab cakes, and oysters (there's an oyster bar). The tastiest dishes are usually the seasonal ones, whose fresh ingredients make the difference.

INEXPENSIVE

✪ **Full Kee.** 509 H St. NW. ☎ **202/371-2233.** Reservations accepted. Lunch main courses $4.25–$9; dinner main courses $6.95–$17. No credit cards. Sun–Thurs 11am–1am, Fri–Sat 11am–3am. Metro: Gallery Place/Chinatown. CHINESE.

This restaurant has the best food in Chinatown. The decor, on the other hand, is forgettable: Full Kee's two rooms are brightly lit and crammed with Chinese-speaking customers sitting on metal-legged chairs at plain rectangular tables. There's no such thing as a no-smoking section. A cook works in the small open kitchen at the front of the room, hanging roasted pig's parts on hooks and wrapping dumplings.

Chefs from some of Washington's best restaurants often congregate here after hours, and here's their advice: Order from the typed back page of the menu. I can personally vouch for at least two of the selections: the jumbo breaded oyster casserole with ginger and scallions and the whole steamed fish. Check out the laminated tent card on the table and find the soups; if you love dumplings, order the Hong Kong–style shrimp dumpling broth: You get either eight shrimp dumplings or four if you order the broth with noodles. Bring your own wine or beer (and your own glasses in which to pour it) if you'd like to have a drink, since Full Kee does not serve any alcohol and accepts no responsibility for helping you imbibe.

3 Downtown, 16th Street NW & West

VERY EXPENSIVE

✪ **Galileo.** 1110 21st St. NW. ☎ **202/293-7191.** www.robertodonna. com. Reservations recommended. Lunch main courses $11–$19; dinner main courses $22–$32. AE, CB, DC, DISC, MC, V. Mon–Fri 11:30am–2pm and 5:30–10pm, Sat 5:30–10:30pm, Sun 5:30–10pm. Free valet parking Mon–Sat nights. Metro: Foggy Bottom. ITALIAN.

Food critics mention Galileo as one of the best Italian restaurants in the country and Roberto Donna as one of our best chefs. The likable Donna opened the white-walled grottolike Galileo in 1984; since then, he has opened several other restaurants in the area, including Il Radicchio and Pesce in Dupont Circle and Barolo on Capitol Hill (see listings), has written a cookbook, and has established himself as an integral part of Washington culture.

Galileo features the cuisine of Donna's native Piedmont region, an area in northern Italy influenced by neighboring France and Switzerland—think truffles, hazelnuts, porcini mushrooms, and veal. The atmosphere is relaxed; diners are dressed in jeans and suits alike. For starters, munch on the Piedmont-style crostini—paper-thin toast dipped in puréed cannellini beans with garlic. Typical entrees include sautéed Chesapeake Bay oysters, served on a bed of leeks and porcini mushrooms; pansotti (a pasta) of truffled potatoes and crispy pancetta in porcini mushroom sauce; and grilled rack of venison with wild berry sauce. Finish with a traditional tiramisù, or, better yet, the warm pear tart with honey vanilla ice cream and caramel sauce—spectacular. The cellar boasts more than 900 vintages of Italian wine (40% Piedmontese). In 1999, Donna opened his Laboratorio del Galileo, a private dining area and kitchen enclosed by glass, where Donna prepares the 10- to 12-course tasting menu and entertains the 30 diners lucky enough to snag a table. There is also a terrace for warm-weather dining.

I Ricchi. 1220 19th St. NW. ☎ **202/835-0459.** www.iricchi.net. Reservations recommended. Lunch main courses $10– $28; dinner main courses $11.95–$32. AE, CB, DC, MC, V. Mon–Fri 11:30am–2pm; Mon–Sat 5:30–10pm. Free valet parking at dinner. Metro: Dupont Circle. ITALIAN.

This restaurant celebrates its 12th year in 2001, and it remains a popular and convivial place to enjoy Italian food à la Tuscany. An open kitchen with a blazing wood-burning grill creates a warming bustle in the large room. The daily specials are great, especially if you're into fish. Those of hearty appetite will be happy with minestrone; the quill pasta with Tuscan meat sauce; and the rolled medallions of pork loin, turkey breast, and veal, each medallion stuffed with spinach and prosciutto. Start with grilled radicchio.

✪ **Prime Rib.** 2020 K St. NW. ☎ **202/466-8811.** www.theprimerib. com. Reservations recommended. Jacket and tie required. Lunch main courses $11–$20; dinner main courses $18–$39. AE, CB, DC, MC, V. Mon–Thurs 11:30am–3pm and 5–11pm, Fri 11:30am–3pm and 5–11:30pm, Sat 5– 11:30pm. Free valet parking after 5pm. Metro: Farragut West. STEAKS/CHOPS/SEAFOOD.

The Prime Rib has plenty of competition now, but it makes no difference. Beef lovers still consider this The Place. It's got a definite men's club feel about it: brass-trimmed black walls, leopard-skin carpeting, comfortable black leather chairs and banquettes. Waiters are in black tie, and a pianist at the baby grand plays show tunes and Irving Berlin classics.

The meat is from the best grain-fed steers and has been aged for 4 to 5 weeks. Steaks and cuts of roast beef are thick, tender, and juicy. For less carnivorous diners, there are about a dozen seafood entrees, including an excellent crab imperial. Mashed potatoes are done right, as are the fried potato skins.

✪ **Restaurant at the Jefferson.** 1200 16th St. NW (at M St.). ☎ **202/833-6206.** Reservations recommended. Breakfast $10–$14; fixed-price lunch $20; lunch main courses $14–$17; dinner main courses $23–$28; Sun brunch $32; tea $16. AE, CB, DC, DISC, JCB, MC, V. Daily 6:30–11am, 11:30am–2:30pm, and 6–10:30pm; tea daily 3–5pm. Free valet parking. Metro: Farragut North. AMERICAN.

Cozy, rather than intimidatingly plush, the Jefferson Hotel's restaurant is actually pretty romantic—ask to be seated in "the snug" (tables 39 or 40). The emphasis on privacy and the solicitous, but not imposing, service also make it a good place to do business.

Chef James Hudock changes his menus seasonally, although some dishes may always be available because of their popularity. Try the appetizer of seared Gulf shrimp with warm beet vinaigrette and roasted garlic mashed potatoes, the chef's signature entree of mushroom-crusted Chilean sea bass with smoked tomato coulis, ricotta gnocchis and wilted pea shoots, and for dessert a divine coffee crème brûlée. An extensive wine list includes many by-the-glass selections.

✪ **Taberna del Alabardero.** 1776 I St. NW (entrance on 18th St. NW). ☎ **202/429-2200.** Reservations recommended. Jacket and tie required.

Lunch main courses $17.25–$20.75; dinner main courses $19–$29.50; tapas $5–$8.75. AE, DC, DISC, MC, V. Mon–Fri 11:30am–2:30pm and 5:30–10:30pm, Sat 5:30–11pm. Free valet parking at dinner. Metro: Farragut West. SPANISH.

Dress up to visit this truly elegant restaurant, where you receive royal treatment from the Spanish staff who are quite used to attending to the real thing: Spain's King Juan Carlos and Queen Sofia and their children regularly dine here when in Washington. In 1999, the Spanish ministry of agriculture named Taberna the best Spanish restaurant in the United States.

The dining room is old-world ornate, with lace covers placed over velvety banquettes and heavy brocadelike drapes framing the large front windows. Order a plate of tapas to start: lightly fried calamari, shrimp in garlic and olive oil, thin smoky ham, and marinated mushrooms. Although the à la carte menu changes with the seasons, four paellas (each feeds a minimum of two) are always available. The lobster and seafood paella served on saffron rice is rich and flavorful. (Ask to have the lobster de-shelled; otherwise, you do the cracking.) Another signature dish is *Txangurro Gratinado* (Basque-style crabmeat).

This is the only Taberna del Alabardero outside of Spain, where there are three. All are owned and operated by Father Luis de Lezama, who opened his first tavern outside the palace gates in Madrid in 1974, as a place to train delinquent boys for employment.

EXPENSIVE

✪ **Georgetown Seafood Grill on 19th St.** 1200 19th St. NW. ☎ **202/530-4430.** www.capitalrestaurants.com. Reservations recommended. Lunch main courses $5–$22; dinner main courses $10–$29; salads and sandwiches $8.95–$12.95. AE, DC, DISC, MC, V. Mon–Thurs 11:30am–10pm, Fri 11:30am–11pm, Sat 5:30–11pm, Sun 4:30–9pm. Metro: Dupont Circle. SEAFOOD.

In the heart of downtown is this hint of the seashore. Two big tanks of lobsters greet you as you enter, and the decor is nautical throughout: aquariums set in walls, canoes fastened to the ceiling, models of tall ships placed here and there. Meanwhile, jazz music from another era wafts in the background. It's enough to make you forget what city you're in.

A bar and tables sit at the front of the restaurant, an open kitchen is in the middle, and tall wooden booths on platforms occupy the rear. The lobster Thermidor special is a mix of Pernod, scallions, mushrooms, and cream mixed with bits of lobster.

But as is the rule in many seafood restaurants, your best bets are the most simply prepared. Besides the lobster, you can choose from a list of at least eight "simply grilled" fish entrees. Raw bar selections list oysters from six different locations daily, including Canada, Virginia, and Oregon, and these may be the freshest in town. Service is excellent.

✪ **The Palm.** 1225 19th St. NW. ☎ **202/293-9091.** www.thepalm.com. Reservations recommended. Lunch main courses $9–$18; dinner main courses $15–$50. AE, DC, MC, V. Mon–Fri 11:45am–10:30pm, Sat 6–10:30pm, Sun 5:30–9:30pm. Free valet parking at dinner. Metro: Dupont Circle. STEAK HOUSE.

The Palm is one in a chain that started 78 years ago in New York— but here in D.C., it feels like an original. The Washington Palm is 29 years old; its walls, like all Palms, are covered with the caricatures of regulars, famous, and not-so. (Look for my friend, Bob Harris.) If you think you see Vernon Jordan or Larry King at a table, you're probably right. You can't go wrong with steak, whether it's the 36-ounce dry-aged New York strip, or sliced in a steak salad. Oversize lobsters are a specialty, and certain side dishes are a must: creamed spinach, onion rings, Palm fries (something akin to deep-fried potato chips), and hash browns. Several of the longtime waiters like to kid with you a bit, but the service is always fast.

✪ **Vidalia.** 1990 M St. NW. ☎ **202/659-1990.** www.vidalia1990.com. Reservations recommended. Lunch main courses $6.75–$18.75; dinner main courses $8–$29. AE, DC, DISC, MC, V. Mon–Fri 11:30am–2:30pm; Mon–Thurs 5:30–10pm, Fri–Sat 5:30–10:30pm, Sun 5–9pm (closed Sun July 4–Labor Day). Free valet parking at dinner. Metro: Dupont Circle. REGIONAL AMERICAN.

Down a flight of steps from the street, the charming Vidalia's tiered dining room has cream stucco walls hung with gorgeous wreaths and works by local artists.

Chef Jeff Buben's regional American menus (focusing on Southern-accented specialties) change frequently, but recommended constants include crisp East Coast lump crab cakes and a fried grits cake with portobello mushrooms. Venture from the regular items and you may delight in a timbale of roasted onion and foie gras. A signature entree is the scrumptious sautéed shrimp on a mound of creamed grits and caramelized onions in a thyme and shrimp-cream sauce. Corn bread and biscuits with apple butter are served at every meal. Vidalia is known for its lemon chess pie, which tastes like pure sugar; I prefer the pecan pie. A carefully chosen wine list highlights American vintages.

🅟 Family-Friendly Restaurants

Baby-boomer parents (and I am one) are so insistent upon taking their children with them everywhere that sometimes it seems all restaurants are forced to be family-friendly, even if you wish certain ones were not. Hotel restaurants, no matter how refined, usually welcome children, since they may be guests of the hotel. The cafeterias at tourist attractions are always a safe bet, since they cater to the multitudes. Inexpensive ethnic restaurants tend to be pretty welcoming to kids, too. Aside from those suggestions, I recommend:

Old Glory Barbecue *(see 93)*   A loud, laid-back place where the waiters are friendly without being patronizing. Go early, since the restaurant becomes more of a bar as the evening progresses. There is a children's menu, but you may not need it; the barbecue, burgers, muffins, fries, and desserts are so good, everyone can order from the main menu.

Austin Grill *(see p. 94)*   Another easygoing, good-service joint, with great background music. Kids will probably want to order from their own menu here, and their drinks arrive in unspillable plastic cups with tops and straws.

Il Radicchio *(see p. 86)*   A spaghetti palace to please the most finicky, at a price that should satisfy the family budget.

America *(see p. 67)*   The cavernous restaurant with its voluminous menu offers many distractions for a restless brood. No children's menu, but why would you need one, when macaroni and cheese, peanut butter and jelly, pizza, and chicken tenders are among the selections offered to everyone?

MODERATE

✪ **Bombay Club.** 815 Connecticut Ave. NW. ☎ **202/659-3727.** Reservations recommended. Main courses $7.50–$18.50; Sun brunch $18.50; pretheater dinner $24. AE, CB, DC, MC, V. Mon–Fri and Sun brunch 11:30am–2:30pm; Mon–Thurs 6–10:30pm, Fri–Sat 6–11pm, Sun 5:30–9pm. Free valet parking after 6pm. Metro: Farragut West. INDIAN.

Dine here and be prepared for Secret Service sweeps of the restaurant, in anticipation of visits by the Clintons or maybe Prince Bandar bin Sultan, the Saudi ambassador. (The White House is just across Lafayette Park.)

The Indian menu ranges from fiery green chile chicken ("not for the fainthearted," the menu warns) to the delicately prepared lobster malabar, a personal favorite. Tandoori dishes, like the chicken marinated in a yogurt, ginger, and garlic dressing, are specialties, as is the vegetarian fare—try the black lentils cooked overnight on a slow fire. Patrons are as fond of the service as the cuisine: Waiters seem straight out of Jewel in the Crown, attending to your every whim. This is one place where you can linger over a meal as long as you like. Slow-moving ceiling fans and wicker furniture accentuate the colonial British ambience.

4 Adams–Morgan

Though the action centers on just 2 or 3 blocks, Adams–Morgan is one of D.C.'s liveliest neighborhoods, filled with ethnic and trendy restaurants and happening nightclubs. At nighttime, it's best to come here via taxi, since parking is difficult and expensive, and the closest Metro stop is a bit of a hike. (During the day, parking is usually not a problem.) If you do take the Metro, exit at Dupont Circle (the North exit) and walk uphill on Connecticut Avenue, picking up Columbia Road (where it forks off Connecticut Avenue), and follow it to Adams–Morgan. Or take the Metro to the Woodley Park–Zoo stop, walk south on Connecticut Avenue to Calvert Street, turn left, and cross the Calvert Street bridge to Adams–Morgan.

EXPENSIVE

✪ **Cashion's Eat Place.** 1819 Columbia Rd. NW (between 18th St. and Mintwood Place). ☎ **202/797-1819.** Reservations recommended. Brunch $6–$9; dinner main courses $14–$21. MC, V. Tues 5:30–10pm, Wed–Sat 5:30–11pm, Sun 11:30am–2:30pm and 5:30–10pm. Valet parking $5. AMERICAN.

Owner/chef Ann Cashion has gained renown for her stints at Nora, Austin Grill, and Jaleo. Her menu features about eight entrees, split between seafood and meat, which could include grilled wild Chesapeake rockfish or rabbit stew with dumplings and vegetables. The side dishes that accompany each entree, such as spiced red cabbage and chestnuts and sautéed foie gras, are worth as much attention. Chocolate cinnamon mousse, lime tartalette, and other desserts are worth saving room for.

The pleasing dining room is centered around a slightly raised, curving bar. In warm weather, the glass-fronted Cashion's opens invitingly to the sidewalk, where you can also dine. Tables at the back offer a view of the small kitchen, where Cashion and her staff work away. In winter, ask for a table away from the front door, which lets in a blast of cold air with each new arrival.

Cities. 2424 18th St. NW (near Columbia Rd.). ☎ **202/328-7194.** Reservations recommended. Main courses $16.50–$24.95. AE, CB, DC, DISC, MC, V. Sun–Thurs 6–11pm, Fri–Sat 6pm–midnight. Bar Sun–Thurs 5pm–2am, Fri–Sat 5pm–3am. Valet parking $10. INTERNATIONAL.

Housed in a century-old former five-and-dime store, Cities is a restaurant-cum-travelogue. A $1.2 million renovation has dressed up the place, with additions like suede drapes, touches of mahogany and Italian leather, and soft lighting provided by hundreds of hanging filament bulbs. Once a year, the restaurant reinvents itself to reflect the cuisine, character, and culture of a different city. The music changes, and even the waiters are attired in native dress or some facsimile thereof. Until spring of 2001 or so, Cities is embracing Venice, with a menu that includes an appetizer of jumbo shrimp with oven-roasted tomatoes, fresh oregano, and melted mozzarella; and entrees of seared rare tuna with risotto crab cake and basil pesto or grilled Piedmontese silver sirloin steak with tomato taleggio pannini. The wine and champagne list complements the menu; premium wines are offered by the glass. On the walls are photographs of Venice. The bar, at the front of the restaurant, is upscale and loungy, and features light fare, starting around $7.50.

Upstairs is Privé at Cities, described by the restaurant as "a private club dedicated to the new age of self-indulgence, available to the restaurant's elite clientele and visiting celebrities." If you think you qualify, talk to your hotel concierge to arrange a visit.

MODERATE

La Fourchette. 2429 18th St. NW. ☎ **202/332-3077.** Reservations recommended on weekends. Main courses $8.95–$23.95. AE, DC, MC, V. Mon–Thurs 11:30am–10:30pm, Fri 11:30am–11pm, Sat 4–11pm, Sun 4–10pm. FRENCH.

The nonsmoking section is upstairs, but even if you don't smoke, you'll want to be downstairs, among the French-speaking clientele and Adams–Morgan regulars. The waiters are suitably crusty and the ambience is as Parisian as you'll get this side of the Atlantic— as is the food. The menu lists escargots, onion soup, bouillabaisse, and mussels Provençal, along with specials like the grilled salmon on spinach mousse and the shrimp Niçoise, ever-so-slightly crusted and sautéed in tomato sauce touched with anchovy.

Adams-Morgan & Dupont Circle Dining

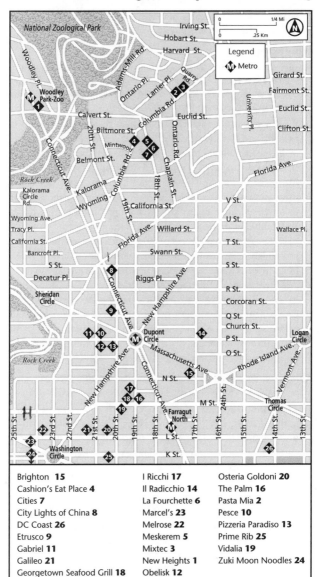

Brighton **15**	I Ricchi **17**	Osteria Goldoni **20**
Cashion's Eat Place **4**	Il Radicchio **14**	The Palm **16**
Cities **7**	La Fourchette **6**	Pasta Mia **2**
City Lights of China **8**	Marcel's **23**	Pesce **10**
DC Coast **26**	Melrose **22**	Pizzeria Paradiso **13**
Etrusco **9**	Meskerem **5**	Prime Rib **25**
Gabriel **11**	Mixtec **3**	Vidalia **19**
Galileo **21**	New Heights **1**	Zuki Moon Noodles **24**
Georgetown Seafood Grill **18**	Obelisk **12**	

A colorful mural covers the high walls; wooden tables and benches push up against bare brick walls.

INEXPENSIVE

Meskerem. 2434 18th St. NW (between Columbia and Belmont rds.). ☎ **202/462-4100.** Reservations recommended. Lunch main courses $5–$10.50; dinner main courses $8.50–$11.50. AE, CB, DC, MC, V. Sun–Thurs noon–midnight, Fri–Sat noon–2am. ETHIOPIAN.

Washington has a number of Ethiopian restaurants, but this is probably the best. It's certainly the most attractive; the three-level high-ceilinged dining room (sunny by day, candlelit at night) has an oval skylight girded by a painted sunburst and walls hung with African art and musical instruments. On the mezzanine level, you sit at messobs (basket tables) on low carved Ethiopian chairs or upholstered leather poufs. Ethiopian music (including live bands after midnight on weekends) enhances the ambience.

Diners share large platters of food, which they scoop up with a sourdough crêpelike pancake called *injera* (no silverware here). Items listed as *watt* are hot and spicy; *alitchas* are milder and more delicately flavored. You might also share an entree—perhaps *yegeb kay watt* (succulent lamb in thick, hot berbere sauce)—along with a platter of five vegetarian dishes served with tomato and potato salads. Some combination platters comprise an array of beef, chicken, lamb, and vegetables. There's a full bar; the wine list includes Ethiopian wine and beer.

✪ **Mixtec.** 1792 Columbia Rd. (just off 18th St.). ☎ **202/332-1011.** Main courses $3.95–$11.95. MC, V. Daily 11am–10pm. MEXICAN REGIONAL.

This cheerful Adams–Morgan spot attracts a clientele of neighborhood folks, D.C. chefs, and Hispanics from all over, all of whom appreciate the delicious authenticity of the regional Mexican cuisine. The kitchen is open, the dining room colorfully decorated, and the Mexican music lively.

Delicious, made-from-scratch corn and flour tortillas enhance whatever they're stuffed with. Small dishes called *antojitos* ("little whims"), in the $2.50 to $4.95 range, include *queso fundido* (a bubbling hot dish of broiled Chihuahua cheese topped with shredded spicy chorizo sausage flavored with jalapeños and cilantro). Also popular are the *enrollados mexicanos,* which are large flour tortillas wrapped around a variety of fillings: grilled chicken, beef, vegetables, salmon. The freshly prepared guacamole is excellent. A house specialty, a full entree served with rice and beans, is *mole Mexicano*—broiled chicken in a rich sauce of five peppers (the kitchen uses some 200 different spices!), sunflower and sesame seeds, onions, garlic, almonds, cinnamon, and chocolate. Choose from 30 kinds of tequila, tequila-mixed drinks, Mexican beers, and fresh fruit juices.

5 Dupont Circle

VERY EXPENSIVE

✪ **Obelisk.** 2029 P St. NW. ☎ **202/872-1180.** Reservations recommended. Fixed-price 5-course dinner $50 Tues–Thurs, $55 Fri–Sat. DC, MC, V. Tues–Sat 6–10pm. Metro: Dupont Circle. ITALIAN.

In this pleasantly spare room decorated with 19th-century French botanical prints and Italian lithographs, owner/chef Peter Pastan presents his small fixed-price menus of simple, yet sophisticated, Italian cuisine that uses the freshest possible ingredients. Pastan says his culinary philosophy is to "get the best stuff we can and try not to screw it up." Each night diners are offered two or three choices for each course. Dinner might begin with mushroom crostini, followed by Tuscan bean soup, and then an artfully arranged dish of pan-cooked cod with fried asparagus and green sauce. Dessert is a choice of cheese or baked specialties, like pear spice cake. Breads and desserts are all baked in-house and are divine. Pastan's carefully crafted wine list represents varied regions of Italy, as well as California vintages. The fixed-price menu is a deal, but wine and coffee can easily double the price per person.

EXPENSIVE

✪ **Brighton.** In the Canterbury Hotel, 1733 N St. NW. ☎ **202/296-0665.** Reservations recommended. Lunch main courses $8–$15; dinner main courses $14–$25. AE, CB, DC, DISC, MC, V. Mon–Fri 11:30am–2pm; Mon–Sat 6– 10pm. Metro: Dupont Circle or Farragut North. AMERICAN.

Brighton lies below street level, and, yet, it is one of the brightest dining rooms you'll find. (If you want cozy, go upstairs to the Union Jack Pub.) Fabric colors are deep salmon and celery, the carpeting a grassy green, the walls lemon yellow. Little vases of fresh-cut yellow roses decorate each table. Locals tend to out-number hotel guests.

The food is sublime. First comes a basket of biscuits, sweet bread, and crusty peasant bread. The appetizers and entrees that follow live up to their dramatically artistic presentation. For a starter, try the iron skillet–roasted mussels with shaved garlic and diced tomato in a Riesling Dijon broth. Entrees include lobster risotto, Maryland crab served Southwestern style, and macadamia nut–encrusted Chilean sea bass in ginger, lime, and coconut sauce—excellent! For dessert, how about the banana macadamia nut spring roll with ginger ice cream and chocolate sauce?

✪ **Gabriel.** In the Radisson Barceló Hotel, 2121 P St. NW. ☎ **202/956-6690.** Reservations recommended. Breakfast $7–$9.25, breakfast buffet $10; lunch main courses $5.50–$12.25, lunch buffet $10.75; dinner main courses $16.50–$22; tapas $3.75–$6.50; Sun brunch buffet $23.75; Wed–Fri Happy Hour buffet $9.25. AE, DC, DISC, MC, V. Mon–Fri 6:30–10:30am, Sat–Sun 7–10:30am; Mon–Fri 11am–2:30pm, Sun brunch 11am–3pm; Sun–Mon 6–9:30pm, Tues–Thurs 6–10pm, Fri–Sat 6–10:30pm. Happy Hour Wed–Fri 5:30–8pm. Free valet parking. Metro: Dupont Circle. LATIN AMERICAN/MEDITERRANEAN.

Like Coco Loco, Gabriel features Latin-accented fare and tapas; while the former is funky/hip, this is a more traditional setting. A large rectangular mahogany bar is the centerpiece of a convivial lounge area; outdoors is a small patio cafe with umbrella tables. Noted Washington chef Greggory Hill spent months studying with major chefs in various parts of Spain and Mexico before creating Gabriel's dazzlingly innovative and ever-changing menu.

Sample a variety of tapas at the bar or make a meal of several of them—plump chorizo-stuffed black figs or gambas al ajillo (shrimp in garlic oil). Entrees might include lamb with mole and sweet potato plantain mash or pork tenderloin with black-bean sauce on basmati rice. There's a well-chosen wine list, with several by-the-glass selections including dry and sweet sherries—the ideal complement to tapas. For dessert, sample the warm phyllo purse stuffed with papaya, pineapple, berries, and pistachio nuts, poised on cinnamon custard.

MODERATE

✪ **Etrusco.** 1606 20th St. NW. ☎ **202/667-0047.** Reservations recommended. Main courses $10–$17. AE, DC, MC, V. Mon–Sat 5:30–10:30pm. Metro: Dupont Circle. TUSCAN ITALIAN.

A good Italian restaurant has always been located at this address and with the same phone number. For nearly 20 years, a man named Vince MacDonald owned and constantly renamed his restaurant: Vincenzo al Sole, Trattoria al Sole, Vincenzo, Sostanza. Under new owner/chef Francesco Ricchi, Etrusco looks exactly the same as it did when Vince owned it, and it remains the sort of place you'd hope to stumble upon as a stranger in town. It's pretty, with a sophisticated but relaxed atmosphere, the food is excellent, and the service is professional. From the slate terrace at street level with umbrella tables, you descend a short flight of steps to the exquisite dining room, which resembles a trattoria with ochre and burnt sienna walls, arched skylight, and tile floor.

On the menu you'll find warm baby octopus salad, ribollita, pappardelle with shredded duck, crumb-coated grilled tuna, and the more traditional veal scaloppine and osso buco. It's very, very good.

✪ **Pesce.** 2016 P St. NW. ☎ **202/466-3474.** Reservations accepted for lunch, 6 or more at dinner. Main courses $12.50–$19. AE, DC, DISC, MC, V. Mon–Fri 11:30am–2:30pm, Sat noon–2:30pm; Mon–Thurs 5:30–10pm, Fri–Sat 5:30–10:30pm, Sun 5–9:30pm. Valet parking $4 at dinner Mon–Sat. Metro: Dupont Circle. SEAFOOD.

Nightly, from about 8:30 to 9:30, a line of people forms inside the cramped waiting area of this restaurant, sometimes trailing out the door, just to enjoy the marvelous grilled or sautéed fresh fish. This small, crowded restaurant has a convivial atmosphere, brought on, no doubt, by the collective anticipation of a pleasant meal. In a simple setting of exposed brick walls adorned with colorfully painted wooden fish, waiters scurry to bring you a basket of crusty bread, your wine selection, and the huge blackboard menu. Among the many appetizers are baked crab cake and several tasty salads. Entrees always list several pastas along with the differently prepared fish. My grilled monkfish was firm but tender and delicious upon its bed of potato purée and wild mushroom ragoût. Owner Regine Palladin brings French savoir faire to the running of her restaurant. *Tip:* Try ordering your wine by the glass; it may cost less for four people than by the bottle.

INEXPENSIVE

City Lights of China. 1731 Connecticut Ave. NW (between R and S sts.). ☎ **202/265-6688.** www.citylightsofchina.com. Reservations recommended. Lunch main courses $4.50–$13; dinner main courses $6.95–$11.95 (though some go as high as $26). AE, DC, DISC, MC, V. Mon–Thurs 11am–10:30pm, Fri 11:30am–11pm, Sat noon–11pm, Sun noon–10:30pm; dinner from 3pm daily. Validated parking after 5pm. Metro: Dupont Circle. CHINESE.

One of Washington's best Chinese restaurants outside of Chinatown, City Lights keeps getting bigger to accommodate its fans, who range from Mick Jagger to Jesse Jackson. White House workaholics frequently order takeout from here. Favorite dishes prepared by Taiwanese chef (and part owner) Kuo-Tai Soug include crisp fried Cornish hen prepared in a cinnamon-soy marinade and served with a tasty dipping sauce, Chinese eggplant in garlic sauce, stir-fried spinach, crisp fried shredded beef, and Peking duck. The setting is pretty but unpretentious: a three-tiered dining room with much of the seating in comfortable pale green leather booths and banquettes. Neat white-linen tablecloths, cloth flower arrangements in lighted niches, and green neon track lighting complete the picture. There's a full bar.

✪ **Il Radicchio.** 1509 17th St. NW. ☎ **202/986-2627.** www.robertodonna. com. Reservations not accepted. Main courses $5.50–$15. AE, CB, DC, MC, V. Mon–Thurs 11:30am–10pm, Fri–Sat 11:30am–11pm, Sun 5–10:30pm. Metro: Dupont Circle, with a 10- to 15-min. walk. ITALIAN.

What a great idea: Order a replenishable bowl of spaghetti for the table at a set price of $6.50, and each of you chooses your own sauce from a long list, at prices that range from $1.50 to $4. Most are standards, like the carbonara of cream, pancetta, black pepper, and egg yolk, and the puttanesca with black olives, capers, garlic, anchovies, and tomato. It's a great deal.

The kitchen prepares daily specials, like Saturday's oven-baked veal stew with polenta, as well as sandwiches, and an assortment of 14 wood-baked pizzas, with a choice of 28 toppings. I'd stick with the pizza, pasta, and salad.

Ingredients are fresh and flavorful, the service quick and solicitous. This branch of the restaurant draws a neighborhood crowd to its long, warm, and cozy room decorated with wall murals of barnyard animals and radicchio leaves. Il Radicchio on Capitol Hill, 223 Pennsylvania Ave. SE (☎ **202/547-5114**), caters to the overworked and underpaid Hill staffers who appreciate the restaurant's food and the price. There's a third Il Radicchio in Arlington at 1801 Clarendon Blvd. (☎ **703/ 276-2627**). Take the Metro to Rosslyn/Courthouse.

✪ **Pizzeria Paradiso.** 2029 P St. NW. ☎ **202/223-1245.** Reservations not accepted. Pizzas $6.75–$15.95; sandwiches and salads $3.25–$6.25. DC, MC, V. Mon–Thurs 11:30am–11pm, Fri 11:30am–midnight, Sat 11am–midnight, Sun noon–10pm. Metro: Dupont Circle. PIZZA/PANINI.

Peter Pastan, master chef/owner of Obelisk, right next door, owns this classy, often crowded, 16-table pizzeria. An oak-burning oven at one end of the charming room produces exceptionally doughy but light pizza crusts. As you wait, you can munch on mixed olives and gaze up at the ceiling painted to suggest blue sky peeking through ancient stone walls. Pizzas range from the plain Paradiso, which offers chunks of tomatoes covered in melted mozzarella, to the robust Siciliano, a blend of nine ingredients including eggplant and red onion. Or you can choose your own toppings from a list of 29. As popular as the pizzas are the panini (sandwiches) of homemade focaccia stuffed with marinated roasted lamb and vegetables and other fillings, and the salads, such as tuna and white bean. Good desserts but a limited wine list.

6 Foggy Bottom/West End

VERY EXPENSIVE

Marcel's. 2401 Pennsylvania Ave. NW. ☎ **202/296-1166.** Reservations recommended. Lunch main courses $13–$21; dinner main courses $19.50–$28. AE, MC, V. Mon–Fri 11:30am–2:30pm; Mon–Thurs 5:30–10:30pm, Fri–Sat 5:30–11pm. Free valet parking evenings. Metro: Foggy Bottom. FRENCH.

When you walk through the front door, look straight ahead into the exhibition kitchen and chances are you'll be staring directly into the eyes of owner/chef Robert Wiedmaier. He is firmly at the helm here, creating French dishes that include nods to his Belgian training: pan-seared skate fish with hotchpot purée (a mix of winter vegetables); duck breast with roulade of duck confit; and, for dessert, seasonal tarts such as spring pear tart with raspberry coulis. The French sommelier is expert.

Marcel's, named after Wiedmaier's young son, occupies the space that most recently was home to the restaurant Provence. When Wiedmaier took it over in spring 1999, he kept that restaurant's winning country French decor: panels of rough-hewn stone framed by rustic shutters, antique hutches displaying provincial pottery, and so on. To the right of the exhibition kitchen is a spacious bar area. Marcel's offers seating on the patio, right on Pennsylvania Avenue, in warm weather.

✪ **Melrose.** In the Park Hyatt Hotel, 1201 24th St. NW (at M St.). ☎ **202/955-3899.** Reservations recommended. Breakfast $9–$18.50; lunch main courses $15–$24; dinner main courses $20–$32; pretheater dinner $32; Sun brunch $40 ($43 with champagne). AE, CB, DC, DISC, JCB, MC, V. Mon–Fri 6:30–10am; Sat–Sun 7–10am; daily 11am–2:30pm and 5:30–10pm. Free valet parking all day. Metro: Foggy Bottom. AMERICAN.

Situated in an upscale hotel, this pretty restaurant offers fine cuisine presented with friendly flourishes. In nice weather, dine outdoors on the beautifully landscaped, sunken terrace whose greenery and towering fountain protect you from traffic noises.

The glass-walled dining room overlooks the terrace and is decorated in accents of marble and brass, with more greenery and grand bouquets of fresh flowers.

Brian McBride is the beguiling executive chef who sometimes emerges from the kitchen to find out how you like the angel-hair pasta with mascarpone and lobster, or his sautéed Dover sole with roasted peppers, forest mushrooms, and mâche. McBride is known for his use of seafood, which makes up most of the entrees and nearly all of the appetizers. Specialties of the house include shrimp ravioli with sweet corn, black pepper, tomato, and lemon-grass beurre blanc, and Melrose crab cakes with grilled vegetables in a rémoulade sauce. Desserts, like the raspberry crème brûlée or the chocolate bread pudding with chocolate sorbet, are excellent. The wine list offers 30 wines by the glass. Sunday night, the restaurant dispenses with corkage fees; feel free to bring your own bottle. Friday and Saturday nights from 7 to 11pm, a quartet plays jazz, swing, and big-band tunes; lots of people get up and dance.

EXPENSIVE

✪ **Kinkead's.** 2000 Pennsylvania Ave. NW. ☎ **202/296-7700.** www. kinkead.com. Reservations recommended. Lunch main courses $10–$18; dinner main courses $18–$26; Sun brunch $7.50–$13; light fare daily 2:20–5:30pm $4–$18. AE, DC, DISC, MC, V. Daily 11:30am–10:30pm. Free valet parking after 5:30pm. Metro: Foggy Bottom. AMERICAN/SEAFOOD.

When a restaurant has been as roundly praised as Kinkead's, you start to think no place can be that good—but Kinkead's is. An appetizer like grilled squid with creamy polenta and tomato fondue leaves you with a permanent longing for squid. The signature dish, pepita-crusted salmon with shrimp, crab, and chiles, provides a nice hot crunch before melting in your mouth. Vegetables you may normally disdain—cabbage, for instance—taste delicious here.

The award-winning chef/owner Bob Kinkead is the star at this three-tier 220-seat restaurant. He wears a headset and orchestrates his kitchen staff in full view of the upstairs dining room, where booths and tables neatly fill the nooks and alcoves of the town house. At street level is a scattering of tables overlooking the restaurant's lower level, the more casual bar and cafe, where a jazz group or pianist performs every evening. *Beware:* If the waiter tries to seat you in the "atrium," you'll be stuck at a table mall-side just outside the doors of the restaurant—yuk.

Kinkead's menu (which changes daily for lunch and again for dinner) features primarily seafood, but always includes at least one meat and one poultry entree. The wine list comprises more than 300 selections. You can't go wrong with the desserts either, like the chocolate dacquoise with cappuccino sauce. If you're hungry, but not ravenous, in late afternoon, stop in for some delicious light fare: fish-and-chips, lobster roll, soups, and salads.

✪ **Osteria Goldoni.** 1120 20th St. NW. ☎ **202/293-1511.** www. goldonirestaurant.com. Reservations recommended. Lunch main courses $10–$19; dinner main courses $16–$27. AE, CB, DC, DISC, MC, V. Mon–Fri 11:30am–2:30pm; Mon–Thurs 5:30–10pm, Fri–Sat 5–11pm, Sun 5–9:30pm. Free valet parking nightly, except Sunday, when street parking is easy. Metro: Farragut North or Farragut West. ITALIAN.

Osteria Goldoni occupies two floors. The downstairs is more casual, with a blue-tiled floor, long marble bar, and murals of circus performers; the upstairs main dining room is red-carpeted and elegant. As dramatic as the decor is the food, which some-times goes overboard in elaborateness—house-made bittersweet chocolate fettuccine with rabbit ragu? In general, lunch meals are simpler.

Still, most dishes are delicious, and service is executed with a flourish. Try the risotto with porcini mushrooms, arugula, and black truffle; or an excellent salad with radicchio, goat cheese, and ground walnuts. You might also sample the restaurant's signature dish: grilled whole fish (we had rockfish, but snapper, sea bass, and others may be available) served on a huge platter with polenta and shiitake mushrooms. Sorbets are a specialty, as is the beautiful tiramisù. Bring a party of people; Osteria Goldoni is a good spot for a celebration.

MODERATE

Zuki Moon Noodles. 824 New Hampshire Ave. NW. ☎ **202/333-3312.** www.zukimoon.com. Reservations recommended. Main courses $9–$17. AE, DC, MC, V. Mon–Fri 11:30am–2:30pm; Mon–Thurs 5–10:30pm, Fri–Sat 5–11pm, Sun 5–10pm. Valet $6 parking. Metro: Foggy Bottom. JAPANESE.

Chef and co-owner Mary Richter, who gained a strong following from her days at Cities, has only acquired more fans since opening Zuki Moon Noodles in the George Washington University Inn. Her menu features Japanese soups filled with soba, udon, or somen noodles and grilled or roasted meats or seafood; delicately done shrimp tempura; grilled squid; spring rolls; and rich sorbets and ice cream for dessert. Soups, sake, and tea come in beautiful handmade pottery. The restaurant is steps away from George Washington University, but students tend to go elsewhere (Burrito Brothers, for example). People from the neighborhood, hotel guests, office workers, and theatergoers (the Kennedy Center is close by) are the patrons here.

7 Georgetown

VERY EXPENSIVE

✪ **Michel Richard's Citronelle.** In the Latham Hotel, 3000 M St. NW. ☎ **202/625-2150.** www.citronelledc.com. Reservations required. Jacket and tie preferred at dinner. Breakfast $3.75–$14; lunch main courses $9–$25; dinner main courses $12–$35; fixed-price dinner $85 and $100. AE, DC, MC, V. Daily 6:30–10:30am; Mon–Fri noon–2pm; Sun–Thurs 6:30–9:30pm, Fri 6:30–10pm, Sat 6–10:30pm. Valet parking at dinner. INNOVATIVE FRENCH.

In March 1998, Citronelle reopened after a $2 million renovation, with much fanfare provided by the enthusiastic Washington foody establishment and Citronelle's ebullient chef/owner Michel Richard. Although Richard originally returned to his flagship restaurant, the famed Citrus in Los Angeles, after opening Citronelle in 1992, the Frenchman has now moved to Washington, happy to please the palates of Washingtonians, whose tastes he believes to be more sophisticated.

In terms of decor, the Citronelle transformation includes a wall that changes colors, a state-of-the-art wine cellar (a glass-enclosed room that encircles the dining room, displaying its 8,000 bottles and a collection of 18th- and 19th-century corkscrews), and a Provençal color scheme of mellow yellow and raspberry red.

Emerging from the bustling kitchen are appetizers like the fricassée of escargots, sweetbreads, porcinis, and crunchy pistachios, and entrees like the crispy lentil-coated salmon. The dessert of choice: Michel Richard's richly layered chocolate "bar" with sauce noisette. Citronelle's extensive wine list offers many premium by-the-glass selections, but with all those bottles staring out at you from the wine cellar, you may want to spring one.

Seasons. In the Four Seasons Hotel, 2800 Pennsylvania Ave. NW. ☎ **202/944-2000.** Reservations recommended. Breakfast $4.75–$17.25; lunch main courses $13.75–$23; dinner main courses $21–$34. AE, DC, JCB, MC, V. Mon–Fri 7–11am and noon–2:30pm, Sat–Sun 8am–noon; daily 6–10:30pm. Free valet parking. Metro: Foggy Bottom. AMERICAN.

Although Seasons is the signature restaurant of one of Washington's most upscale hotels and a major celebrity haunt, it takes a casual approach to formal dining: relaxed atmosphere, no dress code, friendly service. Seasons is candlelit at night, sunlit during the day, with windows overlooking the C&O Canal.

Scottish chef William Douglas McNeill's cuisine focuses on fresh market fare. Stellar entrees range from seared tuna with shiitake mushroom mashed potatoes and peppercorn sauce, to mustard seed–encrusted roast rack of lamb with Provençal veggies. A basket of scrumptious fresh-baked breads might include rosemary flat bread or sun-dried tomato bread drizzled with Parmesan. For dessert, consider a caramelized ginger crème brûlée. For the 12th consecutive year, *Wine Spectator* magazine has named Seasons's vast and carefully researched wine cellar one of the 100 best worldwide, bestowing its wine cellar the Crown Award in 1999.

EXPENSIVE

✪ **Mendocino Grille and Wine Bar.** 2917 M St. NW. ☎ **202/333-2912.** Reservations recommended. Lunch main courses $6.75–$18.75; dinner main courses $17–$29. AE, DC, DISC, MC, V. Mon–Sat 11:30am–3pm; Sun–Thurs 5:30–10pm, Fri–Sat 5:30–11pm. Valet parking after 6:30pm. Metro: Foggy Bottom, with a 20-min. walk. AMERICAN/CALIFORNIAN.

Rough-textured slate walls alternate with painted patches of Big Sur sky to suggest a West Coast winery in California's wine-growing region. The wall sconces resemble rectangles of sea glass and the dangling light fixtures look like turned-over wine glasses. The California-casual works, and so does the food.

Grilled seafood is the highlight: tandoori-seared yellowfin tuna presented on mushroom polenta, nori-seared Chilean sea bass with potato-ginger pot stickers. Nonseafood choices include free-range chicken served on roasted red bliss potatoes and sugar-snap peas, and grilled tenderloin of beef.

All 150 wines on the list are highly rated West Coast selections. Waiters are knowledgeable about the wines, so don't hesitate to ask questions. California-casual doesn't mean cheap: Bottles range from $20 to $525, although most are about $50.

MODERATE

Aditi. 3299 M St. NW. ☎ **202/625-6825.** Reservations recommended. Lunch main courses $4.25–$9.95; dinner main courses $5.95–$14.99. AE, DC, DISC, MC, V. Mon–Sat 11:30am–2:30pm, Sun noon–2:30pm; Sun–Thurs 5:30–10pm, Fri–Sat 5:30–10:30pm. Metro: Foggy Bottom, with a 20-min. walk. INDIAN.

This charming two-level restaurant provides a serene setting in which to enjoy first-rate Indian cooking to the tune of Indian music. A must here is the platter of assorted appetizers—*bhajia* (a deep-fried vegetable fritter), deep-fried cheese-and-shrimp pakoras, and crispy vegetable samosas stuffed with spiced potatoes and peas. Favorite entrees include *lamb biryani,* which is basmati rice pilaf tossed with savory pieces of lamb, cilantro, raisins, and almonds; and the skewered jumbo tandoori prawns, chicken, lamb, or beef—all fresh and fork tender—barbecued in the tandoor (clay oven). Sauces are on the mild side, so if you like your food fiery, inform your waiter. A kachumber salad, topped with yogurt and spices, is a refreshing accompaniment to entrees. For dessert, try *kheer,* a cooling rice pudding garnished with chopped nuts. There's a full bar.

✪ **Bistrot Lepic.** 1736 Wisconsin Ave. NW. ☎ **202/333-0111.** www.bistrolepic.net. Reservations recommended. Lunch main courses $9–$12.25; dinner main courses $14–$19. AE, CB, DC, DISC, MC, V. Tues–Sun 11:30am–2:30pm; Tues–Thurs 5:30–10pm, Fri–Sat 5:30–10:30pm, Sun 5:30–9:30pm. FRENCH.

Tiny Bistrot Lepic is the real thing—a charming French restaurant like you might find on a Parisian side street. The atmosphere is bustling and cheery, and you hear a lot of French spoken—not just by the waiters but by customers. The Bistrot is a neighborhood place, and you'll often see diners waving hellos across the room to each other, or even leaving their table to visit with those at another.

This is traditional French cooking, updated. The seasonal menu offers such entrees as grilled rockfish served with green lentils du Puy and aged balsamic sauce, and roasted rack of lamb with Yukon gold mashed potatoes and garlic sauce. We opted for specials: rare tuna served on fennel with citrus vinaigrette, and grouper with a mildly spicy lobster sauce on a bed of spinach.

The modest French wine list offers a fairly good range. The house wine, Le Pic Saint Loup, is a nice complement to most menu choices and is priced at less than $20 a bottle.

Miss Saigon. 3057 M St. NW. ☎ **202/333-5545.** Reservations recommended, especially weekend nights. Lunch main courses $5.50–$8.95; dinner main courses $6.95–$22.95. AE, DC, MC, V. Mon–Fri 11:30am–11pm (lunch menu served until 3pm), Sat–Sun noon–11pm (dinner menu served all day). Metro: Foggy Bottom, with a 20-min. walk. VIETNAMESE.

This is a charming restaurant, with tables scattered amid a "forest" of tropical foliage, and twinkly lights strewn upon the fronds of the potted palms and ferns.

The food here is delicious and authentic, though the service can be a trifle slow when the restaurant is busy. To begin, there is the crispy calamari, a favorite of Madeline Albright. House specialties include steamed flounder, caramel salmon, and "shaking beef": cubes of tender Vietnamese steak, marinated in wine, garlic, butter, and soy sauce, then sautéed with onions and potatoes and served with rice and salad. There's a full bar. Desserts range from bananas flambé au rhum to ice cream with Godiva liqueur. Not to be missed is drip-pot coffee, brewed tableside and served iced over sweetened condensed milk.

INEXPENSIVE

Ching Ching Cha. 1063 Wisconsin Ave. NW. ☎ **202/333-8288.** Reservations recommended. Tea meal $10; appetizers $1.50–$4.50. AE, DISC, MC, V. Tues–Sat 11:30am–10pm, Sun 11:30am–8pm. Metro: Foggy Bottom, with a 15-min. walk. CHINESE.

Located just below M Street, this skylit Chinese tearoom offers a pleasant respite from the crowds. You can sit on pillows at low tables or on chairs set at rosewood tables. Choices are simple: individual items like a tea-and-spice boiled egg, puff pastry stuffed with lotus seed paste, or five-spice peanuts; or the tea meal, which consists of miso soup, three marinated cold vegetables, rice, a salad, and tastings of either soy-ginger chicken, salmon with mustard-miso sauce, or steamed teriyaki-sauced tofu. Tea choices include several different green, black, medicinal, and oolong teas, plus a Fujian white tea and a ginseng brew.

✪ **Old Glory Barbecue.** 3139 M St. NW. ☎ **202/337-3406.** Reservations accepted for 6 or more Sun–Thurs, reservations not accepted Fri–Sat. Main courses $7.95–$21.95; Sunday brunch buffet $11.95, $5.95 for children 11 and under. AE, DC, DISC, MC, V. Sun–Thurs 11:30am–1am, Fri–Sat 11:30am–3am; Sun brunch 11am–3pm. Metro: Foggy Bottom. BARBECUE.

Raised wooden booths flank one side of the restaurant; an imposing, old-fashioned dark wood bar with saddle-seat stools extends down the other. Blues, rock, and country songs play in the background. Saturday and sometimes Friday nights the music is live (R&B, soul, and swing). Old Glory boasts the city's "largest selection of single-barrel and boutique bourbons," a claim that two buddies at the bar appear to be confirming firsthand. Later in the evening, the two-story restaurant becomes packed with the hard-drinkin' young and restless.

In early evening, though, Old Glory is prime for anyone—singles, families, an older crowd, although it's almost always noisy. Come for the messy, tangy, delicious spare ribs; hickory smoked chicken; tender, smoked beef brisket; or marinated, wood-fried shrimp. Six sauces are on the table, the spiciest being the vinegar-based East Carolina and Lexington. My Southern-raised husband favored the Savannah version, which reminded him of that city's famous Johnny Harris barbecue sauce. The complimentary corn muffins and biscuits, side dishes of collard greens, succotash, and potato salad, and desserts like apple crisp and coconut cherry cobbler all hit the spot.

8 Glover Park

EXPENSIVE
✪ **Sushi-Ko.** 2309 Wisconsin Ave. NW. ☎ **202/333-4187.** Reservations recommended. Main courses $14–$19. AE, MC, V. Tues–Fri noon–2:30pm; Mon 6–10:30pm, Tues–Thurs 6–10:30pm, Fri 6–11pm, Sat 5:30–11pm, Sun 5:30–10pm. Valet parking $4 for dinner. JAPANESE.

Sushi-Ko was Washington's first sushi bar when it opened 20 years ago and it remains the best in town. People know this, so sometimes there's a wait for tables. The sushi chefs are fun to watch—try to sit at the sushi bar. You can expect superb versions of sushi and sashimi standards, but the best items are daily specials: sometimes sea trout napoleon (diced sea trout layered between rice crackers), tuna tartare, seared Maine diver scallops with uni butter and forest mushrooms, or grilled Alaskan halibut with morels, fiddleheads, and wild leeks. The tempuras and teriyakis are also excellent. And there's a long list of sakes.

INEXPENSIVE
✪ **Austin Grill.** 2404 Wisconsin Ave. NW. ☎ **202/337-8080.** www.austingrill.com. Reservations not accepted. Main courses $6–$15. AE, DC, DISC, MC, V. Mon 11:30am–10:30pm, Tues–Thurs 11:30am–11pm, Fri 11:30am–midnight, Sat 11am–midnight, Sun 11am–10:30pm. TEX-MEX.

Owner Rob Wilder opened his grill in 1988 to replicate the easygoing lifestyle, Tex-Mex cuisine, and music he loved when he lived in Austin. The good food and festive atmosphere make this a great place for the kids, a date, or a group of friends. Austin Grill is loud; as the night progresses, conversation eventually drowns out the sound of the taped music (everything from Ry Cooder to Natalie Merchant).

Fresh ingredients are used to create outstanding crabmeat quesadillas, "Lake Travis" nachos (tostadas slathered with red onion, refried beans, and cheese), a daily fish special (like rockfish fajitas), key lime pie, and excellent versions of standard fare (chicken enchiladas, guacamole, pico de gallo, and so on). The margaritas are awesome.

Austin Grill's upstairs overlooks the abbreviated bar area below. An upbeat decor includes walls washed in shades of teal and clay and adorned with whimsical coyotes, cowboys, Indians, and cacti. Arrive by 6pm weekends if you don't want to wait; weekdays are less crowded. This is the original Austin Grill; another District Austin Grill is located near the MCI Center at 750 E St. NW (☎ 202/393-3776).

9 Dining at Sightseeing Attractions

With so many great places to eat in Washington, I have a hard time recommending those at sightseeing attractions. Most are overpriced and too crowded, even if they are convenient. A few, however, are worth mentioning—for their admirable cuisine, noteworthy setting, or both.

Head for the Capitol's numerous restaurants for a chance to rub elbows with your senators and representatives. But keep in mind these spots are usually open only for lunch and can get very crowded; to lessen the chances of a long wait, try going about 30 minutes before the posted closing time. You'll find the **House of Representatives Restaurant** (also called the "Members' Dining Room") in Room H118, at the South end of the Capitol (☎ **202/225-6300**). This fancy chandelier-and-gilt-framed dining room is open to the public but doesn't take reservations (it's also open for breakfast). When the House is in session, however, the dining room closes to the public from 11am to 1:30pm. Senators frequent the **Senate Dining Room** (☎ **202/ 224-2350**), but you'll need a letter from your senator to eat here (jacket and tie required for men, no jeans for men or women). More accommodating is the **Refectory,** first floor, Room S112, Senate side of the Capitol (☎ **202/224-4870**), which serves sandwiches and other light luncheon fare.

Most Hill staffers eat at places like the **Longworth Building Cafeteria,** Independence Avenue and South Capitol Street SE (☎ **202/225-4410**), where they can just grab a bite from a fairly nice food court. But by far the best deal for visitors is the **Dirksen Senate Office Building South Buffet Room,** First and C streets NE (☎ **202/224-4249**). For just $10.45 per adult, $6.85 per child (including a nonalcoholic drink and dessert), you can choose from a buffet that includes a carving station and eight other hot entrees. It's often crowded, but they will take reservations for parties of more than five.

In the same neighborhood, two institutions offering great deals and views (of famous sites or people) are the **Library of Congress**'s Cafeteria (☎ **202/707-8300**), and its more formal Montpelier Room (☎ **202/707-8300**), where the buffet lunch is only $10.50; and the **Supreme Court**'s Cafeteria (☎ **202/479-3246**), where you'll likely spy a justice or two enjoying the midday meal.

Among museum restaurants, the ones that shine are the **Corcoran Gallery of Art**'s Café des Artistes (☎ **202/ 639-1786**); the new six-story Atrium Cafe in the **National Museum of Natural History** (☎ **202/357-2700**); the **National Gallery of Art**'s Terrace Café (☎ **202/216-2492**) and Garden Café (☎ **202/216-2494**); and the **Phillips Collection**'s snug Café (☎ **202/387-2151**).

5

Exploring Washington, D.C.

Washington, D.C., boasts some major attractions. The White House, the U.S. Capitol, and the Supreme Court house the three branches of the world's most powerful government. The Library of Congress is the largest in the world, and the Smithsonian is the largest museum in the world. The National Air and Space Museum holds the record for highest attendance on a single day: 118,437 people on April 14, 1984. The Washington Monument is the world's tallest freestanding work of masonry. The Pentagon, America's military HQ, is the world's largest office building.

For a visitor, all these superlatives can be a bit intimidating. But rest assured; even if you don't have time to see and do it all, the monuments, memorials, and museums will still be there for your next trip. Only the city around them will change. So see as many landmarks as you dare, but leave time for touring one of the wonderful museums off the National Mall, wandering through one of the charming neighborhoods, or jogging or biking the acres and acres of gorgeous parkland.

This chapter should help. Check out the Web sites of individual attractions. Look at the National Park Service site, **www. nps.gov/nacc**, to learn about NPS attractions reviewed on these pages, including the presidential memorials, Rock Creek Park, and the C&O Canal. The Smithsonian Institution) also has its own Web site, **www.si.edu**, which will help you get you to the home pages of its individual museums.

1 The Three Major Houses of Government

Three of the most visited sights in Washington are the buildings housing the executive, legislative, and judicial branches of the U.S. government. All are stunning and offer fascinating lessons in American history and government.

✪ **The White House.** 1600 Pennsylvania Ave. NW (visitor entrance gate at E St. and E. Executive Ave.). ☎ **202/456-7041** or 202/208-1631. www. whitehouse.gov. Free admission. Tues–Sat 10am–noon. Closed some days for official functions; call before you go (the number operates 24 hours a day). Metro: McPherson Square (if you are going straight to the White House) or Federal Triangle (if you are getting tour tickets from the White House Visitor Center).

If you think you're going to get the Monica Lewinsky tour, think again. Whether you visit the White House on a VIP guided tour or go through self-guided, you will see just what your escorts (Secret Service agents, by the way) want you to see, and that doesn't include the Oval Office. So forget the scandal, if you can, and soak up the history of this house that has served as a residence, office, reception site, and world embassy for every U.S. president since John Adams.

White House Tours and Tickets: Tickets to tour the White House are only required in peak season, between mid-March and Labor Day and the month of December. If you're planning to visit the White House at any other time, you simply proceed to the southeast gate of the White House, at E Street and East Executive Avenue NW, and join the line. If you're in line by noon, you should gain admittance.

In peak or off-peak season, you should know a few things before heading out to the president's home. Try first to allow time to tour the **White House Visitor Center,** 1450 Pennsylvania Ave., in the Department of Commerce Building, between 14th and 15th streets (see listing below for more information). White House tours take place mornings only, Tuesday through Saturday. There are no public rest rooms or telephones in the White House, and picture taking and videotaping are prohibited. (The Visitor Center has rest rooms—another reason to stop here first.)

For those visiting the White House during peak season, you must obtain tickets, which can be done in one of two ways: You can obtain advance tickets from your congressperson or senator months in advance (see box). Or you can pick up free tickets at the White House Visitor Center.

Tickets are timed for tours between 10am and noon and are issued on the day of the tour on a first-come, first-served basis starting at 7:30am. During the busy season, people start lining up outside the Visitor Center as early as 4am to snag one of the approximately 4,500 tickets distributed daily. A National Park ranger stamps the hand of each person in line and that person receives up to four tickets. To gain admittance on the tour, some-one in your party must have the magic stamp. (This is to prevent

The White House Area

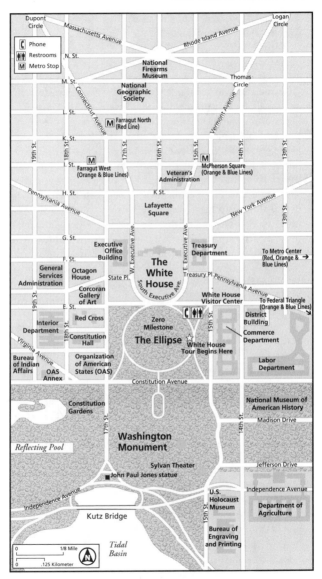

Legend:
- **C** Phone
- **††** Restrooms
- **M** Metro Stop

Dupont Circle
Logan Circle
Massachusetts Avenue
Rhode Island Avenue
N. St.
National Firearms Museum
Thomas Circle
M. St.
National Geographic Society
Connecticut Avenue
L. St.
M Farragut North (Red Line)
K. St.
19th St.
18th St.
17th St.
16th St.
15th St.
14th St.
13th St.
I. St.
M Farragut West (Orange & Blue Lines)
Veteran's Administration
M McPherson Square (Orange & Blue Lines)
Pennsylvania Avenue
H. St.
K St.
New York Avenue
Lafayette Square
13th St.
G. St.
Executive Office Building
W. Executive Ave.
E. Executive Ave.
Treasury Department
To Metro Center (Red, Orange & Blue Lines) →
F. St.
The White House
General Services Administration
Octagon House
State Pl.
South Executive Ave.
Treasury Pl.
Pennsylvania Avenue
Corcoran Gallery of Art
White House Visitor Center
To Federal Triangle (Orange & Blue Lines) ↘
19th St.
E. St.
Red Cross
Zero Milestone
C **††**
15th St.
District Building
Interior Department
18th St.
Commerce Department
Constitution Hall
The Ellipse ☆ White House Tour Begins Here
Virginia Avenue
Bureau of Indian Affairs
Organization of American States (OAS)
Labor Department
OAS Annex
Constitution Avenue
Constitution Gardens
National Museum of American History
17th St.
Madison Drive
Reflecting Pool
Washington Monument
14th St.
Jefferson Drive
Sylvan Theater
■ John Paul Jones statue
U.S. Holocaust Museum
Independence Avenue
Independence Avenue
Department of Agriculture
15th St.
Kutz Bridge
Tidal Basin
Bureau of Engraving and Printing

0 ___ 1/8 Mile
0 ___ .125 Kilometer
(N)

scalping.) The ticket counter closes when the supply for that day is gone. Tickets are valid only for the date and time issued.

Both the VIP tour and the not-so-VIP tour go through the same rooms; on the 25- to 35-minute VIP tour, a Secret Service agent guides you and answers questions at the end; on the 15- to 20-minute self-guided tour, a Secret Service agent posted in each room will answer any questions you have along the way. Highlights of the tour include the following rooms:

The Gold-and-White East Room: This room has been the scene of presidential receptions, weddings (Lynda Bird Johnson, for one), and other dazzling events. This is where the president entertains visiting heads of state and the place where seven of the eight presidents who died in office (all but Garfield) laid in state. It was also where Nixon resigned. The room is decorated in the early-20th-century style of the Theodore Roosevelt renovation; it has parquet Fontainebleau oak floors and white-painted wood walls with fluted pilasters and classical relief inserts. Note the famous Gilbert Stuart portrait of George Washington that Dolley Madison saved from the British torch during the War of 1812.

The Green Room: Thomas Jefferson's dining room is today used as a sitting room. He designed a revolving door with trays on one side so that servants could leave dishes on the kitchen side. Then he would twirl the door and allow guests to help themselves, thus retaining his privacy. Green watered silk fabric covers walls hung with notable paintings by Gilbert Stuart and John Singer Sargent.

The Oval Blue Room: This room, decorated in the French Empire style chosen by James Monroe in 1817, is where presidents and first ladies have officially received guests since the Jefferson administration. The walls, on which hang portraits of five presidents (including Rembrandt Peale's portrait of Thomas Jefferson and G. P. A. Healy's of Tyler), are covered in reproductions of early 19th-century French and American wallpaper. Grover Cleveland, the only president to wed in the White House, was married in the Blue Room. This room was also where the Reagans greeted the 52 Americans liberated after being held hostage in Iran for 444 days, and every year it's the setting for the White House Christmas tree.

The Red Room: Several portraits of past presidents, plus Albert Bierstadt's *View of the Rocky Mountains* and a Gilbert Stuart portrait of Dolley Madison, hang here. It's used as a reception room, usually for afternoon teas.

How to Obtain Advance Tickets for White House Tours

Tuesday through Saturday between 8:15am and 8:45am, the doors of the White House are open for special VIP tours to those with tickets. To obtain these tickets, contact the local or Washington office of your U.S. senator or representative—at least 6 months in advance, because each legislator receives no more than 10 tickets a week to distribute. These early tours guarantee you admission during the busy tourist season, when thousands line up during the 2 hours daily that the White House is open to the public. The VIP tours are no more extensive than the regular tours; it's just that your Secret Service guides provide commentary as you proceed through the ground-floor and state-floor rooms. You should still expect to stand in line to get in, and you will still be one among many (70 or 80). The VIP tour lasts about 25 or 35 minutes and you're not allowed to ask questions until the tour is over.

The State Dining Room: Modeled after late-18th-century neoclassical English houses, this room is a superb setting for state dinners and luncheons. Theodore Roosevelt, a big-game hunter, hung a large moose head over the fireplace and other trophies on the walls. Below G. P. A. Healy's portrait of Lincoln is an inscription written by John Adams on his second night in the White House (FDR had it carved into the mantel): "I Pray Heaven to Bestow The Best of Blessings on THIS HOUSE and on All that shall here-after Inhabit it. May none but Honest and Wise Men ever rule under This Roof."

Note: All visitors, even those with VIP congressional tour passes, should call ☎ 202/456-7041 before setting out in the morning; occasionally the White House is closed to tourists on short notice because of unforeseen events.

✪ **The Capitol.** At the east end of the Mall, entrance on E. Capitol St. and 1st St. NW. ☎ **202/225-6827.** www.aoc.gov, www.house.gov, www.senate.gov. Free admission. Mar–Aug daily 9am–6pm; guided tours Mon–Fri 9:30am–5pm and Sat 9:30am–3:30m, guides posted to assist but not guide you Sun 1–4:30pm. Sept–Feb daily 9am–4:30pm; guided tours Mon–Sat 9am–4pm. Closed Jan 1, Thanksgiving, and Dec 25. Parking at Union Station or on neighborhood streets. Metro: Union Station or Capitol South.

For all tours, whether during the peak season (March through August) or the slow season (September through February), find the east front side of the Capitol, whose sidewalks extend from the Capitol steps and plaza to 1st Street, across from the Library of Congress and Supreme Court.

During the peak season, you have three options if you'd like a guided tour of the Capitol. If you are part of a group of more than 15 people, you can call ☎ **202/224-4910** to reserve a guided tour time, thus avoiding a wait in line. Reservations are very limited, so call months in advance. If you are touring as individuals or as a family, you can try to arrange ahead (try 6 months in advance for spring through August tours) to obtain VIP tour tickets from the office of your representative or senator for the morning tours (departing at intervals between 8 and 8:30am). For these tours, you enter the Capitol through the Law Library door on the east front side of the Capitol, facing the Supreme Court, on the ground level, just to the right of the grand staircase.

The red flag side designates the line for guided tours; the green flag side denotes the self-guided tours line. Guided tours in peak season take place every 30 minutes and admit 50 people at a time. You may have a long wait, especially if you arrive in the morning. Your best bet is midday, late afternoon, or early evening. All tours are free. Whether you are self-guided or Capitol Guide Service–guided, you must have a ticket to enter the Capitol during the peak season, every day but Sunday.

The House and Senate galleries are always open to visitors, but passes are required when these galleries are in session. After 6pm, however, you may enter either gallery without a pass and watch the session to its conclusion. To obtain visitor passes in advance, contact your representative or senator, either in your home state, or by calling the Capitol switchboard at ☎ **202/224-3121.** You'll know the House and/or the Senate is in session if you see flags flying over their respective wings of the Capitol, or you can check the weekday "Today in Congress" column in the *Washington Post* for details on times of the House and Senate sessions and committee hearings.

Note: Different sections of the Capitol are currently undergoing renovation. Call ahead (☎ **202/225-6827**) to find out whether the work underway means that the building or the areas of the building you wish to visit are closed to tourists.

✪ **The Supreme Court of the United States.** One 1st St. NE (between E. Capitol St. and Maryland Ave. NE). ☎ **202/479-3000.** www. supremecourtus.gov. Free admission. Mon–Fri 9am–4:30pm. Closed all federal holidays. Metro: Capitol South or Union Station.

Capitol Hill

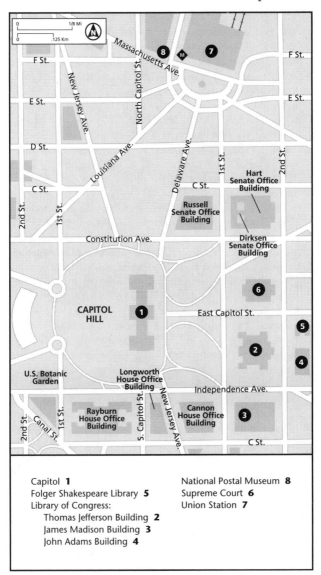

Capitol **1**
Folger Shakespeare Library **5**
Library of Congress:
    Thomas Jefferson Building **2**
    James Madison Building **3**
    John Adams Building **4**

National Postal Museum **8**
Supreme Court **6**
Union Station **7**

The highest tribunal in the nation, the Supreme Court is charged with deciding whether actions of Congress, the president, the states, and lower courts are in accord with the Constitution and with applying the Constitution's enduring principles to novel situations and a changing country. The Supreme Court's chief justice and eight associate justices have the power of judicial review: authority to invalidate legislation or executive action that conflicts with the Constitution. Out of the 7,500 cases submitted to it each year, the Supreme Court hears only about 100 cases, many of which deal with issues vital to the nation. The Court's rulings are final, reversible only by another Supreme Court decision, or in some cases, an Act of Congress or a constitutional amendment.

Until 1935 the Supreme Court met in the Capitol. Architect Cass Gilbert designed the stately Corinthian marble palace that houses the Court today. The building was considered rather grandiose by early residents: One justice remarked that he and his colleagues ought to enter such pompous precincts on elephants.

If you're in town when the Court is in session, try to see a case being argued (call ☎ **202/479-3211** for details). The Court meets Monday through Wednesday from 10am to noon, and, on occasion, from 1 to 2pm, starting the first Monday in October through late April, alternating in approximately 2-week intervals between "sittings" to hear cases and deliver opinions and "recesses" for consideration of business before the Court. Mid-May to late June, you can attend brief sessions (about 15 minutes) at 10am on Monday, when the justices release orders and opinions. Arrive at least an hour early—even earlier for highly publicized cases—to line up for seats, about 150 of which are allotted to the general public.

Contact your senator or congressperson (at least 2 months in advance) to arrange a guided tour of the Court; on a self-guided tour you won't be able to go everywhere the guided tour does.

2 The Presidential Memorials

Tributes to American presidents appear in various guises all over the city. There's the Washington Monument, the Lincoln and Jefferson Memorials, Theodore Roosevelt Island, and the Franklin Delano Roosevelt Memorial, the most recent addition. Unfortunately, none of these lies directly on a Metro line, so you can expect a bit of a walk from the specified station. Alternatively, you can go by Tourmobile (see "Organized Tours," near the end of this chapter).

Washington Monument. Directly south of the White House (at 15th St. and Constitution Ave. NW). ☎ **202/426-6841.** Free admission. Early Apr–Labor Day daily 8am–midnight; early Sept–early Apr daily 9am–5pm. Last elevators depart 15 min. before closing (arrive earlier). Closed Dec 25, open until noon July 4. Metro: Smithsonian, with a 10-min. walk.

Although admission to the Washington Monument is free, you'll still have to get a ticket. The ticket booth is located at the bottom of the hill from the monument, on 15th Street NW between Independence and Constitution avenues. The tickets grant admission at half-hour intervals between the stated hours. You can obtain tickets on the day of the tour; if you want to save yourself the trouble and get them in advance (up to six tickets per person), call Ticketmaster (☎ **800/505-5040**), but you'll pay $1.50 per ticket plus a 50¢ service charge per transaction.

After a 2-year restoration, the 555-foot Washington Monument stands proud, its mortar and masonry exterior now shining clean, its elevator refurbished, new climate-control system installed, 897 interior steps scrubbed, and 193 carved commemorative stones polished. The repair work was the monument's first major restoration since it opened in 1888.

Though most of the massive restoration was completed in 2000, there is a chance that final interior work may take place in winter 2001. To be safe, call ahead just to make sure the monument is open on the day you plan to visit.

The monument stands at the very center of Washington, D.C., landmarks, and the 360-degree views from the top are spectacular. Due east are the Capitol and Smithsonian buildings; due north is the White House; due west is the Lincoln Memorial (with Arlington National Cemetery beyond); and due south is the Jefferson Memorial, overlooking the Tidal Basin and the Potomac River. It's like being at the center of a compass, and it provides a marvelous orientation to the city.

Climbing the 897 steps is verboten, but the large elevator whisks visitors to the top in just 70 seconds. If, however, you're avid to see more of the interior, "Down the Steps" tours are given, subject to staff availability, weekends at 10am and 2pm.

✪ **Lincoln Memorial.** Directly west of the Mall in Potomac Park (at 23rd St. NW, between Constitution and Independence aves.). ☎ **202/426-6842.** Free admission. Daily 8am–midnight. Closed Dec 25. Metro: Foggy Bottom, with a 30-min. walk.

Washington, D.C., Attractions

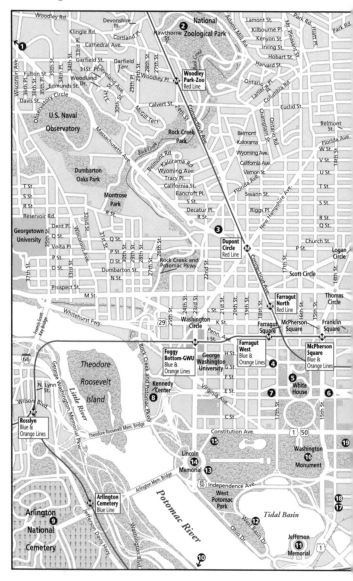

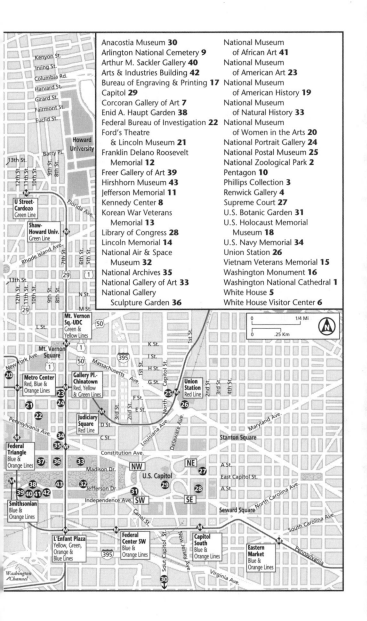

Anacostia Museum **30**
Arlington National Cemetery **9**
Arthur M. Sackler Gallery **40**
Arts & Industries Building **42**
Bureau of Engraving & Printing **17**
Capitol **29**
Corcoran Gallery of Art **7**
Enid A. Haupt Garden **38**
Federal Bureau of Investigation **22**
Ford's Theatre
 & Lincoln Museum **21**
Franklin Delano Roosevelt
 Memorial **12**
Freer Gallery of Art **39**
Hirshhorn Museum **43**
Jefferson Memorial **11**
Kennedy Center **8**
Korean War Veterans
 Memorial **13**
Library of Congress **28**
Lincoln Memorial **14**
National Air & Space
 Museum **32**
National Archives **35**
National Gallery of Art **33**
National Gallery
 Sculpture Garden **36**

National Museum
 of African Art **41**
National Museum
 of American Art **23**
National Museum
 of American History **19**
National Museum
 of Natural History **33**
National Museum
 of Women in the Arts **20**
National Portrait Gallery **24**
National Postal Museum **25**
National Zoological Park **2**
Pentagon **10**
Phillips Collection **3**
Renwick Gallery **4**
Supreme Court **27**
U.S. Botanic Garden **31**
U.S. Holocaust Memorial
 Museum **18**
U.S. Navy Memorial **34**
Union Station **26**
Vietnam Veterans Memorial **15**
Washington Monument **16**
Washington National Cathedral **1**
White House **5**
White House Visitor Center **6**

107

This beautiful and moving testament to the nation's greatest president attracts millions of visitors annually. Like its fellow presidential memorials, this one was a long time in the making. Although it was planned as early as 1867—2 years after Lincoln's death—it was not until 1912 that Henry Bacon's design was completed, and the memorial itself was dedicated in 1922.

The neoclassical templelike structure, similar in architectural design to the Parthenon in Greece, has 36 fluted Doric columns representing the states of the Union at the time of Lincoln's death, plus two at the entrance. On the attic parapet are 48 festoons symbolizing the number of states in 1922, when the monument was erected. Hawaii and Alaska are noted in an inscription on the terrace. Due east is the Reflecting Pool, lined with American elms and stretching 2,000 feet toward the Washington Monument and the Capitol beyond.

The memorial chamber has limestone walls inscribed with the Gettysburg Address and Lincoln's Second Inaugural Address. Most powerful, however, is Daniel Chester French's 19-foot-high seated statue of Lincoln, which disappears from your sightline as you get close to the base of the memorial, then emerges slowly into view as you ascend the stairs.

Limited free parking is available along Constitution Avenue and south along Ohio Drive.

Jefferson Memorial. South of the Washington Monument on Ohio Dr. (at the south shore of the Tidal Basin). ☎ **202/426-6841.** Free admission. Daily 8am–midnight. Closed Dec 25. Metro: Smithsonian, with a 20- to 30-min. walk, or by Tourmobile.

The site for the Jefferson Memorial was of extraordinary importance. The Capitol, the White House, and the Mall were already located in accordance with architect Pierre L'Enfant's master plan for the city, but there was no spot for such a project that would maintain L'Enfant's symmetry. So the memorial was built on land reclaimed from the Potomac River, now known as the Tidal Basin. Franklin Delano Roosevelt, who laid the cornerstone in 1939, had all the trees between the Jefferson Memorial and the White House cut down so that he could see the memorial every morning.

The memorial is a columned rotunda in the style of the Pantheon in Rome, whose classic architecture Jefferson himself introduced to this country (he designed his home, Monticello, and the earliest University of Virginia buildings in Charlottesville). On the Tidal Basin side, the sculptural group above the entrance depicts Jefferson with Benjamin Franklin, John Adams, Roger Sherman, and Robert Livingston, all of whom worked on drafting the Declaration of Independence. The domed interior of the memorial contains the 19-foot bronze statue of Jefferson standing on a 6-foot pedestal of black Minnesota granite.

Rangers present 20- to 30-minute programs throughout the day as time permits. There's free 1-hour parking.

✪ **Franklin Delano Roosevelt Memorial.** In West Potomac Park, about midway between the Lincoln and Jefferson Memorials, on the west shore of the Tidal Basin. ☎ **202/426-6841.** Free admission. Ranger staff on duty daily 8am–midnight. Closed Dec 25. Free parking along W. Basin and Ohio drs. Metro: Smithsonian, with a 30-min. walk or by Tourmobile.

The FDR Memorial has proven to be the most popular of the presidential memorials since it opened on May 2, 1997, attracting twice as many visitors as any other. Its popularity has to do as much with the design as the man it honors. This is a 7½-acre outdoor memorial that lies beneath a wide-open sky. It stretches out, rather than rising up, across the stone-paved floor. Granite walls define the four "galleries," each representing a different term in FDR's presidency from 1933 to 1945.

One drawback of the FDR memorial is the noise. Planes on their way to or from nearby Reagan National Airport zoom overhead, and the many displays of cascading water can sound thunderous.

The memorial is probably the most accessible tourist attraction in the city; as at most of the National Park Service locations, wheelchairs are available for free use on-site. If you don't see a posting of tour times, look for a ranger and request a tour; the rangers are happy to oblige.

3 The Smithsonian Museums

The Smithsonian's collection of nearly 141 million objects spans the entire world and all of its history, its peoples and animals (past and present), and our attempts to probe into the future. The sprawling institution comprises 14 museums (9 of them on the Mall), as well as the National Zoological Park in Washington, D.C. (there are 2 additional museums in New York City).

It all began with a $500,000 bequest from James Smithson, an English scientist who had never visited the U.S. When he died in 1829, he willed his entire fortune to his nephew, stipulating that should the nephew die without heirs (which he did in 1835), the estate should go to the U.S. to found "at Washington . . . an establishment for the increase and diffusion of knowledge." In 1846, Congress created a corporate entity to carry out Smithson's will, and the federal government agreed to pay 6% interest on the bequeathed funds in perpetuity. Since then, private donations have swelled Smithson's original legacy many times over.

To find out information about any of the Smithsonian museums, you call the same number: ☎ **202/357-2700** or TTY 202/357-1729. The information specialists who answer are very professional and always helpful.

Smithsonian Information Center (the "Castle"). 1000 Jefferson Dr. SW. ☎ **202/357-2700** or TTY 202/357-1729. www.si.edu. E-mail: info@info. si.edu. Daily 9am–5:30pm, info desk 9am–4pm. Closed Dec 25. Metro: Smithsonian.

Make this your first stop. Built in 1855, this Norman-style red sandstone building, popularly known as the "Castle," is the oldest building on the Mall, yet it holds the impressively high-tech and comprehensive Smithsonian Information Center.

The main information area here is the Great Hall, where a 20-minute video overview of the institution runs throughout the day in two theaters. There are two large schematic models of the Mall (as well as a third in Braille), and two large electronic maps of Washington allow visitors to locate nearly 100 popular attractions and Metro and Tourmobile stops. Interactive videos, some at children's heights, offer extensive information about the Smithsonian and other capital attractions and transportation (the menus seem infinite).

Parking Near the Mall

Don't drive; use the Metro. If you're hell-bent on driving on a weekday, though, set out early to nab one of the Independence or Constitution avenues spots that become legal at 9:30am, when rush hour ends. Arrive about 9:15 and just sit in your car until 9:30am (to avoid getting a ticket), then hop out and stoke the meter. So many people do this, that if you arrive at 9:30 or later, you'll find most of the street parking spots gone.

The Mall

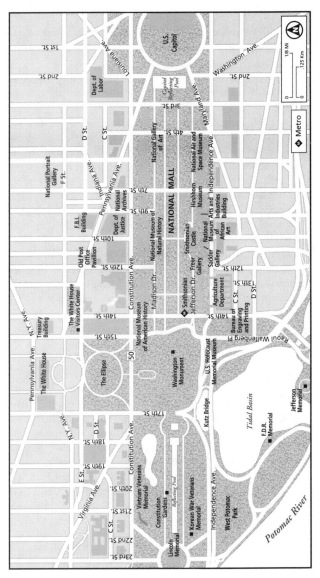

The entire facility is accessible to persons with disabilities. Daily Smithsonian events appear on monitors. Most of the museums are within easy walking distance of the facility.

Anacostia Museum. 1901 Fort Place SE (off Martin Luther King Jr. Ave.). ☎ **202/357-2700.** www.si.edu/anacostia. Free admission. Daily 10am–5pm. Closed Dec 25. Metro: Anacostia, then take a W1 or W2 bus directly to the museum.

Note: This museum is being renovated, but should open again to the public by spring 2001.

This unique Smithsonian establishment was created in 1967 as a neighborhood museum. Expanding its horizons over the years, the museum today is devoted to the identification, documentation, protection, and interpretation of the African-American experience, focusing on Washington, D.C., and the Upper South. The permanent collection includes about 7,000 items, ranging from videotapes of African-American church services to art, sheet music, historic documents, textiles, glassware, and anthropological objects. In addition, the Anacostia produces a number of shows each year and offers a comprehensive schedule of free educational programs and activities in conjunction with exhibit themes.

Arthur M. Sackler Gallery. 1050 Independence Ave. SW. ☎ **202/357-2700.** www. si.edu/asia. Free admission. Daily 10am–5:30pm; in summer, museum stays open Thurs until 8pm, but call to confirm. Closed Dec 25. Metro: Smithsonian.

Opened in 1987, this national museum of Asian art presents traveling exhibitions from major cultural institutions in Asia, Europe, and the United States. In the recent past, these have focused on such wide-ranging areas as 15th-century Persian art and culture; contemporary Japanese woodblock prints and ceramics; photographs of Asia; and art highlighting personal devotion in India. Art from the permanent collection supplements the traveling shows: It includes Khmer ceramics; ancient Chinese jades, bronzes, paintings, and lacquerware; 20th-century Japanese ceramics and works on paper; ancient Near Eastern works in silver, gold, bronze, and clay; and stone and bronze sculptures from South and Southeast Asia. Since the museum's opening, 11th- to 19th-century Persian and Indian paintings, manuscripts, calligraphies, miniatures, and bookbindings from the collection of Henri Vever have enhanced Sackler's original gift.

The Sackler is part of a museum complex that also houses the National Museum of African Art. It shares its staff and research facilities with the adjacent Freer Gallery, to which it is connected via an underground exhibition space.

The Sackler offers museum programs (including many wonderful experiences for children and families), free daily highlight tours (highly recommended), films, events, and temporary exhibits.

Arts & Industries Building. 900 Jefferson Dr. SW (on the south side of the Mall). ☎ 202/357-2700. www.si.edu/ai. Free admission. Daily 10am–5:30pm. Closed Dec 25. Metro: Smithsonian.

Completed in 1881 as the first U.S. National Museum, this red brick and sandstone structure was the scene of President Garfield's Inaugural Ball. (It looks quite similar to the Castle, so don't be confused; from the Mall, the Arts & Industries Building is the one on the left.) From 1976 through the mid-1990s, it housed exhibits from the 1876 U.S. International Exposition in Philadelphia—a celebration of America's centennial that featured the latest advances in technology. Some of these Victorian tools, products, art, and other objects are on permanent display. The building displays rotating exhibits, such as "Speak to My Heart: Communities of Faith and Contemporary African-American Life," on view through February 28, 2001.

Singers, dancers, puppeteers, and mimes perform in the **Discovery Theater** (open all year except August, with performances weekdays and on selected Saturdays). Call ☎ **202/357-1500** for show times and ticket information; admission of about $5 is charged. Don't miss the charming Victorian motif shop on the first floor. Weather permitting, a 19th-century carousel operates across the street, on the Mall.

☼ Freer Gallery of Art. On the south side of the Mall (at Jefferson Dr. and 12th St. SW). ☎ **202/357-2700.** www.si.edu/asia. Free admission. Daily 10am–5:30pm; in summer, gallery stays open Thurs until 8pm, but call to confirm. Closed Dec 25. Metro: Smithsonian (Mall or Independence Ave. exit).

Charles Lang Freer, a collector of Asian and American art from the 19th and early 20th centuries, gave the nation 9,000 of these works for his namesake gallery's opening in 1923. Freer's original interest was, in fact, American art, but his good friend James McNeill Whistler encouraged him to collect Asian works as well. Eventually, the latter became predominant. Freer's gift included funds to construct a museum and an endowment to add objects of the highest quality to the Asian collection only, which now numbers more than 28,000 objects. It includes Chinese and Japanese sculpture, lacquer, metalwork, and ceramics; early Christian illuminated manuscripts; Iranian manuscripts, metalwork, and miniatures; ancient Near Eastern metalware; and South Asian sculpture and paintings.

Among the American works are more than 1,200 pieces (the world's largest collection) by Whistler, including the famous **Peacock Room.** Originally a dining room designed for the London mansion of F. R. Leyland, the Peacock Room displayed a Whistler painting called *The Princess from the Land of Porcelain.* But after his painting was installed, Whistler was dissatisfied with the room as a setting for his work. When Leyland was away from home, Whistler painted over the very expensive leather interior and embellished it with paintings of golden peacock feathers. Not surprisingly, a rift ensued between Whistler and Leyland. After Leyland's death, Freer purchased the room, painting and all, and had it shipped to his home in Detroit. It is now permanently installed here. Other American painters represented in the collections are Thomas Wilmer Dewing, Dwight William Tryon, Abbott Henderson Thayer, John Singer Sargent, and Childe Hassam.

Housed in a grand granite and marble building that evokes the Italian Renaissance, the pristine Freer has lovely skylit galleries. The main exhibit floor centers on an open-roof garden court. An underground exhibit space connects the Freer to the neighboring Sackler Gallery, and both museums share the **Meyer Auditorium,** which is used for free chamber music concerts, dance performances, Asian feature films, and other programs. Inquire about these, as well as children's activities and free tours given daily, at the information desk.

Hirshhorn Museum & Sculpture Garden. On the south side of the Mall (at Independence Ave. and 7th St. SW). ☎ **202/357-2700.** www.si. edu/hirshhorn. Free admission. Museum daily 10am–5:30pm; in summer, museum stays open Thurs until 8pm, but call to confirm. Sculpture Garden daily 7:30am–dusk. Closed Dec 25. Metro: L'Enfant Plaza (Smithsonian Museums/Maryland Ave. exit).

This museum of modern and contemporary art is named after Latvian-born Joseph H. Hirshhorn, who, in 1966, donated his vast art collection—more than 4,000 drawings and paintings and some 2,000 pieces of sculpture—to the United States "as a small repayment for what this nation has done for me and others like me who arrived here as immigrants." At his death in 1981, Hirshhorn bequeathed an additional 5,500 artworks to the museum, and numerous other donors have greatly expanded his legacy.

Constructed 14 feet above ground on sculptured supports, the donut-shaped concrete and granite building shelters a verdant plaza courtyard where sculpture is displayed. The light and airy interior follows a simple circular route that makes it easy to see every exhibit without getting lost in a honeycomb of galleries. Natural light from floor-to-ceiling windows makes the inner galleries the perfect venue for viewing sculpture, second only, perhaps, to the beautiful tree-shaded sunken Sculpture Garden across the street (don't miss it). Paintings and drawings are installed in the outer galleries, along with intermittent sculpture groupings.

A rotating show of about 600 pieces is on view at all times. The collection features just about every well-known 20th-century artist and touches on most of the major trends in Western art since the late 19th century, with particular emphasis on our contemporary period. Among the best-known pieces are Rodin's *The Burghers of Calais* (in the Sculpture Garden), Hopper's *First Row Orchestra,* de Kooning's *Two Women in the Country,* and Warhol's *Marilyn Monroe's Lips.*

Pick up a free calendar when you enter to find out about free films, lectures, concerts, and temporary exhibits. An outdoor cafe is open during the summer. Free tours of the collection and the Sculpture Garden are given daily; call about them.

National Air & Space Museum. On the south side of the Mall (between 4th and 7th sts. SW), with entrances on Jefferson Dr. or Independence Ave. ☎ **202/357-2700** or 202/357-1686 for IMAX ticket information. www.nasm.si.edu. Free admission. Daily 10am–5:30pm. Free 1½-hour highlight tours daily at 10:15am and 1pm. Closed Dec 25. Metro: L'Enfant Plaza (Smithsonian Museums/Maryland Ave. exit).

This museum chronicles the story of the mastery of flight, from Kitty Hawk to outer space. Plan to spend several hours here. During the tourist season and on holidays, arrive before 10am to make a rush for the film ticket line when the doors open. The not-to-be-missed IMAX films shown here are immensely popular, and tickets to most shows sell out quickly. You can purchase tickets up to 2 weeks in advance, but they are available only at the

Langley Theater box office on the first floor. Five or more films play each day, most with aeronautical or space exploration themes: *To Fly, Cosmic Voyage, Mission to Mir,* and *Michael Jordan to the Max* (celebrating a different kind of flying) are four that were playing in 2000. Tickets cost $5.50 for adults, $4.25 for ages 2 to 21 and seniors 55 and older; they're free for children under 2. You can also see IMAX films most evenings after the museum's closing (call for details and ticket prices, which are higher than daytime prices). At the same time, purchase tickets for a show at the Albert Einstein Planetarium.

Popular from the day it opened in 1976, the Air and Space Museum has suffered a lot of wear and tear over the years. Its design, too, has made it vulnerable to the elements—those skylights and walls of windows leak, it turns out. Repair work began in 2000 and will continue into 2001, closing some galleries you might wish to visit, so call ahead.

Highlights of the first floor include famous airplanes (such as the *Spirit of St. Louis*) and spacecraft (the *Apollo 11* Command Module); the world's only touchable moon rock; numerous exhibits on the history of aviation and air transportation; galleries in which you can design your own jet plane and study astronomy; and rockets, lunar exploration vehicles, manned spacecraft, and guided missiles. (See "Washington Women" box in this chapter about attractions that highlight women's achievements.)

How Things Fly, a gallery that opened in 1996 to celebrate the museum's 20th anniversary, includes wind and smoke tunnels, a boardable Cessna 150 airplane, and dozens of interactive exhibits that demonstrate principles of flight, aerodynamics, and propulsion. All the aircraft, by the way, are originals.

Kids love the walk-through **Skylab orbital workshop** on the second floor. Other galleries here highlight the solar system; U.S. manned space flights, sea-air operations, aviation during both world wars, and artists' perceptions of flight. An important exhibit is **Beyond the Limits: Flight Enters the Computer Age,** illustrating the primary applications of computer technology to aerospace.

An attractive cafeteria and a restaurant are on the premises.

National Museum of African Art. 950 Independence Ave. SW. ☎ **202/ 357-4600.** www.si.edu/nmafa. Free admission. Daily 10am–5:30pm. Closed Dec 25. Metro: Smithsonian.

Founded in 1964, and part of the Smithsonian since 1979, the National Museum of African Art moved to the Mall in 1987 to share a subterranean space with the Sackler Gallery (see above) and the Ripley Center. Its aboveground domed pavilions reflect the arch motif of the neighboring Freer.

The museum collects and exhibits ancient and contemporary art from the entire African continent, but its permanent collection of more than 7,000 objects (shown in rotating exhibits) highlights the traditional arts of the vast sub-Saharan region. Most of the collection dates from the 19th and 20th centuries. Also among the museum's holdings are the **Eliot Elisofon Photographic Archives,** comprising 300,000 photographic prints and transparencies and 120,000 feet of film on African arts and culture. Permanent exhibits include **"The Ancient West African City of Benin, A.D. 1300–1897"; "The Ancient Nubian City of Kerma, 2500–1500 B.C."** (ceramics, jewelry, and ivory animals); **"The Art of the Personal Object"** (everyday items such as chairs, headrests, snuffboxes, bowls, and baskets); and **"Images of Power and Identity."**

Inquire at the desk about special exhibits, workshops (including excellent children's programs), storytelling, lectures, docent-led tours, films, and demonstrations. A comprehensive events schedule provides a unique opportunity to learn about the diverse cultures and visual traditions of Africa.

National Museum of American Art. 8th and G sts. NW. ☎ **202/ 357-2700.** www.nmaa.si.edu. Free admission. Daily 10am–5:30pm. Closed Dec 25. Metro: Gallery Place–Chinatown.

This museum and the adjoining National Portrait Gallery are closed for a major renovation until 2003. What you're missing is the largest collection of American Art in the world: more than 37,500 works representing 2 centuries of the nation's national art history. Some of the collection is on display at the Renwick Gallery (see below).

✪ **National Museum of American History.** On the north side of the Mall (between 12th and 14th sts. NW), with entrances on Constitution Ave. and Madison Dr. ☎ **202/357-2700.** www.americanhistory.si.edu. Free admission. Daily 10am–5:30pm. Closed Dec 25. Metro: Smithsonian or Federal Triangle.

This is the museum that deals with "everyday life in the American past" and the external forces that have helped to shape our national character. Its massive contents range from General Washington's Revolutionary War tent to Archie Bunker's chair.

At press time, many changes were anticipated, especially on the first floor, to include the creation of an extensive visitor center and the replacement of the longtime **"A Material World"** exhibit. In its place will be the important new **"American Legacies,"** which will explain to visitors the importance of the museum's collections. The exhibit, which will probably still be under construction through 2001, plans to explore themes of telling stories with artifacts, collecting the nation's history, and exploring American identity.

Here's what you *can* count on seeing. On the first floor are exhibits that explore the development of farm machinery, power machinery, transportation, timekeeping, phonographs, and typewriters. The **"Palm Court"** on this level includes the interior of Georgetown's Stohlman's Confectionery Shop as it appeared around 1900 and part of an actual 1902 Horn and Hardart Automat, where you can stop and have an ice cream. You can have your mail stamped "Smithsonian Station" at a post office that had been located in Headsville, West Virginia, from 1861 to 1971, when it was brought, lock, stock, and barrel, to the museum.

If you enter from the Mall, you'll find yourself on the second floor. Here, you have the intriguing opportunity to see expert textile conservationists painstakingly working to preserve the huge, original Star-Spangled Banner, 30 by 42 feet. This is the very flag that inspired Francis Scott Key to write the U.S. national anthem in 1814. Now it lies outstretched, flat, behind glass, in a lab specially designed for this restoration work, which will continue through 2002.

The museum holds many other major exhibits. **"After the Revolution"** focuses on the everyday activities of ordinary 18th-century Americans. **"Field to Factory"** tells the story of African-American migration from the south between 1915 and 1940. One of the most popular exhibits on the second floor is **"First Ladies: Political Role and Public Image,"** which displays the first ladies' gowns and tells you a bit about each of these women. Infinitely more interesting, I think, is the neighboring exhibit, **"From Parlor to Politics: Women and Reform in America, 1890–1925,"** which chronicles the changing roles of women as they've moved from domestic to political and professional pursuits.

Yet another wonderful new exhibit, this one on the third floor, is **"The American Presidency."** It explores the power and meaning of the presidency by studying those who have held the position. Here, too, is the first American flag to be called Old Glory (1824).

The gift shop is vast—it's the largest of the Smithsonian shops.

✪ **National Museum of Natural History.** On the north side of the Mall (at 10th St. and Constitution Ave. NW), with entrances on Madison Dr. and Constitution Ave. ☎ **202/357-2700** or 202/633-7400 for information about IMAX films. www.mnh.si.edu. Free admission. Daily 10am–5:30pm. Closed Dec 25. Free highlight tours Mon–Thurs 10:30am and 1:30pm, Fri 10:30am. Metro: Smithsonian or Federal Triangle.

Before you step inside the museum, stop outside first, on the Ninth Street side of the building, to visit the new butterfly garden. Four habitats—wetland, meadow, wood's edge, and urban garden—are on view, designed to beckon butterflies and visitors alike. The garden is at its best in warm weather, but it's open year-round.

Now go inside. Children refer to this Smithsonian showcase as the dinosaur museum (there's a great dinosaur hall), or sometimes the elephant museum (a huge African bush elephant is the first amazing thing you see if you enter the museum from the Mall). Whatever you call it, the National Museum of Natural History is the largest of its kind in the world, and one of the most visited museums in Washington. It contains more than 120 million artifacts and specimens, everything from Ice Age mammoths to the legendary **Hope Diamond.**

On the Mall Level, off the Rotunda, is the **fossil collection,** which traces evolution back billions of years and includes a 3.5-billion-year-old stromatolite (blue-green algae clump) fossil—one of the earliest signs of life on Earth—and a 70-million-year-old dinosaur egg. **"Life in the Ancient Seas"** features a 100-foot-long mural depicting primitive whales, a life-size walk-around diorama of a 230-million-year-old coral reef, and more than 2,000 fossils that chronicle the evolution of marine life. The **"Dinosaur Hall"** displays giant skeletons of creatures that dominated the Earth for 140 million years before their extinction about 65 million years ago. Here, too, you'll find a spectacular living coral reef in a 3,000-gallon tank, a second 1,800-gallon tank housing a subarctic sea environment typical of the Maine coast, and a giant squid exhibit focusing on the world's largest invertebrates.

Upstairs is the popular **"O. Orkin Insect Zoo,"** where kids will enjoy looking at tarantulas, centipedes, and the like, and crawling through a model of an African termite mound. The **"Ocean Planet"** exhibit gives a video tour of what lies beneath the ocean surface and teaches you about ocean conservation. The new hall, the **Janet Annenberg Hooker Hall of Geology, Gems, and Minerals,** includes all you want to know about earth science, from volcanology to the importance of mining in our daily lives. Interactive computers, animated graphics, and a multimedia presentation of the "big picture" story of the Earth are some of the things that have brought the exhibit and museum up-to-date.

Don't miss **Discovery Center,** funded by the Discovery Channel, and featuring an IMAX theater with a six-story-high screen for 2-D and 3-D. The theater box office is on the first floor of the museum; purchase tickets at least 30 minutes before the screening. Ticket prices are $6.50 for adults and $5.50 for children (2 to 17) and seniors (adults over 55).

National Portrait Gallery. 8th and F sts. NW. ☎ **202/357-2700.** www.npg.si.edu. Free admission. Daily 10am–5:30pm. Closed Dec 25. Metro: Gallery Place–Chinatown.

Note: This museum and the National Museum of American Art are closed for renovations until 2003. Check the museum Web site to keep abreast of renovation progress. The gallery enshrines those who have made "significant contributions to the history, development, and culture of the United States."

✪ **National Postal Museum.** 2 Massachusetts Ave. NE (at 1st St.). ☎ **202/633-9360.** www.si.edu/postal. Free admission. Daily 10am–5:30pm. Closed Dec 25. Metro: Union Station.

Opened in 1993, this most recent addition to the Smithsonian complex occupies the lower level of the palatial beaux arts quarters of the City Post Office Building, which was designed by architect Daniel Burnham and is situated next to Union Station. This museum is, somewhat surprisingly, a hit for the whole family.

Bring your address book and you can send postcards to the folks back home through an interactive exhibit that issues a cool postcard and stamps it. That's just one feature that makes the museum visitor-friendly. Many of its exhibits involve easy-to-understand activities, like postal-themed video games.

The museum documents America's postal history from 1673 (about 170 years before the advent of stamps, envelopes, and mailboxes) to the present. (*Fun fact:* Did you know that a dog sled was used to carry mail in Alaska until 1963 when it was replaced by an airplane?) In the central gallery, titled **Moving the Mail,** three planes that carried mail in the early decades of the 20th century are suspended from a 90-foot atrium ceiling. In **Binding the Nation,** historic correspondence illustrates how mail kept families together in the developing nation. Several exhibits deal with the famed Pony Express, a service that lasted less than 2 years but was romanticized to legendary proportions by Buffalo Bill and others. In the Civil War section you'll learn about Henry "Box" Brown, a slave who had himself "mailed" from Richmond to a Pennsylvania abolitionist in 1856. **The Art of Cards and Letters** gallery displays rotating exhibits of personal (sometimes wrenching, always interesting) correspondence taken from different periods in history, as well as greeting cards and postcards. And an 800-square-foot gallery, called **Artistic License: The Duck Stamp Story,** focuses on federal duck stamps (first issued in 1934 to license waterfowl hunters), with displays on the hobby of duck hunting and the ecology of American water birds. In addition, the museum houses a vast research library for philatelic researchers and scholars, a stamp store, and a museum shop. Inquire about free walk-in tours at the information desk.

National Zoological Park. Adjacent to Rock Creek Park, main entrance in the 3000 block of Connecticut Ave. NW. ☎ **202/673-4800** (recording) or 202/673-4717. www.si. edu/natzoo. Free admission. Daily May to mid-Sept (weather permitting): grounds 6am–8pm, animal buildings 10am–6pm. Daily mid-Sept to May: grounds 6am–6pm, animal buildings 10am–4:30pm. Closed Dec 25. Metro: Woodley Park–Zoo or Cleveland Park.

Established in 1889, the National Zoo is home to some 500 species, many of them rare and/or endangered. A leader in the care, breeding, and exhibition of animals, it occupies 163 beautifully landscaped and wooded acres and is one of the country's most delightful zoos. Among the animals you'll see are cheetahs, zebras, camels, elephants, tapirs, antelopes, brown pelicans, kangaroos, hippos, rhinos, giraffes, apes, and, of course, lions, tigers, and bears (oh my). Be sure to catch **Amazonia,** where you can hang out for an hour peering up into the trees and still not spy the sloth—do yourself a favor and ask the attendant where it is.

Zoo facilities include stroller-rental stations, a number of gift shops, a bookstore, and several paid-parking lots. The lots fill up quickly, especially on weekends, so arrive early or take the Metro.

Renwick Gallery of the National Museum of American Art. Pennsylvania Ave. and 17th St. NW. ☎ **202/357-2700.** www.nmaa.si.edu. Free admission. Daily 10am–5:30pm. Closed Dec 25. Metro: Farragut West or Farragut North.

A department of the National Museum of American Art (though nowhere near it), the Renwick is a showcase for American creativity in crafts, housed in a historic mid-1800s landmark building of the French Second Empire style. The original home of the Corcoran Gallery, it was saved from demolition by First Lady Jacqueline Kennedy in 1963, when she recommended that it be renovated as part of the Lafayette Square restoration. In 1965, it became part of the Smithsonian and was renamed for its architect, James W. Renwick, who also designed the Smithsonian Castle. Although the setting—especially the magnificent Victorian Grand Salon with its wainscoted plum walls and 38-foot skylight ceiling—evokes another era, the museum's contents are mostly contemporary. The rich and diverse displays boast changing crafts exhibits and contemporary works from the museum's permanent collection. Typical exhibits range from **"Uncommon Beauty: The Legacy of African-American Craft Art"** to **"Calico and Chintz: Antique Quilts from the Patricia Smith Collection."** The **Grand Salon** on the second floor, styled in 19th-century opulence, is newly refurbished and currently displays 170 paintings and sculpture from the closed-for-renovation American Art Museum. The great thing about this room, besides its fine art and grand design, is its cushiony, velvety banquettes; perfect resting stops for the weary sightseer.

The Renwick offers a comprehensive schedule of crafts demonstrations, lectures, and films. Inquire at the information desk. And check out the museum shop near the entrance for books on crafts, design, and decorative arts, as well as craft items, many of them for children. *Note:* It is the main branch of the National Museum of American Art that is closed for renovation, not this offshoot.

4 Elsewhere on the Mall

National Archives. Constitution Ave. NW (between 7th and 9th sts.; enter via Constitution Ave.). ☎ **202/501-5000** for information on exhibits and films or 202/501-5400 for research information. www.nara.gov. Free admission. Exhibition Hall: Apr–Aug daily 10am–9pm; Sept–Mar daily 10am–5:30pm. Free tours Mon–Fri 10:15am and 1:15pm by appointment only; call (way ahead) ☎ **202/501-5205.** Call for research hours. Closed Dec 25. Metro: Archives/Navy Memorial.

Note: The Rotunda of the National Archives will close for renovation July 5, 2001, and will reopen in 2003.

Keeper of America's documentary heritage, the National Archives display our most cherished treasures in appropriately awe-inspiring surroundings. On permanent display in the **Rotunda of the Exhibition Hall** are the nation's three most important documents—the Declaration of Independence, the Constitution of the United States, and the Bill of Rights—as well as the 1297 version of the Magna Carta.

High above and flanking the documents are two larger-than-life murals painted by Barry Faulkner. One, entitled *The Declaration of Independence,* shows Thomas Jefferson presenting a draft of the Declaration to John Hancock, the presiding officer of the Continental Congress; the other, entitled *The Constitution,* shows James Madison submitting the Constitution to George Washington at the Constitutional Convention. In the display cases on either side of the Declaration are exhibits that rotate over a 3-year period, for instance, **"American Originals,"** which features 26 compelling American historical documents ranging from George Washington's Revolutionary War expense account to the Louisiana Purchase Treaty signed by Napoléon.

The Archives serve as much more than a museum of cherished documents. Famous as a center for genealogical research—Alex Haley began his work on *Roots* here—it is sometimes called "the nation's memory." This federal institution is charged with sifting through the accumulated papers of a nation's official life—billions of pieces a year—and determining what to save and what to destroy. The Archives' vast accumulation of census figures, military records, naturalization papers, immigrant passenger lists, federal documents, passport applications, ship manifests, maps, charts, photographs, and motion picture film (and that's not the half of it) spans 2 centuries. And it's all available for the perusal of anyone age 16 or over (call for details). If you're casually thinking about tracing your roots, stop by Room 400, where a staff member can advise you about the time and effort that will be involved, and, if you decide to pursue it, exactly how to proceed.

✪ **National Gallery of Art.** 4th St. and Constitution Ave. NW, on the north side of the Mall (between 3rd and 7th sts. NW). ☎ **202/737-4215.** www.nga.gov. Free admission. Mon–Sat 10am–5pm, Sun 11am–6pm. Closed Jan 1 and Dec 25. Metro: Archives, Judiciary Square, or Smithsonian.

Most people don't realize it, but the National Gallery of Art is not part of the Smithsonian complex. Housing one of the world's foremost collections of Western painting, sculpture, and graphic arts from the Middle Ages through the 20th century, the National Gallery has a dual personality. The original West Building, designed by John Russell Pope (architect of the Jefferson Memorial and the National Archives), is a neoclassic marble masterpiece with a domed rotunda over a colonnaded fountain and high-ceilinged corridors leading to delightful garden courts. It was a gift to the nation from Andrew W. Mellon, who also contributed the nucleus of the collection, including 21 masterpieces from the Hermitage, two Raphaels among them. The ultramodern East Building, designed by I. M. Pei and opened in 1978, is composed of two adjoining triangles with glass walls and lofty tetrahedron skylights. The pink Tennessee marble from which both buildings were constructed was taken from the same quarry; it forms an architectural link between the two structures.

The West Building: On the main floor of the West Building, about 1,000 paintings are always on display. To the left (as you enter off the Mall) is the **Art Information Room,** housing the **Micro Gallery,** where those so inclined can design their own tours of the permanent collection and enhance their knowledge of art via user-friendly computers. Continuing to the left of the rotunda are galleries of 13th- through 18th-century Italian paintings and sculpture, including what is generally considered the finest Renaissance collection outside Italy; here you'll see the only painting by Leonardo da Vinci housed outside Europe: *Ginevra de'Benci.* Paintings by El Greco, Ribera, and Velázquez highlight the Spanish galleries; Grünewald, Dürer, Holbein, and Cranach can be seen in the German; Van Eyck, Bosch, and Rubens in the Flemish; and Vermeer, Steen, and Rembrandt in the Dutch. To the right of the rotunda, galleries display 18th- and 19th-century French paintings (including one of the world's greatest impressionist collections), paintings by Goya, works of late-18th- and 19th-century Americans—such as Cole, Stuart, Copley, Homer, Whistler, and Sargent—and of somewhat earlier British artists, such as Constable, Turner, and Gainsborough. Room decor reflects the period and country of the art shown: Travertine marble adorns the Italian gallery, and somber oak panels define the Dutch galleries. Down a flight of stairs are prints and drawings, 15th- through 20th-century sculpture (with many pieces by Daumier, Degas, and Rodin), American native 18th- and 19th-century paintings, Chinese porcelains, small Renaissance bronzes, 16th-century Flemish tapestries, and 18th-century decorative arts.

On May 23, 1999, the long-awaited National Gallery Sculpture Garden, just across 7th Street from the West Wing, opened to the public. The park takes up 2 city blocks and features open lawns; a central pool with a spouting fountain (the pool turns into an ice rink in winter); an exquisite glassed-in pavilion housing a cafe; 17 sculptures by renowned artists, like Roy Lichtenstein and

Avoiding the Crowds at the National Gallery of Art

The best time to visit the National Gallery is Monday morning; the worst is Sunday afternoon.

Ellsworth Kelly (and Scott Burton, whose "Six-Part Seating" you're welcome to sit upon); and informally landscaped shrubs, trees, and plants. It continues to be a hit, especially in warm weather, when people sit on the wide rim of the pool and dangle their feet in the water while they eat their lunch.

The East Building: This wing was conceived as a showcase for the museum's collection of 20th-century art, including Picasso, Miró, Matisse, Pollock, and Rothko, and to house the art history research center. Always on display are the massive aluminum Calder mobile dangling under a seven-story skylight and an exhibit called **"Small French Paintings,"** which I love.

Pick up a floor plan and calendar of events at an information desk to find out about National Gallery exhibits, films, tours, lectures, and concerts. Highly recommended are the free highlight tours (call for exact times) and audio tours. The gift shop is a favorite. The gallery offers several good dining options, the best being the Terrace Café, which sometimes tailors its menu to complement a particular exhibit.

✪ **United States Holocaust Memorial Museum.** 100 Raoul Wallenberg Place (formerly 15th St. SW; near Independence Ave., just off the Mall). ☎ **202/488-0400.** www. ushmm.org. Free admission. Daily 10am–5:20pm. Closed Yom Kippur and Dec 25. Metro: Smithsonian.

When this museum opened in 1993, officials thought perhaps 500,000 people might visit annually. In fact, 2 million come here every year. And if you arrive without a reserved ticket specifying an admission time, you'll have to join the line of folks seeking to get one of the 1,575 day-of-sale tickets the museum makes available each day (see "Holocaust Museum Touring Tips"). The museum opens its doors at 10am, and the tickets are usually gone by 10:30am. Get in line early in the morning (around 8am).

The noise and bustle of so many visitors can be disconcerting and certainly at odds with the experience that follows. But things settle down as you begin your tour. When you enter, you will be issued an identity card of an actual victim of the Holocaust. By 1945, 66% of those whose lives are documented on these cards were dead.

The tour begins on the fourth floor, where exhibits portray the events of 1933 to 1939, the years of the Nazi rise to power. On the third floor (documenting 1940 to 1944), exhibits illustrate the narrowing choices of people caught up in the Nazi machine. You board a Polish freight car of the type used to transport Jews from the Warsaw ghetto to Treblinka and hear recordings of survivors telling what life in the camps was like. This part of the museum documents the details of the Nazis' "Final Solution" for the Jews.

The second floor recounts a more heartening story: It depicts how non-Jews throughout Europe, by exercising individual action and responsibility, saved Jews at great personal risk. Denmark—led by a king who swore that if any of his subjects wore a yellow star, so would he—managed to hide and save 90% of its Jews. Exhibits follow on the liberation of the camps, life in Displaced Persons camps, emigration to Israel and America, and the Nuremberg trials. A highlight at the end of the permanent exhibition is a 30-minute film called *Testimony,* in which Holocaust survivors tell their personal stories. The tour concludes in the hexagonal Hall of Remembrance, where you can meditate on what you've experienced and light a candle for the victims.

The museum recommends not bringing children under 11; for older children, it's advisable to prepare them for what they'll see. There's a cafeteria and museum shop on the premises.

You can see some parts of the museum without tickets. These include two special areas on the first floor and concourse: **Daniel's Story: Remember the Children** and the **Wall of Remembrance** (Children's Tile Wall), which commemorates the 1.5 million children killed in the Holocaust, and the **Wexner Learning Center.**

5 Other Government Agencies

Bureau of Engraving & Printing. 14th and C sts. SW. ☎ **202/874-3188** or 202/874-2330. www.bep.treas.gov. Free admission. Mon–Fri 9am–2pm (last tour begins at 1:40pm); in summer, extended hours 5–6:40pm. Closed Dec 25–Jan 1 and federal holidays. Metro: Smithsonian (Independence Ave. exit).

This is where they will literally show you the money. A staff of 2,600 works around the clock churning it out at the rate of about $700 million a day. Everyone's eyes pop as they walk past rooms overflowing with new greenbacks. But although the money draws everyone in, it's not the whole story. The bureau prints many other products, including 25 billion postage stamps a year, presidential portraits, and White House invitations.

As many as 5,000 people line up each day to get a peek at all that moola, so arriving early, especially during the peak tourist season, is essential. Consider securing VIP tickets from your senator or congressperson; VIP tours are offered Monday through Friday at 8am and 8:15am, with an additional 4pm tour added in summer, and last about 45 minutes. Write at least 3 months in advance for tickets.

Tickets for general public tours are required April through September. Obtain a same-day ticket specifying a tour time from the ticket booth on Raoul Wallenburg Place to enter the building at its 14th Street entrance. Booth hours are from 8am to 2pm all year long and reopening in summer from 3:30 to 6:30pm. October through March, you simply proceed to the 14th Street entrance where a staff person will gather you up with others for the next tour.

The 40-minute guided tour begins with a short introductory film. Then you'll see, through large windows, the processes that go into the making of paper money: the inking, stacking of bills, cutting, and examination for defects. Most printing here is done from engraved steel plates in a process known as *intaglio,* the hardest to counterfeit because the slightest alteration will cause a noticeable change in the portrait in use. Additional exhibits include bills no longer in use, counterfeit money, and a $100,000 bill designed for official transactions (since 1969, the largest denomination printed for the general public is $100).

Federal Bureau of Investigation. J. Edgar Hoover FBI Building, E St. NW (between 9th and 10th sts.). ☎ **202/324-3447.** www.fbi.gov. Free admission. Mon–Fri 8:45am–4:15pm. Closed Jan 1, Dec 25, and other federal holidays. Metro: Metro Center or Federal Triangle.

More than half a million visitors (many of them kids) come here annually to learn why crime doesn't pay. Tours begin with a short videotape presentation about the priorities of the bureau: organized crime, white-collar crime, terrorism, foreign counterintelligence, illegal drugs, and violent crimes. En route, you'll learn about this organization's history (it was established in 1908) and its activities over the years. You'll see some of the weapons used by big-time gangsters such as Al Capone, John Dillinger, Bonnie and Clyde, and "Pretty Boy" Floyd; and an exhibit on counterintelligence operations. There are photographs of the 10 most-wanted

---

FBI Touring Tips

To beat the crowds, arrive before 8:45am or write to a senator or congressperson for a scheduled reservation as far in advance as possible. Guided congressional tours take place at 9:45am, 11:45am, 1:45pm, and 3:15pm, with an additional 2:45pm tour added in summer. Contact your senator or representative at least 3 months ahead to schedule an appointment for constituent groups of six or fewer. Tours last 1 hour and are conducted every 20 to 30 minutes, depending upon staff availability. The building closes at 4:15pm, so you must arrive at least 1 hour before closing if you want to make the last tour (arrive even earlier in high season). Once inside, you'll undergo a security check.

---

fugitives (2 were recognized at this exhibit by people on the tour, and 10 have been located via the FBI-assisted TV show *America's Most Wanted*).

Other exhibits deal with white-collar crime, organized crime, terrorism, drugs, and agent training. On display are more than 5,000 weapons, most of them confiscated from criminals.

You'll also visit the **DNA lab** (the very same where tests did indeed conclude that the stains on Monica Lewinsky's dress were (a) semen and (b) "to a reasonable degree of scientific certainty" genetically linked to Bill Clinton). Other stops include the **Firearms Unit** (where agents determine whether a bullet was fired from a given weapon); the **Material Analysis Unit** (where the FBI can deduce the approximate make and model of a car from a tiny piece of paint); the unit where hairs and fibers are examined; and a **Forfeiture and Seizure Exhibit**—a display of jewelry, furs, and other proceeds from illegal narcotics operations. The tour ends with a bang, lots of them in fact, when an agent gives a sharpshooting demonstration and discusses the FBI's firearm policy and gun safety.

If you're coming between April and August, try to arrange for tickets ahead of time. At the height of this season, you could get in line at 8 in the morning and still not get in. Even if you call for advance tickets, the tour office might tell you that they won't confirm your tickets until a week before your visit.

✪ **Library of Congress.** 1st St. SE (between Independence Ave. and E. Capitol St.). ☎ **202/707-8000.** www/loc.gov. Free admission. Madison

Building Mon–Fri 8:30am–9:30pm, Sat 8:30am–6pm. Jefferson Building Mon–Sat 10am–5:30pm. Closed federal holidays. Stop at the information desk inside the Jefferson Building's west entrance on 1st St. to obtain same-day free tickets to tour the Library. Tours of the Great Hall: Mon–Sat 11:30am, and 1, 2:30, and 4pm. Metro: Capitol South.

The question most frequently asked by visitors to the Library of Congress is: Where are the books? The answer is: on the 532 miles of shelves located throughout the library's three buildings. Established in 1800, "for the purchase of such books as may be necessary for the use of Congress," the library today serves the nation, with holdings for the visually impaired (for whom books are recorded on cassette and/or translated into Braille), research scholars, and college students. Its first collection of books was destroyed in 1814 when the British burned the Capitol (where the library was then housed) during the War of 1812. Thomas Jefferson then sold the institution his personal library of 6,487 books as a replacement, and this became the foundation of what would grow to become the world's largest library.

Today, the collection contains a mind-boggling 113 million items. Its buildings house more than 17 million catalogued books, over 49 million manuscripts, over 13 million prints and photographs, more than 2 million audio holdings (discs, tapes, talking books, and so on), more than 700,000 movies and video-tapes, musical instruments from the 1700s, and the letters and papers of everyone from George Washington to Groucho Marx. The library offers a year-round program of free concerts, lectures, and poetry readings, and houses the Copyright Office.

As impressive as the scope of the library's effects and activities is the building that holds them: the ornate Italian Renaissance–style Thomas Jefferson Building, which reopened to the public May 1, 1997, after an $81.5 million, 12-year overhaul. The Jefferson Building was erected between 1888 and 1897 to hold the burgeoning collection and establish America as a cultured nation with magnificent institutions equal to anything in Europe. Fifty-two painters and sculptors worked for 8 years on its interior. There are floor mosaics of Italian marble, allegorical paintings on the overhead vaults, more than 100 murals, and numerous ornamental cornucopias, ribbons, vines, and garlands within. The building's exterior has 42 granite sculptures and yards of bas-reliefs. Especially impressive are the exquisite marble **Great Hall** and the **Main Reading Room,** the latter under a

160-foot dome. Originally intended to hold the fruits of at least 150 years of collecting, the Jefferson was, in fact, filled up in 13. It is now supplemented by the James Madison Memorial Building and the John Adams Building. On permanent display in the Jefferson Building's Great Hall is an exhibit called **"Treasures of the Library of Congress,"** which rotates a selection of more than 200 of the rarest and most interesting items from the library's collection—like Thomas Jefferson's rough draft of the Declaration of Independence with notations by Benjamin Franklin and John Adams in the margins, and the contents of Lincoln's pockets when he was assassinated.

If you have to wait for a tour, take in the 12-minute orientation film in the Jefferson's new visitors' theater or browse in its new gift shop. Pick up a calendar of events when you visit. Free concerts take place in the Jefferson Building's elegant Coolidge Auditorium; find out more about them on the LOC concert Web site: **lcweb.loc.gov/rr/perform/concert**. The **Madison Building** offers interesting exhibits and features classic, rare, and unusual films in its Mary Pickford Theater.

6 War Memorials

Korean War Veterans Memorial. Just across from the Lincoln Memorial (east of French Dr., between 21st and 23rd sts. NW). ☎ **202/426-6841.** Free admission. Rangers on duty daily 8am–midnight except Dec 25. Ranger-led interpretive programs are given throughout the day. Metro: Foggy Bottom.

This privately funded memorial founded in 1995 honors those who served in Korea, a 3-year conflict (1950–1953) that produced almost as many casualties as Vietnam. It consists of a circular "Pool of Remembrance" in a grove of trees and a triangular "Field of Service," highlighted by lifelike statues of 19 infantrymen, who appear to be trudging across fields. In addition, a 164-foot-long black granite wall depicts the array of combat and support troops that served in Korea (nurses, chaplains, airmen, gunners, mechanics, cooks, and others); a raised granite curb lists the 22 nations that contributed to the U.N.'s effort there; and a commemorative area honors KIAs, MIAs, and POWs. Limited parking is available along Ohio Drive.

United States Navy Memorial and Naval Heritage Center. 701 Pennsylvania Ave. NW. ☎ **800/821-8892** or 202/737-2300. www.lonesailor.org. Free admission. Mon–Sat 9:30am–5pm. Closed Jan 1, Thanksgiving, and Dec 25. Metro: Archives–Navy Memorial.

Authorized by Congress in 1980 to honor the men and women of the U.S. Navy, this memorial comprises a 100-foot-diameter plaza bearing a granite world map flanked by fountains and waterfalls salted with waters from the seven seas. A statue of *The Lone Sailor* watching over the map represents all who have served in the U.S. Navy.

The building adjoining the memorial houses a naval heritage center. The center's museum includes interactive video kiosks proffering a wealth of information about Navy ships, aircraft, and history; the **Navy Memorial Log Room,** a computerized record of past and present Navy personnel; the **Presidents Room,** honoring the six U.S. presidents who served in the Navy and the two who became Secretary of the Navy; the **Ship's Store,** filled with nautical and maritime merchandise; and a wide-screen 70mm Surroundsound film called *At Sea,* which lets viewers experience the adventure of going to sea on a Navy ship. The 35-minute film plays every Monday through Saturday at 11am and 1pm; admission is $4 for adults, $3 for seniors and students 18 and under.

Guided tours are available from the front desk, subject to staff availability. The plaza is the scene of many free band concerts in spring and summer; call for details.

✪ **Vietnam Veterans Memorial.** Just across from the Lincoln Memorial (east of Henry Bacon Dr. between 21st and 22nd sts. NW). ☎ **202/ 426-6841.** Free admission. Rangers on duty daily 8am–midnight except Dec 25. Ranger-led programs are given throughout the day. Metro: Foggy Bottom.

The Vietnam Veterans Memorial is possibly the most poignant site in Washington: two long, black granite walls in the shape of a V, each inscribed with the names of the men and women who gave their lives, or remain missing, in the longest war in American history. Even if no one close to you died in Vietnam, it's wrenching to watch visitors grimly studying the directories to find out where their loved ones are listed, or rubbing pencil on paper held against a name etched into the wall. The walls list close to 60,000 people, many of whom died very young.

Because of the raging conflict over U.S. involvement in the war, Vietnam veterans had received almost no recognition of their service before the memorial was conceived by Vietnam veteran Jan Scruggs. The nonprofit Vietnam Veterans Memorial Fund raised $7 million and secured a 2-acre site in tranquil Constitution Gardens to erect a memorial that would make no political statement about the war and would harmonize with neighboring memorials.

Yale senior Maya Lin's design was chosen in a national competition open to all citizens over 18 years of age. The two walls are angled at 125° to point to the Washington Monument and the Lincoln Memorial. The wall's mirrorlike surface reflects surrounding trees, lawns, and monuments. The names are inscribed in chronological order, documenting an epoch in American history as a series of individual sacrifices from the date of the first casualty in 1959 to the last death in 1975.

The park rangers at the Vietnam Veterans Memorial are very knowledgeable and are usually milling about—be sure to seek them out if you have any questions. Limited parking is available along Constitution Avenue.

7 Other Attractions

✪ **Arlington National Cemetery.** Just across the Memorial Bridge from the base of the Lincoln Memorial. ☎ **703/607-8052.** www.arlingtoncemetery. org or www.mdw.army.mil/cemetery.htm. Free admission. Apr–Sept daily 8am–7pm; Oct–Mar daily 8am–5pm. Metro: Arlington National Cemetery. If you come by car, parking is $1.25 an hour for the first 3 hours, $2 an hour thereafter. The cemetery is also accessible via Tourmobile.

Upon arrival, head over to the Visitor Center, where you can view exhibits, pick up a detailed map, use the rest rooms (there are no others until you get to Arlington House), and purchase a Tourmobile ticket ($4.75 per adult, $2.25 for children 4 to 11) allowing you to stop at all major sights in the cemetery and then reboard whenever you like. Service is continuous and the narrated commentary is informative; this is the only guided tour of the cemetery offered. If you've got plenty of stamina, consider doing part or all of the tour on foot. Remember as you go that this is a memorial frequented not just by tourists but by those visiting the graves of beloved relatives and friends who are buried here.

The Tomb of the Unknowns, containing the unidentified remains of service members from both world wars and the Korean War. The entire tomb is an unembellished, massive white marble block, moving in its simplicity. A 24-hour honor guard watches over the tomb, with the changing of the guard taking place every half hour April to September, every hour on the hour October to March, and every 2 hours at night.

Within a 20-minute walk, all uphill, from the Visitor Center is **Arlington House** (☎ 703/557-0613). From 1831 to 1861, this

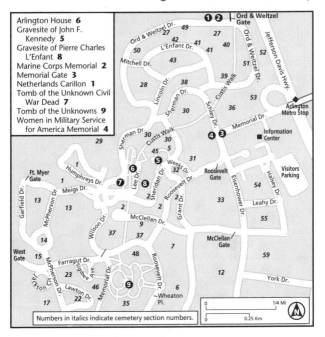

Arlington House **6**
Gravesite of John F.
  Kennedy **5**
Gravesite of Pierre Charles
  L'Enfant **8**
Marine Corps Memorial **2**
Memorial Gate **3**
Netherlands Carillon **1**
Tomb of the Unknown Civil
  War Dead **7**
Tomb of the Unknowns **9**
Women in Military Service
  for America Memorial **4**

Numbers in italics indicate cemetery section numbers.

was the legal residence of Robert E. Lee, where he and his family lived off and on until the Civil War. During the Civil War, the estate was taken over by Union forces and troops were buried here. A year before the defeat of the Confederate forces at Gettysburg, the U.S. government bought the estate. You tour the house on your own; park rangers are on-site to answer your questions. Admission is free. It's open daily from 9:30am to 4:30pm (closed January 1 and December 25).

Pierre Charles L'Enfant's grave was placed near Arlington House at a spot that is believed to offer the best view of Washington, the city he designed.

Below Arlington House, an 8-minute walk from the Visitor Center, is the **Gravesite of John Fitzgerald Kennedy.** Jacqueline Kennedy Onassis rests next to her husband and Robert Kennedy is buried close by. The Kennedy graves attract streams of visitors. Arrive close to 8am to contemplate the site quietly; otherwise, it's mobbed.

About 1½ miles from the Kennedy graves, the **Marine Corps Memorial,** the famous statue of the marines raising the flag on Iwo Jima, stands near the north (or Orde & Weitzel Gate) entrance. On Tuesday evenings in summer, there are military parades on the grounds at 7pm.

In October 1997, the ✪ **Women in Military Service for America Memorial** (☎ **800/222-2294** or 703/533-1155; www.womensmemorial.org) was added to Arlington Cemetery to honor the more than 1.8 million women who have served in the armed forces from the American Revolution to the present. The impressive new memorial lies just beyond the gated entrance to the cemetery, a 3-minute walk from the Visitor Center.

Hours are 8am to 5pm (until 7pm April through September), every day but Christmas.

✪ **Corcoran Gallery of Art.** 500 17th St. NW (between E St. and New York Ave.). ☎ **202/639-1700.** www.corcoran.org. Free admission. Wed and Fri–Mon 10am–5pm, Thurs 10am–9pm. Suggested contribution $3 adults, $1 students and senior citizens, $5 for families; free for children 12 and under. Free 45-min. tours daily at noon, with a second tour offered each Thurs 7:30pm, Sat and Sun 2:30. Closed Jan 1 and Dec 25. Metro: Farragut West or Farragut North.

This elegant art museum is a favorite party site in the city, hosting everything from inaugural balls to wedding receptions.

The first art museum in Washington, the Corcoran Gallery was housed from 1869 to 1896 in the redbrick and brownstone building that is now the Renwick. The collection outgrew its quarters and was transferred in 1897 to its present beaux arts building, designed by Ernest Flagg.

The collection, shown in rotating exhibits, focuses chiefly on American art. A prominent Washington banker, William Wilson Corcoran, was among the first wealthy American collectors to realize the importance of encouraging and supporting this country's artists. Enhanced by further gifts and bequests, the collection comprehensively spans American art from 18th-century portraiture to 20th-century moderns like Nevelson, Warhol, and Rothko. Nineteenth-century works include Bierstadt's and Remington's imagery of the American West; Hudson River School artists; expatriates like Whistler, Sargent, and Mary Cassatt; and two giants of the late 19th century, Homer and Eakins.

The Corcoran is not exclusively an American art museum. On the first floor is the collection from the estate of Senator William Andrews Clarks, an eclectic grouping of Dutch and Flemish masters; European painters; French impressionists; Barbizon landscapes; Delft porcelains; a Louis XVI *salon dore* transported in toto from Paris; and more. Clark's will stated that his diverse collection, which any curator would undoubtedly want to disperse among various museum departments, must be shown as a unit. He left money for a wing to house it and the new building opened in 1928. Don't miss the small walnut-paneled room known as "Clark Landing," which showcases 19th-century French impressionist and American art; a room of exquisite Corot landscapes; another of medieval Renaissance tapestries; and numerous Daumier lithographs donated by Dr. Armand Hammer.

Ford's Theatre & Lincoln Museum. 517 10th St. NW (between E and F sts.). ☎ **202/426-6925.** www.nps.gov/foth. Free admission. Daily 9am–5pm. Closed Dec 25. Metro: Metro Center.

On April 14, 1865, President Abraham Lincoln was in the audience of Ford's Theatre, one of the most popular playhouses in Washington. Everyone was laughing at a funny line from Tom Taylor's celebrated comedy, *Our American Cousin,* when John Wilkes Booth crept into the president's box, shot the president, and leapt to the stage, shouting "Sic semper tyrannis" (Thus ever to tyrants). With his left leg broken from the vault, Booth mounted his horse in the alley and galloped off. Doctors carried Lincoln across the street to the house of William Petersen, where the president died the next morning.

The theater was closed after Lincoln's assassination and used as an office by the War Department. In 1893, 22 clerks were killed when three floors of the building collapsed. It remained in disuse until the 1960s, when it was remodeled and restored to its appearance on the night of the tragedy. Except when rehearsals or matinees are in progress (call before you go), visitors can see the theater and trace Booth's movements on that fateful night. Free 15-minute talks on the history of the theater and the story of the assassination are given throughout the day. Be sure to visit the Lincoln Museum in the basement, where exhibits—including the Derringer pistol used by Booth and a diary in which he outlines his rationalization for the deed—focus on events surrounding Lincoln's assassination and the trial of the conspirators.

John F. Kennedy Center for the Performing Arts. New Hampshire Ave. NW (at Rock Creek Pkwy.). ☎ **800/444-1324** or 202/416-8341 for information or tickets. www.kennedy-center.org. Free admission. Daily 10am–midnight. Free guided tours Mon–Fri 10am–5pm, Sat–Sun 10am–1pm. Metro: Foggy Bottom (there's a free shuttle service from the station). Bus: no. 80 from Metro Center.

Opened in 1971, the Kennedy Center is both our national performing arts center and a memorial to John F. Kennedy. Set on 17 acres overlooking the Potomac, the striking $73 million facility, designed by noted architect Edward Durell Stone, encompasses an opera house, a concert hall, two stage theaters, a theater lab, and a film theater. The best way to see the Kennedy Center is to take a free 50-minute guided tour (which takes you through some restricted areas). You can beat the crowds by writing in advance to a senator or congressperson for passes for a free VIP tour, given year-round Monday through Friday at 9:30am and 4:30pm, and at 9:30am only on Saturday. Call ☎ **202/ 416-8303** for details.

If you'd like to attend performances during your visit, call the toll-free number above and request the current issue of *Kennedy Center News Magazine,* a free publication that describes all Kennedy Center happenings and prices.

National Museum of Women in the Arts. 1250 New York Ave. NW (at 13th St.). ☎ **202/783-5000.** www.nmwa.org. Suggested contribution $3 adults, $2 students and seniors. Daily 10am–5pm. Closed Jan 1, Thanksgiving, and Dec 25. Metro: Metro Center, 13th St. exit.

Celebrating "the contribution of women to the history of art," this relatively new museum is Washington's 72nd but a national first. Its 10th anniversary in 1997 saw the opening of the **Elizabeth A. Kasser Wing,** which adds 5,300 square feet and two new galleries to the museum. Founders Wilhelmina and Wallace Holladay, who donated the core of the permanent collection—more than 200 works by women from the 16th through the 20th centuries—became interested in women's art in the 1960s. After discovering that no women were included in H. W. Janson's *History of Art,* a standard text (which, by the way, did not change until 1986!), the Holladays began collecting art by women, and the concept of a women's art museum soon evolved.

Since its opening, the collection has grown to more than 2,000 works by artists including Rosa Bonheur, Frida Kahlo, Helen Frankenthaler, Barbara Hepworth, Georgia O'Keeffe, Camille Claudel, Lila Cabot Perry, Mary Cassatt, Elaine de Kooning,

Käthe Kollwitz, and many other lesser-known artists from earlier centuries.

✪ **Phillips Collection.** 1600 21st St. NW (at Q St.). ☎ **202/387-2151.** www.phillipscollection.org. Admission Sat–Sun $7.50 adults, $4 students and seniors, free for children 18 and under; contribution suggested Tues–Fri. Special exhibits may require an additional fee. Tues–Sat 10am–5pm year-round (Thurs until 8:30pm); Sun noon–7pm Sept–May and noon–5pm June–Aug. Free tours Wed and Sat 2pm. Closed Jan 1, July 4, Thanksgiving, and Dec 25. Metro: Dupont Circle (Q St. exit).

Conceived as "a museum of modern art and its sources," this intimate establishment, occupying an elegant 1890s Georgian Revival mansion and a more youthful wing, houses the exquisite collection of Duncan and Marjorie Phillips, avid collectors and proselytizers of modernism. Carpeted rooms with leaded- and stained-glass windows, oak paneling, plush chairs and sofas, and fireplaces establish a comfortable, homelike setting. Today the collection includes more than 2,500 works. Among the highlights: superb Daumier, Dove, and Bonnard paintings; some splendid small Vuillards; five van Goghs; Renoir's *Luncheon of the Boating Party;* seven Cézannes; and six works by Georgia O'Keeffe. Ingres, Delacroix, Manet, El Greco, Goya, Corot, Constable, Courbet, Giorgione, and Chardin are among the "sources" or forerunners of modernism represented. Modern notables include Rothko, Hopper, Kandinsky, Matisse, Klee, Degas, Rouault, Picasso, and many others. It's a collection no art lover should miss.

✪ **Washington National Cathedral.** Massachusetts and Wisconsin aves. NW (entrance on Wisconsin Ave.). ☎ **202/537-6200.** www.cathedral.org. Suggested donation $2 adults, $1 children. Fees for specialty tours (see below). Cathedral daily 10am–4:30pm; May 1–Labor Day, the nave level stays open Mon–Fri until 9pm. Gardens daily until dusk. Regular tours Mon–Sat 10–11:30am and 12:45–3:15pm, Sun 12:30–2:45pm; suggested donation $3 adults, $1 children. No tours on Palm Sunday, Easter, Thanksgiving, Dec 25, or during services. Worship services vary throughout the year but you can count on a daily Evensong service at 4:30pm, a noon service Mon–Sat, and an 11am service every Sun; call for other service times. Metro: Tenleytown, with a 20-min. walk. Bus: Any N bus up Massachusetts Ave. from Dupont Circle or any 30-series bus along Wisconsin Ave. This is a stop on the Old Town Trolley Tour.

Pierre L'Enfant's 1791 plan for the capital city included "a great church for national purposes," but possibly because of early America's fear of mingling church and state, more than a century elapsed before the foundation for Washington National Cathedral was laid. Its actual name is the Cathedral Church of St. Peter and St. Paul. The church is Episcopal, but it has no local congregation and seeks to serve the entire nation as a house of prayer for all people. It has been the setting for every kind of religious observance from Jewish to Serbian Orthodox.

A church of this magnitude—it's the sixth largest cathedral in the world—took a long time to build. Its principal (but not original) architect, Philip Hubert Frohman, worked on the project from 1921 until his death in 1972. The foundation stone was laid in 1907 using the mallet with which George Washington set the Capitol cornerstone. Construction was interrupted by both world wars and by periods of financial difficulty. The cathedral was completed with the placement of the final stone atop a pinnacle on the west front towers on September 29, 1990, 83 years to the day it was begun.

English Gothic in style (with several distinctly 20th-century innovations, such as a stained-glass window commemorating the flight of *Apollo 11* and containing a piece of moon rock), the cathedral is built in the shape of a cross, complete with flying buttresses and gargoyles. It is, along with the Capitol and the Washington Monument, one of the dominant structures on the Washington skyline. Its 57-acre landscaped grounds have two lovely gardens (the lawn is ideal for picnicking), four schools, a greenhouse, and two gift shops.

Over the years, the cathedral has seen much history. Services to celebrate the end of World Wars I and II were held here. It was the scene of President Wilson's funeral (he and his wife are buried here), as well as President Eisenhower's. Helen Keller and her companion, Anne Sullivan, were buried in the cathedral at her request. And during the Iranian crisis, a round-the-clock prayer vigil was held in the Holy Spirit Chapel throughout the hostages' captivity. When they were released, the hostages came to a service here.

The best way to explore the cathedral is to take a 30- to 45-minute guided tour; they leave continually from the west end of the nave. You can also walk through on your own.

GARDENS

Enid A. Haupt Garden. 10th St. and Independence Ave. SW. ☎ **202/357-2700.** Free admission. Late May–Aug daily 7am–8pm; Sept to mid-May daily 7am–5:45pm. Closed Dec 25. Metro: Smithsonian.

Named for its donor, a noted supporter of horticultural projects, this stunning garden presents elaborate flower beds and borders, plant-filled turn-of-the-20th-century urns, 1870s cast-iron furnishings, and lush baskets hung from reproduction 19th-century lampposts. Although on ground level, the garden is actually a 4-acre rooftop garden above the subterranean Sackler and African Art museums. An "Island Garden" near the Sackler Gallery, entered via a 9-foot moon gate, has benches backed by English boxwoods under the shade of weeping cherry trees.

A "Fountain Garden" outside the African Art Museum provides granite seating walls shaded by hawthorn trees. Three small terraces, shaded by black sour-gum trees, are located near the Arts & Industries Building. And five majestic linden trees shade a seating area around the Downing Urn, a memorial to American landscapist Andrew Jackson Downing. Elaborate cast-iron carriage gates made according to a 19th-century design by James Renwick, flanked by four red sandstone pillars, have been installed at the Independence Avenue entrance to the garden.

✪ **United States Botanic Garden.** 100 Maryland Ave. (at 1st St. SW at the east end of the Mall). ☎ **202/225-8333.** www.nationalgarden.org. Free admission. Daily 9am–5pm. Metro: Federal Center SW.

The Botanic Garden is at last open after a major renovation. The grand conservatory devotes half of its space to exhibits that focus on the importance of plants to people, and half to exhibits that focus on ecology and the evolutionary biology of plants. A jungle exists where there used to be a palm house, and the new National Garden outside the conservatory includes a First Ladies Water Garden, a formal rose garden, and a lawn terrace.

Also visit the garden annex across the street, **Bartholdi Park.** The park is about the size of a city block, with a stunning cast-iron classical fountain created by Frédéric Auguste Bartholdi, designer of the Statue of Liberty. Charming flower gardens bloom amid tall ornamental grasses, benches are sheltered by vine-covered bowers, and a touch and fragrance garden contains such herbs as pineapple-scented sage.

PARKS
POTOMAC PARK

West and East Potomac Parks, their 720 riverside acres divided by the Tidal Basin, are most famous for their spring display of cherry blossoms and all the hoopla that goes with it. So much attention is lavished on Washington's cherry blossoms that the National Park Service devotes a home page to the subject: **www.nps.gov/ nacc/cherry**. You can access this site to find out forecasts for the blooms and assorted other details. You can also call the National Park Service (☎ **202/485-9880**) for details.

In all, there are 3,363 cherry trees planted along the Tidal Basin, with another 337 blooming on the grounds of the Washington Monument and in other pockets of the city. To get to the Tidal Basin by car (not recommended in cherry blossom season), you want to get on Independence Avenue and follow the signs posted near the Lincoln Memorial that show you where to turn to find parking and the FDR Memorial. If you're walking, you'll want to cross Independence Avenue where it intersects with W. Basin Drive (there's a stoplight and crosswalk) and follow the path to the Tidal Basin. There is no convenient Metro stop near here.

West Potomac Park encompasses Constitution Gardens, the Vietnam, Korean, Lincoln, Jefferson, and FDR Memorials, a small island where ducks live, and the Reflecting Pool. It has 1,628 trees bordering the Tidal Basin. The blossoming of the cherry trees is the focal point of a week-long celebration. The trees bloom for a little less than 2 weeks beginning somewhere between March 20 and April 17; April 5 is the average date. Planning your trip around the blooming of the cherry blossoms is an iffy proposition, and I wouldn't advise it. All it takes is one good rain and those cherry blossoms are gone. The cherry blossoms are not illuminated at night.

East Potomac Park has 1,681 cherry trees in 11 varieties. The park also has picnic grounds, tennis courts, three golf courses, a large swimming pool, and biking and hiking paths by the water, all of which are described in "Outdoor Activities," below.

ROCK CREEK PARK

Created in 1890, ✪ **Rock Creek Park** (**www.nps.gov/rocr**) was purchased by Congress for its "pleasant valleys and ravines, primeval forests and open fields, its running waters, its rocks clothed with rich ferns and mosses, its repose and tranquillity, its light and shade, its ever-varying shrubbery, its beautiful and extensive views." A 1,750-acre valley within the District of Columbia, extending 12 miles from the Potomac River to the Maryland border, it's one of the biggest and finest city parks in the nation. Parts of it are still wild; it's not unusual to see a deer scurrying through the woods in more remote sections.

For full information on the wide range of park programs and activities, visit the Rock Creek Nature Center and Planetarium, 5200 Glover Rd. NW (☎ 202/426-6829), Wednesday through Sunday from 9am to 5pm; or Park Headquarters, 6545 Williamsburg Rd. NW (☎ 202/282-1063), Monday through Friday from 7:45am to 4:15pm. To get to the Nature Center by public transportation, take the Metro to Friendship Heights and transfer to bus no. E2 or E3 to Military Road and Oregon Avenue/Glover Road.

There's convenient free parking throughout the park.

8 Organized Tours

ON FOOT

TourDC, Walking Tours of Georgetown, Dupont Circle & Embassy Row (☎ 301/588-8999; www.tourdc.com) conducts 90-minute ($12) walking tours of Georgetown, telling about the neighborhood's history up to the present and taking you past the homes of notable residents.

✪ **Guided Walking Tours of Washington** (☎ 301/294-9514) offers 2-hour walks through the streets of Georgetown, Adams–Morgan, and other locations, guided by author/historian Anthony S. Pitch. Rates are $10 per person, $6 for seniors and students.

BY BUS

If you're looking for an easy-on/easy-off tour of major sites, consider ✪ **Tourmobile Sightseeing** (☎ 888/868-7707 or 202/554-5100; www.tourmobile.com), whose comfortable red, white, and blue sightseeing trams travel to as many as 25 sites, as far out as Arlington National Cemetery and even Mount Vernon. (See "Getting Around: By Tourmobile" in chapter 2 for details).

BY BOAT

Since Washington is a river city, why not see it by boat? Potomac cruises allow sweeping vistas of the monuments and memorials, Georgetown, the Kennedy Center, and other Washington sights. Read the information carefully, since not all boat cruises offer guided tours.

Some of the following boats leave from the Washington waterfront and some from Old Town Alexandria:

Spirit of Washington Cruises, Pier 4 at 6th and Water Streets SW (☎ **202/554-8000;** www.spiritcruises.com; Metro: Waterfront), offers a variety of trips daily, including evening dinner, lunch, and brunch, and moonlight dance cruises, as well as a half-day excursion to Mount Vernon and back. Lunch and dinner cruises include a 40-minute high-energy musical revue. Prices range from $26.50 for a sightseeing (no meals) excursion to Mount Vernon, which takes 5½ hours, including a 2-hour tour break, to $72.45 for a Saturday dinner cruise, drinks not included. Call to make reservations.

The **Capitol River Cruise**'s *Nightingale II* (☎ **800/405-5511** or 301/460-7447; www.capitolrivercruises.com) is a historic 65-foot steel riverboat that can accommodate up to 90 people. The *Nightingale II*'s narrated jaunts depart Georgetown's Washington Harbour every hour on the hour, from 11am to 9pm, April through October. The 50-minute narrated tour travels past the monuments and memorials as you head to National Airport and back. A snack bar on board sells light refreshments, beer, wine, and sodas; you're welcome to bring your own picnic aboard. The price is $10 per adult, $5 per child ages 3 to 12. To get here, take the Metro to Foggy Bottom and then walk into Georgetown, following Pennsylvania Avenue, which becomes M Street. Turn left on 31st Street NW, which dead-ends at the Washington Harbour complex.

9 Outdoor Pursuits

BIKING   Thompson's Boat Center (see "Boating," below) and **Fletcher's Boat House** (Reservoir and Canal roads, (☎ **202/ 244-0461;** www.fletchersboathouse.com), rent both bikes and boats. As does **Big Wheel Bikes,** 1034 33rd St. NW, right near the C&O Canal just below M Street (☎ **202/337-0254**). The rate is $5 per hour, with a 3-hour minimum, or $25 for the day. Shop opens at 10am daily and closing times vary. Photo ID and a major credit card are required to rent bicycles.

Rock Creek Park has an 11-mile paved bike route from the Lincoln Memorial through the park into Maryland. Or you can follow the bike path from the Lincoln Memorial and go over the Memorial Bridge to pedal to Old Town Alexandria and to Mount Vernon. The C&O Canal and the Potomac Parks, described earlier in "Parks & Gardens," also have extended bike paths.

A new 7-mile path, the **Capital Crescent Trail,** takes you from Georgetown to the suburb of Bethesda, Maryland.

BOATING   Thompson's Boat Center, 2900 Virginia Ave. at Rock Creek Parkway NW (☎ **202/333-4861** or 202/333-9543; www.guestservices.com. Metro: Foggy Bottom, with a 10-minute walk), rents canoes, kayaks, rowing shells (recreational and racing), and bikes. They also offer sculling and sweep-rowing lessons. Photo ID and a credit card are required for rentals. They're open for boat and bike rentals usually from March through November daily from 6am to 8pm. Boat rentals range from $6 an hour for a canoe to $32 for a day's rental of a double kayak. Bike rentals range from $4 per hour for a single-speed cruiser to $22 for a day's rental of an all-terrain 15-speed bike.

Late March to mid-September, you can rent paddleboats on the north end of the Tidal Basin off Independence Avenue (☎ **202/479-2426**). Four-seaters rent for $14 an hour; two-seaters are $7 an hour. You can rent boats daily from 10am to about an hour before sunset.

JOGGING   There's a par course jogging path in Rock Creek Park. Its 1½-mile oval route, beginning near the intersection of Calvert Street NW and Rock Creek Parkway (directly behind the Omni Shoreham Hotel), includes 18 calisthenics stations with instructions on prescribed exercises. There's another par course, with only four stations, at 16th and Kennedy streets NW. Other popular jogging areas are the C&O Canal and the Mall.

6

Shopping the District

*G*reat shopping areas in the District include **Adams–Morgan,** good for secondhand bookshop and eclectic collectibles stores; **Connecticut Avenue,** for high-end retailers like Brooks Brothers, Talbots, and Burberry's; **Dupont Circle,** for art galleries, book and record shops, and gay and lesbian boutiques; **Downtown,** for department stores and mall-type shopping; **Georgetown,** with both chain and one-of-a-kind shops, chic as well as thrift lining the crowded intersection of Wisconsin and M Streets; **Upper Wisconsin Avenue Northwest,** a quarter-mile shopping district in a residential area, with stores ranging from Banana Republic to Neiman Marcus; and **Union Station,** a mall with more than 100 specialty shops.

ANTIQUES

While you won't find many bargains in Washington area antiques stores, you will see beautiful and rare decorative furniture, silver, jewelry, art, and fabrics, from Amish quilts to Chinese silks. Antiques shops dot the greater Washington landscape, with the richest concentrations found in Old Town Alexandria, Capitol Hill, Georgetown, Adams–Morgan, and Kensington (in Maryland).

✪ **Antiques-on-the-Hill.** 701 North Carolina Ave. SE. ☎ **877/509-377** or 202/543-1819. Metro: Eastern Market.

A Capitol Hill institution since the 1960s, this place sells silver, furniture, glassware, jewelry, porcelain, and lamps.

✪ **Brass Knob Architectural Antiques.** 2311 18th St. NW. ☎ **202/332-3370.** www.thebrassknob.com. Metro: Woodley Park or Dupont Circle.

When early homes and office buildings are demolished in the name of progress, these savvy salvage merchants spirit away saleable treasures, from chandeliers to wrought-iron fencing. Cross the street to its other location: the **Brass Knob's Back Doors Warehouse,** 2329 Champlain St. NW (☎ **202/265-0587**).

Georgetown Antiques Center. 2918 M St. NW. Metro: Foggy Bottom, with a 20-min. walk.

The Cherub Antiques Gallery (☎ 202/337-2224) specializes in art nouveau and art deco, art glass (signed Tiffany, Steuben, Lalique, and Gallé), Liberty arts and crafts, and Louis Icart etchings. Sharing the premises is **Michael Getz Antiques** (☎ 202/338-3811), which sells American, English, and continental silver; porcelain lamps; and many fireplace accessories.

Susquehanna Antiques. 3216 O St. NW. ☎ **202/333-1511.** www.susquehannaantiques.com. Metro: Foggy Bottom, with a 25-min. walk.

This Georgetown store specializes in American, English, and European furniture, paintings, and garden items of the late 18th and early 19th centuries.

ART GALLERIES

Art galleries abound in Washington, but are especially prolific in the Dupont Circle and Georgetown neighborhoods, and along 7th Street downtown. For a complete listing of local galleries, get your hands on a copy of *"Galleries,"* a monthly guide to major galleries and their shows; the guide is available free at many hotel concierge desks and at each of the galleries listed in the publication. Here's a selection of top places.

DUPONT CIRCLE

Anton Gallery. 2108 R St. NW. ☎ **202/328-0828.** www.antongallery.com. Metro: Dupont Circle.

Expect to find contemporary American paintings, with maybe a little sculpture or photography. Nearly all of the artists shown live locally but hail from around the world.

GEORGETOWN

✪ **Addison/Ripley Fine Art.** 1670 Wisconsin Ave. NW. ☎ **202/338-5180.** www.artnet.com. Metro: Foggy Bottom.

This gallery represents both nationally and regionally recognized artists, from the 19th century to the present.

Govinda Gallery. 1227 34th St. NW. ☎ **202/333-1180.** www.govindagallery.com. Metro: Foggy Bottom.

You read about this one in the newspaper a lot since it often shows artwork by famous musicians (like the 1999 exhibit of paintings and prints by Rolling Stones guitarist Ronnie Wood) and pictures of celebrity musicians taken by well-known photographers.

SEVENTH STREET ARTS CORRIDOR

A couple of these galleries predate the renaissance taking place in this downtown neighborhood. To get here, take the Metro to either the Archives/Navy Memorial (Blue–Orange Line) or Gallery Place/Chinatown/MCI Center (Red–Yellow Line) stations.

406 Art Galleries. 406 7th St. NW, between D and E sts.

Several first-rate art galleries, some of them interlopers from Dupont Circle, occupy this historic building, with its 13-foot-high ceilings and spacious rooms. The first floor of the building is a furniture store, so keep going to the next level. Galleries include: **David Adamson Gallery** (☎ **202/628-0257;** www.artnet.com/ adamsonexhibitions), which is probably the largest gallery space in D.C., with two levels featuring the works of contemporary artists, like locals Kevin MacDonald and Renee Stout, and national artists KiKi Smith and William Wegman; and **Touchstone Gallery** (☎ **202/347-2787**), which is a self-run co-op of 36 artists who take turns exhibiting their work.

BOOKS

Washingtonians are readers, so bookstores constantly pop up throughout the city. An increasingly competitive market means that chain bookstores do a brisk business, even in a town that can claim more general-interest independent bookstores than any other city. Here are my favorites.

Barnes & Noble. 3040 M St. NW. ☎ **202/965-9880.** www.barnesandnoble. com. Metro: Foggy Bottom, with a 20-min. walk.

This wonderful three-story shop discounts hardcover best-sellers by 30% and paperback best-sellers by 20%. It has sizable software, travel book, and children's title sections. A cafe on the second level hosts concerts. Other area locations include 4801 Bethesda Ave., in Bethesda, Maryland (☎ **301/986-1761**); 12089 Rockville Pike, in Rockville, Maryland (☎ **301/881-0237**); 3651 Jefferson Davis Highway, in Alexandria, Virginia (☎ **703/ 299-9124**); and 6260 Seven Corners Center, in Falls Church, Virginia (☎ **703/536-0774**).

Borders Books & Music. 1800 L St. NW. ☎ **202/466-4999.** www. borders.com. Metro: Farragut North.

Other Borders stores in the District include 5333 Wisconsin Ave. NW (☎ **202/ 686-8270**), in upper northwest D.C., and Hamilton Square, at 14th and F streets NW (phone number not available at this writing).

Kramerbooks & Afterwords Café. 1517 Connecticut Ave. NW. ☎ **202/ 387-1400.** Metro: Dupont Circle.

The first bookstore/cafe in the Dupont Circle area, this place has launched countless romances. It's jammed and often noisy, stages live music Wednesday through Saturday evenings, and is open all night weekends. Paperback fiction takes up most of its inventory, but the store carries a little of everything. No discounts.

✪ **Olsson's Books and Records.** 1239 Wisconsin Ave. NW, between M and N sts. ☎ **202/338-9544.** www.olssons.com. Metro: Foggy Bottom, with a 20-min. walk.

This 27-year-old independent, quality bookstore chain has about 60,000 to 70,000 books on its shelves. Members of its helpful staff know what they're talking about and will order books they don't have in stock. Some discounts are given on books, tapes, and CDs, and their regular prices are pretty good, too.

Travel Books & Language Center. 4437 Wisconsin Ave. NW. ☎ **800/ 220-2665** or 202/237-1322. www.travelbks.com. Metro: Tenleytown.

Its move in November 1997 to new digs tripled the space of this travel bookstore, which has the best-in-the-area assortment of guidebooks and maps covering the entire world, as well as language dictionaries and learning tapes, travel diaries, memoirs, and novels famous for their evocation of particular places.

Trover Shop. 221 Pennsylvania Ave. SE. ☎ **202/547-BOOK.** www.trover. com. Metro: Capitol South.

The only general-interest bookstore on Capitol Hill, Trover specializes in its political selections and its magazines. The store discounts 20% on the top 10 *Washington Post* hardcover fiction and nonfiction best-sellers.

CAMERAS

Ritz Camera Centers. 1740 Pennsylvania Ave. NW. ☎ **202/466-3470.** Metro: Farragut West.

This place sells camera equipment for the average photographer and offers 1-hour film processing. Call for other locations—there are many throughout the area.

CRAFTS

✪ **American Hand Plus.** 2906 M St. NW. ☎ **202/965-3273.** www. americanhandplus.com. Metro: Foggy Bottom, with a 20-min. walk.

This store features exquisite contemporary handcrafted American ceramics and jewelry, plus international objets d'art.

Appalachian Spring. 1415 Wisconsin Ave. NW, at P St. ☎ **202/337-5780.** Metro: Foggy Bottom, with a 25-min. walk, or take one of the 30-series buses (nos. 30, 32, 34, 36) from downtown into Georgetown.

Here you'll find country crafts in citified Georgetown. They sell pottery, jewelry, newly made pieced and appliqué quilts, stuffed dolls and animals, candles, rag rugs, hand-blown glassware, an incredible collection of kaleidoscopes, glorious weavings, and wooden kitchenware. Everything in the store is made by hand in the United States. There's another branch in Union Station (☎ **202/682-0505**).

Indian Craft Shop. Department of the Interior, 1849 C St. NW, Room 1023. ☎ **202/208-4056.** Weekday hours only. www.indiancraftshop.com. Metro: Farragut West or Foggy Bottom.

The Indian Craft Shop has represented authentic Native American artisans since 1938, selling their handwoven rugs and handcrafted baskets, jewelry, figurines, paintings, pottery, and other items. You need a photo ID to enter the building.

✪ **The Phoenix.** 1514 Wisconsin Ave. NW. ☎ **202/338-4404.** Metro: Foggy Bottom, with a 30-min. walk, or take one of the 30-series buses (nos. 30, 32, 34, 36) from downtown into Georgetown.

Around since 1955, the Phoenix still sells those embroidered Mexican peasant blouses popular in hippie days; Mexican folk and fine art; handcrafted sterling silver jewelry from Mexico and all over the world; clothing in natural fibers from Mexican and American designers like Eileen Fisher and Flax; collectors' quality masks; and decorative doodads in tin, brass, copper, and wood.

DEPARTMENT STORES

Hecht's. Metro Center, 1201 G St. NW. ☎ **202/628-6661.** Metro: Metro Center.

Everything from mattresses to electronics, children's underwear to luggage, can be bought at this mid-priced emporium.

Lord & Taylor. 5255 Western Ave. NW. ☎ **202/362-9600.** Metro: Friendship Heights.

This is another, lesser version of a New York chain, although lately the store has vastly improved its selections. The staff, too, seems more professional and helpful than in the past. Its women's clothing and accessories departments are probably its strong suit; go elsewhere for gadgets and gifts.

Nordstrom. Fashion Center at Pentagon City. 1400 S. Hayes St., Arlington, VA. ☎ **703/415-1121.** Metro: Pentagon City.

This Seattle-based retailer's reputation for exceptional service is well deserved. In keeping with the store's beginnings as a shoe store, this location has three entire departments devoted to women's footwear: designer, dressy, and just plain fun. If you can't find your size or color, they'll order it.

FARMERS' & FLEA MARKETS

Alexandria Farmers' Market. 301 King St., at Market Square in front of the city hall, in Alexandria. ☎ **703/838-4770.** Metro: King St., then take the DASH bus (AT2 or AT5) eastbound to Market Square.

The oldest continuously operating farmers' market in the country (since 1752), this market offers the usual assortment of locally grown fruits and vegetables, along with delectable baked goods, cut flowers, and plants. Open Saturday from 5:30 to 10am.

✪ **Eastern Market.** 225 7th St. SE, between North Carolina Ave. and C St. SE. ☎ **202/546-2698.** Metro: Eastern Market.

This is the one everyone knows about, even if they've never been here. Located on Capitol Hill, Eastern Market is an inside/outside bazaar of stalls, where greengrocers, butchers, bakers, farmers, artists, craftspeople, florists, and other merchants vend their wares on weekends. Saturday morning is the best time to go. On Sunday, the food stalls become a flea market. Open Saturday and Sunday from 10am to 5pm.

✪ **Georgetown Flea Market.** In the Hardy Middle School parking lot bordering Wisconsin Ave., between S and T sts. NW. Metro: Foggy Bottom, with a 30- to 40-min. walk, or take one of the 30-series buses (nos. 30, 32, 34, 36) from downtown into Georgetown.

Grab a coffee at Starbucks across the lane and get ready to barter. The Georgetown Flea Market is frequented by all types of Washingtonians looking for a good deal—they often get it—on antiques, painted furniture, vintage clothing, and decorative garden urns. Nearly 50 vendors sell their wares here. Open March through December on Sunday from 9am to 5pm. The school recently converted part of its parking lot into an athletic field, sending another 50 of its original 100 vendors to set up at a new location: Georgetown Flea Market at U Street, 1345 U St. NW, which is open every Saturday and Sunday from 9am to 5pm.

MEN'S CLOTHES

Beau Monde. International Square, 1814 K St. NW. ☎ **202/466-7070.** Metro: Farragut West.

This boutique sells all Italian-made clothes, some double-breasted traditional suits, but mostly avant-garde.

Britches of Georgetowne. 1247 Wisconsin Ave. NW. ☎ **202/338-3330.** Metro: Foggy Bottom, with a 20-min. walk.

See where Washington men go for that straight-laced look. Britches sells moderately priced to expensive dress apparel, both designer wear and from its own label. Its sportswear selections are more extensive than in the past. Another location is at 1776 K St. NW (☎ **202/347-8994**).

Brooks Brothers. 1201 Connecticut Ave. NW. ☎ **202/659-4650.** Metro: Dupont Circle or Farragut North.

Brooks sells traditional men's clothes, as well as the fine line of Peal's English shoes. This store made the news as the place where Monica Lewinsky bought a tie for President Clinton. It also sells an extensive line of women's clothes. Other locations are at Potomac Mills (see "Malls," below) and at 5500 Wisconsin Ave., in Chevy Chase, Maryland (☎ **301/654-8202**).

MUSIC

12″ Dance Records. 2010 P St. NW, 2nd floor. ☎ **202/659-2010.** www.12inchdance.com. Metro: Dupont Circle.

Disco lives. If you ever moved to it on a dance floor, Wresch Dawidjian and his staff of deejays have it or they can get it. There's always a deejay mixing it up live in the store and they pump the beats out into the street.

POLITICAL MEMORABILIA

Capitol Coin and Stamp Co. Inc. 1701 L St. NW. ☎ **202/296-0400.** Metro: Farragut North.

A museum of political memorabilia—pins, posters, banners—and all of it is for sale. This is also a fine resource for the endangered species of coin or stamp collectors.

✪ **Political Americana.** Union Station. ☎ **202/547-1685.** Metro: Union Station.

This is another great place to pick up souvenirs. The store sells political novelty items, books, bumper stickers, old campaign buttons, and historical memorabilia. Another location is at 14th Street and Pennsylvania Avenue NW (☎ **202/737-7730**).

WOMEN'S CLOTHES

If Washington women don't dress well, it isn't for lack of stores. The following boutiques range in styles from baggy grunge to the crisply tailored, from Laura Ashley to black leather. There are also outlets of **Ann Taylor** at Union Station (☎ **202/371-8010**), 1720 K St. NW (☎ **202/466-3544**), 600 13th St. NW (☎ **202/737-0325**), and Georgetown Park, 3222 M St. NW (☎ **202/338-5290**). **Talbots** stores can be found at 1122 Connecticut Ave. NW (☎ **202/887-6973**) and Georgetown Park, 3222 M St. NW (☎ **202/338-3510**). **Victoria's Secret** also has stores in Union Station (☎ **202/682-0686**) and Georgetown Park (☎ **202/965-5457**), as well as at Connecticut and L streets NW (☎ **202/293-7530**).

Betsy Fisher. 1224 Connecticut Ave. NW. ☎ **202/785-1975.** Metro: Dupont Circle.

A walk past the store is all it takes to know that this shop is a tad different. Its windows and racks show off whimsically feminine fashions by new American designers.

✪ **Commander Salamander.** 1420 Wisconsin Ave. NW. ☎ **202/337-2265.** Metro: Foggy Bottom, with a 25-min. walk.

Loud music, young crowd, and funky clothes. Commander Salamander has a little bit of everything, including designer items, some of which are quite affordable: Moschino dresses, $1 ties, and handmade jackets with Axl jewelry sewn on. Too cool.

7

Washington, D.C., After Dark

*W*hen the sun goes down, Washington still heats up. You'll find a cornucopia of entertainment options, from a Shakespeare play, to a comedy club, to a thriving bar and club scene. Washingtonians are theatergoers, so it may be hard to get a seat at a popular show; if there's something you simply must see, call for tickets in advance. U Street, Adams–Morgan, Georgetown, and Dupont Circle are all good neighborhoods to cruise at night. Even skinflints will find lots to do after dark in Washington. Many of the museums often stage free or inexpensive cultural performances. Most notable is the Kennedy Center's Millennium stage performances, which are free, take place every evening from 6 to 7pm, and feature a different artist nightly: maybe a group like Los Lobos or the National Symphony Orchestra.

Look over the listings that follow and check the Friday "Weekend" section of the *Washington Post,* which will inform you about children's theater, sports events, flower shows, and all else. The *City Paper,* available free at restaurants, bookstores, and other places around town, is another good source. Go online, if you can, to check out the *Post*'s nightlife information, especially the Weekend section's "Nightwatch" column.

TICKETS

TICKETplace, Washington's only discount day-of-show ticket outlet, has one location: in the Old Post Office Pavilion, 1100 Pennsylvania Ave. NW (Metro: Federal Triangle). Call ☎ **202/TICKETS** for information. On the day of performance only (except Sunday and Monday, see below), you can buy half-price tickets (with cash, select debit and credit cards, or traveler's checks) to performances with tickets still available at most major Washington area theaters and concert halls, as well as for performances of the opera, ballet, and other events. TICKET-place is open Tuesday through Saturday from 11am to 6pm; half-price tickets for Sunday and Monday shows are sold on Saturday.

You'll have to pay a service charge of 10% of the full face value of the ticket.

Full-price tickets for most performances in town can be bought through **Ticketmaster** (☎ **202/432-SEAT**) at Hecht's Department Store, 12th and G streets NW, and at George Washington University's Marvin Center, across from Lisner Auditorium, at 21st Street and H Street NW (Metro: Foggy Bottom). These locations are open from 10am to 8pm. You can purchase tickets to Washington theatrical, musical, and other events before you leave home by calling ☎ **800/551-SEAT.** Another similar ticket outlet is Tickets.com (formerly Protix). You can order tickets by calling ☎ **800/955-5566** or 703/218-6500, or by accessing its Web site www.tickets.com.

1 Theater

D.C.'s theatrical productions are first-rate and varied. Almost anything on Broadway has either been previewed here or will eventually come here. The city also has several nationally acclaimed repertory companies and a theater specializing in Shakespearean productions.

✪ **Arena Stage.** 6th St. and Maine Ave. SW. ☎ **202/488-3300.** www. arenastage.org. Tickets $27–$50; discounts available for students, people with disabilities, groups, and senior citizens. A limited number of $10 tickets, called HOTTIX, are available for cash only, 90 min. before most performances (call for details). $6 limited parking on-site, satellite lots, as well as street parking. Metro: Waterfront.

Founded by the brilliant Zelda Fichandler, the Arena Stage celebrates its 50th anniversary with the presentation of its 2000–2001 season. Arena is home to one of the oldest acting ensembles in the nation. Several works nurtured here have moved to Broadway, and many graduates have gone on to commercial stardom, including Ned Beatty, James Earl Jones, and Jane Alexander.

Arena presents eight productions annually on two stages: the Fichandler (a theater-in-the-round) and the smaller, fan-shaped Kreeger. In addition, the Arena houses the Old Vat, a space used for new play readings and special productions.

Ford's Theatre. 511 10th St. NW (between E and F sts.). ☎ **202/ 347-4833,** TDD 202/347-5599 for listings, 800/955-5566 or 703/218-6500 to charge tickets. www.fordstheatre.org. Tickets $27–$43; discounts available for families, also for seniors at matinee performances and any time on the "day of" for evening shows; students with ID can get "rush" tickets an hour before performances if tickets are available. Metro: Metro Center or Gallery Place.

This is the actual theater where, on the evening of April 14, 1865, actor John Wilkes Booth shot President Lincoln. The assassination marked the end of what had been John T. Ford's very popular theater; it remained closed for more than a century. In 1968, Ford's reopened, completely restored to its 1865 appearance, based on photographs, sketches, newspaper articles, and samples of wallpaper and curtain material from museum collections.

Ford's season is more or less year-round (it's closed for a while in the summer). Several of its productions have gone on to Broadway and off-Broadway. Recent shows have included Marcel Marceau, Frank McCourt and his brother Malachy in *A Couple of Blaguards* and *Reunion: A Musical Epic in Miniature*. A big event here is the nationally televised "A Festival at Ford's": a celebrity-studded bash usually held in the fall and attended by the president and first lady.

National Theatre. 1321 Pennsylvania Ave. NW. ☎ **202/628-6161,** or 800/447-7400 to charge tickets. www.nationaltheatre.org. Tickets $30–$75; discounts available for students, seniors, military personnel, and people with disabilities. Metro: Metro Center.

The luxurious Federal-style National Theatre is the oldest continuously operating theater in Washington (since 1835). It's exciting just to see the stage on which Sarah Bernhardt, John Barrymore, Helen Hayes, and so many other notables have performed. The 1,672-seat National is the closest thing Washington has to a Broadway-style playhouse. Managed by New York's Shubert Organization, it presents star-studded hits, often pre- or post-Broadway, most of the year.

The National also offers free public-service programs: Saturday morning children's theater (puppets, clowns, magicians, dancers, and singers) and Monday night showcases of local groups and performers September through May. Call ☎ **202/783-3372** for details.

✪ **Shakespeare Theatre.** 450 7th St. NW (between D and E sts.). ☎ **202/ 547-1122.** www.shakespearedc.org. Tickets $17.50–$56, $10 for standing-room tickets sold 1 hour before sold-out performances; discounts available for students, seniors, and groups. Metro: Archives–Navy Memorial or Gallery Place.

This internationally renowned classical ensemble company offers five productions, usually three Shakespearean and two modern classics each September-to-June season.

Source Theatre Company. 1835 14th St. NW (between S and T sts.).
☎ **202/462-1073** for information or 301/738-7073 to charge tickets.
www.sourcetheatre.org. Tickets $20–$25, Washington Theatre Festival shows $15.

The Source is Washington's major producer of new plays, also
mounting works by established playwrights. The theater presents
top local artists in a year-round schedule of dramatic and
comedy plays, both at the above address and during the summer
at various spaces around town. Annual events here include the
Washington Theatre Festival each July, a 4-week showcase of
about 50 new plays.

2 Other Performing Arts

The following places offer a potpourri of theater, opera, classical
music, headliners, jazz, rock, dance, and comedy. Here you'll find
some of the top entertainment choices in the District.

Carter Barron Amphitheater. 16th St. and Colorado Ave. NW. ☎ **202/
260-6836.** Take Metro to Silver Spring, transfer to S2 or S4 bus, with Federal
Triangle destination sign, and let the driver know you wish to hop off at the
16th St. bus stop nearest the Carter Barron; the amphitheater is a 5-min. walk
from that stop.

Way out on 16th Street (close to the Maryland border) is this
4,250-seat outdoor amphitheater in Rock Creek Park. Summer
performances include a range of gospel, blues, and classical entertainment. You can always count on Shakespeare: The **Shakespeare
Theatre Free For All** takes place at the Carter Barron usually for
2 weeks in June, Tuesday through Sunday evenings; the free tickets
are available the day of performance only, on a first-come, first-
serve basis (call ☎ **202/334-4790** for details). The 2000 Free
For All featured *The Merchant of Venice.*

DAR Constitution Hall. 18th and D sts. NW. ☎ **202/628-4780**; 800/
551-SEAT or 202/432-SEAT to charge tickets. Tickets $15–$50. Metro: Farragut
West.

Housed within a beautiful turn-of-the-20th-century beaux
arts–style building is this fine 3,746-seat auditorium. Its excellent
acoustics have supported an eclectic (and I mean eclectic) group
of performers: Sting, the Buena Vista Social Club, John Hiatt, the
Count Basie Orchestra, the Los Angeles Philharmonic, Diana
Ross, Jay Leno, Ray Charles, Trisha Yearwood, Kathleen Battle,
and Marilyn Horne.

Folger Shakespeare Library. 201 E. Capitol St. SE. ☎ **202/544-7077.**
www.folger.edu. Students and seniors receive discounts with proof of ID. Call

for information about ticket prices, which are $8–$50, depending upon the event. Metro: Capitol South or Union Station.

The Folger Shakespeare Library is open year-round, featuring exhibits and tours of its Tudor-style great rooms. Among the offerings are the Folger Consort, an early music ensemble, which performs medieval, Renaissance, and baroque music, troubadour songs, madrigals, and court ensembles; between October and May, they give 30 concerts over the course of seven weekends. The Folger also presents plays and musical performances, lectures, readings, and other events in its Elizabethan Theatre, which is styled after the inn-yard theater of Shakespeare's time.

On selected evenings, readings feature such poets as Seamus Heany, Gwendolyn Brooks, and John Ashbery. Another exciting program is the Friday-night PEN/Faulkner series of fiction readings by noted authors such as John LeCarre, Joyce Carol Oates, and Joan Didion. And the Folger offers Saturday programs for children, ranging from medieval treasure hunts to preparing an Elizabethan feast.

✪ **John F. Kennedy Center for the Performing Arts.** At the southern end of New Hampshire Ave. NW and Rock Creek Pkwy. ☎ **800/444-1324** or 202/467-4600. www.kennedy-center.org. 50% discounts are offered (for most attractions) to students, seniors 65 and over, people with permanent disabilities, enlisted military personnel, and persons with fixed low incomes (call ☎ 202/416-8340 for details). Garage parking $9. Metro: Foggy Bottom (though it's a fairly short walk, there's a free shuttle between the station and the Kennedy Center, departing every 15 min. from 7am to midnight). Bus: 80 from Metro Center.

The hub of Washington's cultural and entertainment scene is actually made up of six different national theaters,

The Kennedy Center's free concert series, known as "Millennium Stage," features daily performances by area musicians and sometimes national artists, staged each evening at 6pm in the center's Grand Foyer. These free performances are so popular (as many as 7,000 people have shown up at a time, although 400 is a more typical number) that in 1999 the Kennedy Center expanded the Millennium Stage area to include two new spaces and debuted broadcasts of the nightly performances on the Internet: http://kennedy-center.org/stage/millennium. The Friday "Weekend" section of the *Washington Post* lists the free performances scheduled for the coming week; the daily "Style" section lists nightly performances under Free Events, in the Guide to the Lively Arts column.

Opera House: This plush red-and-gilt 2,300-seat theater is designed for ballet, modern dance, musical comedy, and opera, and it's also the setting for occasional gala events such as the Kennedy Center Honors, which you've probably seen on TV (Neil Simon, B. B. King, Lauren Bacall, and Bob Dylan have been honorees). Other offerings have included performances by the Joffrey Ballet, the Bolshoi Ballet, the Kirov Ballet, the Royal Ballet, and the American Ballet Theatre. The Washington Opera (**www.dc-opera.org**) stages many of its performances here and in the Eisenhower Theater. Tickets often sell out before the season begins.

Concert Hall: This is the home of the National Symphony Orchestra, which presents concerts from September to June. Tickets are available by subscription and for individual performances. Guest artists have included Itzhak Perlman, Vladimir Ashkenazy, Zubin Mehta, Jean-Pierre Rampal, and Isaac Stern. Headliners like Ray Charles and Patti LuPone also appear here.

Terrace Theater: Small chamber works, choral recitals, musicals, comedy revues, cabarets, and theatrical and modern dance performances are among the varied provinces of the 500-seat Terrace Theater, a bicentennial gift from Japan.

Eisenhower Theater: A wide range of dramatic productions can be seen here. The Eisenhower is also the setting for smaller productions of the Washington Opera from December to February, solo performances by the likes of Harry Belafonte, dance presentations by the Paul Taylor Dance Company, and others.

Theater Lab & More: By day, the Theater Lab is Washington's premier stage for children's theater. By night, it becomes a cabaret, now in a long run of *Shear Madness,* a comedy whodunit (tickets are $25 to $29).

The 29-year-old Kennedy Center is in the middle of a $50 million overhaul scheduled to continue until the year 2007. Limited underground parking is $9 for the entire night after 2pm; if that lot is full, go to the Columbia Plaza Garage at 2400 Virginia Ave. NW, which runs a free shuttle back to the facility.

MCI Center. 601 F St. NW, where it meets 7th St. ☎ **202/628-3200.** www.mcicenter.com. To charge tickets by phone, call ☎ 800/551-SEAT or 202/432-SEAT. Very limited parking; take the Metro: Gallery Place (stop lies just beneath the building).

Set on 5 acres of prime downtown real estate, the MCI Center is Washington's premier indoor sports arena (home to the NBA

Wizards, WNBA Mystics, NHL Capitals, and Georgetown NCAA basketball). The 20,600-seat arena also hosts rock and country concerts and business conferences.

Robert F. Kennedy Memorial Stadium/D.C. Armory. 2400 E. Capitol St. SE. ☎ **202/ 547-9077;** 800/551-SEAT or 202/432-SEAT to charge tickets. Metro: Stadium–Armory.

The erstwhile home of the Washington Redskins continues as an outdoor event facility, packing crowds of 55,000-plus into its seats for concert festivals. The D.C. Armory, right next door, is a year-round venue for antique shows and other large-scale events.

Warner Theatre. 1299 Pennsylvania Ave. NW (entrance on 13th St., between E and F sts.). ☎ **202/783-4000** for information; 800/551-SEAT, 202/ 783-4000, or 202/432-SEAT to charge tickets. www.warnertheatre.com. Tickets $20–$60. Metro: Metro Center. Parking is available in the Warner Building PMI lot on 12th St. NW.

Opened in 1924 as the Earle Theatre (a movie/vaudeville palace) and restored to its original appearance in 1992 at a cost of $10 million, this stunning neoclassical-style theater features a gold-leafed grand lobby and auditorium. Everything is plush and magnificent, from the glittering crystal chandeliers to the gold-tasseled velvet draperies. It's worth coming by just to see its ornately detailed interior. The 2,000-seat auditorium offers year-round entertainment, alternating dance performances (from Baryshnikov to the Washington Ballet's Christmas performance of *The Nutcracker*), and Broadway/off-Broadway shows (*Cabaret, Lord of the Dance, Godspell*) with headliner entertainment (Sheryl Crow, Natalie Merchant, Wynton Marsalis).

✪ **Wolf Trap Farm Park for the Performing Arts.** 1551 Trap Rd., Vienna, VA. ☎ **703/ 255-1868;** Tickets are available through Tickets.com (☎ 800-955-5566; www.tickets.com). www.wolf-trap.org. Filene Center seats $16–$70, lawn $7–$20; Barns tickets average $14–$20. Take I-495 (the Beltway) to exit 12W (Dulles Toll Rd.); follow the signs and exit (after paying a 50¢ toll) at the Wolf Trap ramp. Stay on the local exit road (you'll see a sign) until you come to Wolf Trap. The park is also accessible from exit 67 off I-66 west. There's plenty of parking. Metro (summer only): West Falls Church stop. From there, the Wolf Trap Shuttle ($3.50 round-trip) runs every 20 min. starting 2 hours before performance time and (return trip) 20 min. after the performance ends or 11pm (whichever comes first).

The country's only national park devoted to the performing arts, Wolf Trap, just 30 minutes by car from downtown D.C., offers a star-studded Summer Festival Season from late May to mid-September. The 2000 season featured performances by the

National Symphony Orchestra (it's their summer home), Mary Chapin Carpenter, Natalie Merchant, and the Joffrey Ballet.

Performances take place in the 7,000-seat Filene Center, about half of which is under the open sky. You can also buy cheaper lawn seats on the hill, which is sometimes the nicest way to go. If you do, arrive early (the lawn opens 90 minutes before the performance), and bring a blanket and a picnic dinner—it's a tradition.

Wolf Trap also hosts a number of very popular festivals. The park features a day-long Irish music festival in May; the Louisiana Swamp Romp Cajun Festival and a weekend of jazz and blues in June; and the International Children's Festival each September.

From late fall until May, the 350-seat Barns of Wolf Trap, just up the road at 1635 Trap Rd., features jazz, pop, country, folk, bluegrass, and chamber musicians, and the Wolf Trap Opera Company. Call ☎ **703/938-2404** for information.

3 The Club & Music Scene

The best nightlife districts are Adams–Morgan; the area around U and 14th streets NW, a still developing district that's in a somewhat dangerous part of town; the 7th Street NW corridor near Chinatown and the MCI Center; and Georgetown. As a rule, while club-hopping—even in Georgetown—stick to the major thoroughfares and steer clear of deserted side streets. The best source of information about what's doing at bars and clubs is *City Paper,* available free at bookstores, movie theaters, drugstores, and other locations.

COMEDY

In addition to The Improv, large auditoriums, like DAR Constitution Hall, also feature big-name comedians from time to time.

The Improv. 1140 Connecticut Ave. NW (between L and M sts.). ☎ **202/ 296-7008.** www.dcimprov.com. Cover $12 Sun–Thurs, $15 Fri–Sat, plus a 2-drink minimum (waived if you dine). Parking garage next door $5. Metro: Farragut North.

The Improv features top performers on the national comedy club circuit as well as comic plays and one-person shows. *Saturday Night Live* performers David Spade, Chris Rock, and Adam Sandler have all played here, as have comedy bigs Ellen DeGeneres, Jerry Seinfeld, and Robin Williams. Shows are about 1½ hours long and include three comics (an emcee, feature act, and headliner).

Show times are 8:30pm from Sunday to Thursday, 8pm and 10:30pm on Friday and Saturday. The best way to snag a good seat is to have dinner here (make reservations), which allows you to enter the club as early as 7pm. Drinks average $4.95. You must be 18 to get in.

POP/ROCK

Black Cat. 1831 14th St. NW (between S and T sts.). ☎ **202/667-7960.** www.burn-one.com. Cover $5–$15 for concerts; no cover in the Red Room. Metro: U St.–Cardozo.

This comfortable, low-key bar draws a black-clad crowd to its large, funky, red-walled living-roomy lounge with booths, pinball machines, a pool table, and a jukebox stocked with a really eclectic collection. A college crowd collects on weekends, but you can count on seeing a 20- to 30-something bunch here most nights, including members of various bands who like to stop in for a drink. There's live music in the adjoining room, essentially a large dance floor (it accommodates about 400 people) with stages at both ends. Entertainment is primarily alternative rock, with a little jazz, swing, folk, and occasional poetry readings thrown in. The Red Room Bar is open until 2am from Sunday to Thursday, and until 3am Friday and Saturday. Concerts take place 4 or 5 nights a week, beginning at about 8:30pm (call for details). Light fare, such as kabob dinners, is available; the bar has European and microbrew beers on tap.

✪ **Chief Ike's Mambo Room.** 1725 Columbia Rd. NW. ☎ **202/332-2211.** www.greatidea.com/chiefike. Cover $5 Thurs–Sat. Open daily 4pm to 2 or 3am. Metro: Woodley Park–Zoo, with a 20-min. walk.

Chief Ike's served as a location shot for a scene in Will Smith's 1998 movie, *Enemy of the State*. Its more usual role though is as a party scene, with live music (jazz, blues, rock) playing Thursday and a deejay on weekends. Chief Ike's, unlike other clubs, sets great store by its grub: regional American. Happy hour lasts weeknights from 4 to 8pm. The crowd is (for the most part) young, with lots of politicos and local artists stopping in. You'll find the dancing downstairs; upstairs is for kibitzing and pool-playing.

Metro Café. 1522 14th St. NW. ☎ **202/518-7900.** For advance tickets, call ☎ 202/884-0060. Cover $5 until 12:30am. Shows start at 9:30pm Sun–Thurs, about 10:30pm Fri–Sat. Free parking across the street. Metro: Dupont Circle, about 5 blocks away.

The Metro holds about 100 people in a room with a big stage, an L-shaped bar, red velvet curtains, and tall ceilings. Acts range from hip-hop to good local rock bands to national acts like Andy Summers, one-time guitarist for The Police. The club attracts all ages, everyone in black. Like several other nightclubs, State of the Union for one (see below), the Metro is also into drama, presenting short plays on various nights.

Nation. 1015 Half St. SE (at K St.). ☎ **202/554-1500.** www.nation-dc.com. Cover $7–$15. Metro: Navy Yard.

A $2 million renovation in 1999 transformed the "Ballroom" into a more functional concert/dance space, with separate areas for live music, dance music, and lounging, and a three-tiered outdoor patio. This is primarily a Gen-X mecca (though some performers attract an older crowd). It's also D.C.'s largest club, accommodating about 2,000 people a night. Wednesday is rave night in one part of the club and goth night in the other; Thursday is hip-hop night; Friday night features deejays playing techno, house, and jungle music from 10pm to 6am. Saturday is given over to a gay dance party called "velvet nation." You can buy tickets in advance via Ticketmaster (☎ **202/432-SEAT**). The game room and state-of-the-art lighting/laser/sound systems are a plus. The Nation is in a pretty bad neighborhood, so make sure you have good directions to get there; the building itself is very secure.

✪ **9:30 Club.** 815 V St. NW. ☎ **202/393-0930.** Tickets $5–$40, depending on the performer. Metro: U St.–Cardozo.

Housed in yet another converted warehouse, this major live-music venue hosts frequent record company parties and features a wide range of top performers. In 1998, the concert trade publication, *Pollstar,* named The 9:30 the nightclub of the year. You might catch Sheryl Crow, the Wallflowers, Smashing Pumpkins, Bodeans, even Tony Bennett. It's only open when there's a show on (call ahead). The sound system is state of the art. There are four bars: two on the main dance-floor level, one in the upstairs VIP room (anyone is welcome here unless the room is being used for a private party), and another in the distressed-looking cellar. The 9:30 Club is a stand-up place, literally—there are no seats. Tickets to most shows are available through Tickets.com (☎ **800/955-5566** or 703/218-6500; www.tickets.com).

Polly Esther's. 605 12th St. NW. ☎ **202/737-1970.** Cover $7 Thurs, $10 Fri–Sat. Thurs 8pm–2am, Fri–Sat 8pm–3am. Metro: Metro Center.

Decor and music from the '70s reign here, with artifacts from that decade hanging on the walls (a John Travolta memorial, anything to do with the Brady Bunch) and disco music (think "YMCA," ABBA, the BeeGees) blaring from the sound system. Another dance floor features '90s music. And downstairs is more culture-clubbish, where you dance to '80s tunes by artists like Madonna and Prince.

State of the Union. 1357 U St. NW. ☎ **202/588-8810;** www.stateoftheu. com. Cover generally $5–$7. Open until 2am Sun–Thurs, 3am Fri–Sat. Metro: U St.–Cardozo.

Deejay and live music highlight reggae, hip-hop, and acid jazz sounds in this nightclub that plays on a Soviet Union theme: hammer and sickle sconces, a bust of Lenin over the bar, and a big painting of Rasputin on a back wall. The hip crowd is diverse ("different every half hour," says a bartender), ranging from mid-20s to about 35, interracial, and international. The music, both live and deejay-provided, is cutting edge: renowned D.C. deejays playing rare grooves, funk, soul, hip-hop, and house; live reggae; live jazz; and straight, funk, and acid jazz. Weather permitting, the back room has an open-air screen (actually more like a cave wall). There's an interesting selection of beers and over 30 flavored vodkas.

JAZZ/BLUES

BET on Jazz Restaurant. 730 11th St. NW. ☎ **202/393-0975.** www.betonjazz.com. No cover. Metro: Metro Center.

Despite its name, BET on Jazz is primarily a restaurant. But stop here for dinner any night and you'll be treated to good Caribbean cuisine and the sounds of, say, Brazilian jazz. This is an elegant place (see review in chapter 6), and you must dress up to get in.

Blues Alley. 1073 Wisconsin Ave. NW (in an alley below M St.). ☎ **202/ 337-4141.** www.bluesalley.com. Cover $15–$50, plus $7 food or drink minimum, plus $1.75 surcharge.

Blues Alley, in Georgetown, has been Washington's top jazz club since 1965, featuring such artists as Nancy Wilson, McCoy Tyner, Wynton Marsalis, and Maynard Ferguson. There are usually two shows nightly at 8 and 10pm; some performers also do midnight shows on weekends. Reservations are essential (call after noon); since seating is on a first-come, first-serve basis, it's best to arrive no later than 7pm and have dinner. Drinks are $5.35 to $9. The decor is of the classic jazz club genre: exposed brick walls, beamed ceiling, and small candlelit tables.

Columbia Station. 2325 18th St. NW. ☎ **202/462-6040.** No cover but $6 minimum. Weeknights 9:30pm–1:30am, weekends 9:30pm–2:30am. Metro: Dupont Circle (North exit) or Woodley Park–Zoo, with a 20- to 30-min. walk.

Another fairly intimate club in Adams–Morgan, this one showcases live blues and jazz nightly. The performers are pretty good, which is amazing, considering there's no cover. Columbia Station is also a bar/restaurant, with the kitchen usually open until midnight, serving semi-Cajun cuisine.

✪ **Madam's Organ Restaurant and Bar.** 2461 18th St. NW. ☎ **202/667-5370.** www.madamsorgan.com. Cover $2–$5. Sun–Thurs 5pm–2am, Fri–Sat 5pm–3am. Metro: Dupont Circle (North exit) or Woodley Park–Zoo, with a 20- to 30-min. walk.

This beloved Adams–Morgan hangout fulfills owner Bill Duggan's definition of a good bar: great sounds and sweaty people. The great sounds feature One Night Stand, a jazz group, on Monday; bluesman Ben Andrews on Tuesday; bluegrass open mike on Wednesday; and the salsa sounds of Patrick Alban and Noche Latina on Thursday, which is also Ladies Night. Friday and Saturday feature regional blues groups and the place is packed. The club includes a wide-open bar decorated eclectically with a 150-year-old gilded mirror, stuffed fish and animal heads, and paintings of nudes. The second-floor bar is called Big Daddy's Love Lounge & Pick-Up Joint, which tells you everything you need to know.

New Vegas Lounge. 1415 P St. NW. ☎ **202/483-3971.** Cover $7–$10. Tues–Thurs until 2am, Fri–Sat until 3am. Metro: Dupont Circle.

When the Vegas Lounge is good, it's very good. When it's bad, it's laughable. This dark one-room joint is crowded with tables filled with a mix of Washingtonians, college kids, and their elders. If you're lucky, you might find a blues band out of Chicago covering Otis Redding so well that everyone's on their feet dancing. On other nights, you're likely to hear a neighborhood group that has no business appearing in public. Thursdays are college nights.

✪ **One Step Down.** 2517 Pennsylvania Ave. NW. ☎ **202/955-7141.** Cover $5 Mon–Thurs, typically $12.50 or $13.50 Sat–Sun, but sometimes much higher, with 2-drink minimum every night. Mon–Thurs 5:30pm–1am, Fri–Sat 5:30pm–2am. Metro: Foggy Bottom.

This quintessential, hole-in-the-wall jazz club is the constant on this stretch of Pennsylvania Avenue just outside of Georgetown. The One Step showcases the talents of names you often recognize—sax player Paul Bollenbeck, the Steve Wilson Quartet, Ronnie Wells, and Ron Elliston—and some you don't. Blues night is the last Thursday of every month (cover $5). Live music plays here 6 nights a week. The people who come to the One Step tend to be heavy jazz enthusiasts who stay quiet during the sets.

INTERNATIONAL SOUNDS

Chi Cha Lounge. 1624 U St. NW. ☎ **202/234-8400.** www.chi-cha.com. Cover $15 (minimum). Sun–Thurs 5:30pm– 1:30am, Fri–Sat 5:30pm–2:30am. Metro: U St.–Cardozo.

You can sit around on couches, eat Ecuadoran tapas, and listen to live Latin music, featured Sunday through Wednesday. Or you can sit around on couches and smoke Arabic tobacco through a 3-foot-high arguileh pipe. Or you can just sit around. It's a neighborhood place and it's popular.

✪ **Coco Loco.** 810 7th St. NW (between H and I sts.). ☎ **202/289-2626.** Cover $10 after 10pm. Metro: Gallery Place.

This is one of D.C.'s liveliest clubs. Friday, Saturday, and sometimes Thursday nights, come for a late tapas or mixed-grill dinner and stay for international music and dancing, with occasional live bands. On Friday and Saturday nights, the entertainment includes a sexy 11pm floor show featuring Brazilian exhibition dancers who begin performing in feathered and sequined Rio Rita costumes and strip down to a bare minimum. Laser lights and other special effects enhance the show, which ends with a conga line and a limbo contest. Dancing to deejay music follows the show, Latin music in one room, and international music in the other—until 3am. Come here on Thursday nights at 9pm for a free salsa lesson, followed by dancing until 2am. Coco Loco draws an attractive, upscale, international crowd of all ages, including many impressively talented dancers.

✪ **Habana Village.** 1834 Columbia Rd. NW. ☎ **202/462-6310.** Cover $5 Fri–Sat after 9:30pm (no cover for women). Wed–Thurs 6:30pm–1am, Fri–Sat 6:30pm–3am. Metro: Dupont Circle, with a 15-min. walk, or Woodley Park–Zoo, with a 20-min. walk.

This two-story nightclub has a bar/restaurant on the first floor and a bar/dance floor on the second level. Salsa and merengue lessons are given Wednesday, Thursday, and Friday evenings from 7 to 9pm, tango lessons every Saturday evening, same time; each lesson is $10. Otherwise, a deejay plays danceable Latin jazz tunes.

Zanzibar on the Waterfront. 700 Water St. SW. ☎ **202/554-9100.** www.zanzibar-otw.com. Cover typically $10 (more for live shows). Sun–Thurs 5pm–2am, Fri–Sat 5pm–3am. Metro: Waterfront.

One day Washington will get its act together and develop the waterfront neighborhood in which you find Zanzibar. In the meantime, this area is pretty deserted at night, except for a handful of restaurants and Arena Stage. It really doesn't matter, though, because inside the nightclub you're looking out at the Potomac. In keeping with current trends, Zanzibar has lots of couches and chairs arranged just so. A Caribbean and African menu is available. Every night brings something different, from jazz and blues to oldies. Wednesday is salsa night, with free lessons from 7 to 8pm, though a cover still applies: $5 to get in before 10pm and $10 after. An international crowd gathers here to dance or just hang out.

GAY CLUBS

Dupont Circle is the gay hub of Washington, D.C., with at least 10 gay bars within easy walking distance of one another. The Saturday night "Velvet Nation" party at Nation (see above) is a gay event.

Badlands. 1415 22nd St. NW, near P St. ☎ **202/296-0505.** www.badlandsdc.com. Sometimes a cover: $3 to $10, depending on event. Tues and Thurs–Sat 8pm–2am. Metro: Dupont Circle.

Badlands is an old favorite dance club for gay men. In addition to the parquet dance floor in the main room, the club has at least six bars throughout the first level. Upstairs is the Annex bar/lounge/pool hall, and a show room where karaoke performers commandeer the mike Friday night and a drag show takes place Saturday night.

J.R.'s Bar and Grill. 1519 17th St. NW (between P and Q sts.). ☎ **202/328-0090.** www.jrsdc.com. No cover. Sun–Thurs 11:30am–2am, Fri–Sat 11:30–3am. Metro: Dupont Circle.

This casual and intimate all-male Dupont Circle club draws a friendly, upscale, and very attractive crowd. The big screen over the bar area is used to air music videos, showbiz sing-alongs, and Ally McBeal–watching on Monday, favorite TV shows on Tuesday, disco and retro night Wednesday. Thursday is all-you-can-drink for $7 from 5 to 8pm; at midnight you get free shots. The balcony, with two pool tables, is a little more laid-back. Food is served daily, until 5pm Sunday and until 7pm all other days.

4 The Bar Scene

If you're in the mood for a sophisticated setting, seek out a bar in one of the nicer hotels, like the Jefferson, the Willard, or the St. Regis.

Asylum. 2471 18th St. NW. ☎ **202/319-8353.** No cover. Sun–Tues 8pm–2am, Wed–Thurs 5pm–2am, Fri 5pm–3am, Sat 7pm–3am. Metro: Dupont Circle, with a 15-min. walk, or Woodley Park–Zoo, with a 20-min. walk across the Calvert St. Bridge.

This below-street joint has room for about 100 people, plays rock CDs, has a pool table, tables for sitting and drinking, a heavy goth decorative scheme, and a stream of underage youth trying to get served at the bar.

Big Hunt. 1345 Connecticut Ave. NW (between N St. and Dupont Circle). ☎ **202/785-2333.** No cover. Sun–Thurs until 2am, Fri–Sat until 3am. Metro: Dupont Circle.

This casual and comfy Dupont Circle hangout for the 20- to 30-something crowd bills itself as a "happy hunting ground for humans" (read: meat market). It has a kind of Raiders of the Lost Ark/jungle theme. A downstairs room (where music is the loudest) is adorned with exotic travel posters and animal skins. Amusing murals grace the balcony level, which adjoins a room with pool tables. The candlelit basement is the spot for quiet conversation. The menu offers typical bar food; and the bar offers close to 30 beers on tap, most of them microbrews. An outdoor patio lies off the back pool room.

Brickskeller. 1523 22nd St. NW. ☎ **202/293-1885.** No cover. Mon–Thurs 11:30am–2am, Fri 11:30am–3am, Sat 6pm–3am, Sun 6pm–2am. Metro: Dupont Circle or Foggy Bottom.

If you like beer and you like choices, head for Brickskeller, which has been around for nearly 40 years and offers about 800 beers from around the world. The tavern draws students, college professors, embassy types, and people from the neighborhood. Brickskeller is a series of interconnecting rooms filled with gingham tableclothed tables; upstairs rooms are only open weekend nights. The food is generally okay; more than okay are the burgers, which include the excellent Brickburger, topped with bacon, salami, onion, and cheese.

✪ **Café Milano.** 3251 Prospect St. NW. ☎ **202/333-6183.** No cover. Sun–Thurs 11:30–1am, Fri–Sat 11:30–2am. Metro: Foggy Bottom, with a 25-min. walk.

Located just off Wisconsin Avenue in lower Georgetown, Café Milano has gained a reputation for attracting beautiful people. You might see a few famous faces—or those on the prowl for famous faces. It's often crowded, especially Thursday through Saturday nights. The food is rather good; salads and pastas are excellent.

Dubliner. In the Phoenix Park Hotel, 520 N. Capitol St. NW, with its own entrance on F St. NW. ☎ **202/737-3773.** No cover. Sun–Thurs 7am–1am, Fri–Sat 11am–2:30am. Metro: Union Station.

This is your typical old Irish pub. It's got the dark wood paneling and tables, the etched- and stained-glass windows, an Irish-accented staff from time to time, and, most importantly, the Auld Dubliner Amber Ale. You'll probably want to stick to drinks here, but you can grab a burger, grilled chicken sandwich, or roast duck salad. The Dubliner is frequented by Capitol Hill staffers and journalists who cover the Hill. Irish music groups play nightly.

Lucky Bar. 1221 Connecticut Ave. NW. ☎ **202/331-3733.** No cover. Mon–Thurs 3pm–2am, Fri–Sat noon–3am, Sun noon–3pm. Metro: Dupont Circle or Farragut North.

Lucky Bar is a good place to kick back and relax. But it also features dance lessons: salsa on Monday night and swing on Saturday night. Sometimes the music is live and sometimes it's a deejay. Other times the jukebox plays, but never so loud that you can't carry on a conversation. The bar has a front room overlooking Connecticut Avenue and a back room with couches and a pool table.

MCCXXIII. 1223 Connecticut Ave. NW. ☎ **202/822-1800.** www.1223.com. Cover for men only: Mon $5, Tues $10; other nights, no cover. Sun–Thurs until 2am, Fri–Sat until 3am. Metro: Dupont Circle or Farragut North.

This is about as swank and New York as Washington gets: hipsters lined up at the velvet rope, a doorman who decides whether you pass the dress code, outrageously high food and drink prices (with amounts in deceptive Roman numerals), a soaring ceiling and opulent interior, beautiful women servers who purr at you, more beautiful people milling about. Monday is Latin night; Tuesday hip-hop deejays play.

Mr. Smith's of Georgetown. 3104 M St. NW. ☎ **202/333-3104.** No cover. Sun–Thurs 11:30am–1:30am, Fri–Sat 11:30am–2:30am. Metro: Foggy Bottom, with a 15-min. walk.

Mr. Smith's bills itself as "The Friendliest Saloon in Town," but the truth is that it's so popular among regulars, you're in danger of being ignored if the staff doesn't know you. The bar, which opened about 30 years ago, has a front room with original brick walls, wooden seats, and a long bar, at which you can count on finding pairs of newfound friends telling obscene jokes, loudly. At the end of this room is a large piano around which customers congregate each night to accompany the pianist. An interior light-filled garden room adjoins an outdoor garden area.

Nathans. 3150 M St. NW. ☎ **202/338-2600.** No cover. Mon–Thurs 11:30am–2am, Fri–Sat 11am–3am, Sun 11am–2am. Metro: Foggy Bottom, with a 20-min. walk.

Nathans is on the corner of M Street and Wisconsin Avenue in the heart of Georgetown. If you pop in here in mid-afternoon, it's a quiet place to grab a beer or glass of wine and watch the action on the street. Visit at night, though, and it's the more typical bar scene, crowded with locals, out-of-towners, students, and a sprinkling of couples in from the 'burbs. That's the front room. The back room at Nathans is a civilized, candlelit restaurant serving classic American fare. After dinner on Friday and Saturday, this room turns into a dance hall, playing deejay music and attracting the 20-somethings Friday night, an older crowd Saturday night.

✪ **Politiki.** 319 Pennsylvania Ave. SE. ☎ **202/546-1001.** No cover. Daily 4pm–1:30am, later on weekends. Metro: Capitol South.

This funny, funky bar with a Polynesian theme is a welcome addition to the more traditional pubs along this stretch of Capitol Hill. It's a theme you can build upon: Think Scorpion Bowl and piña colada drinks, pu-pu platters, and hula dancer figurines. The basement has pool tables, a bar, and a lounge area; the street level has booths and a bar.

The Rock. 717 6th St. NW. ☎ **202/842-7625.** www.soccer-nation.com. No cover. Mon–Tues 3pm–2am, Wed–Sat noon–3am, Sun noon–2am. Metro: Gallery Place.

The Rock has the best location a sports bar could have: across the street from the MCI Center. The three-floor bar fills a former warehouse, its decor a montage of preexisting exposed pipes and concrete floors, and TV screens, pool tables, and sports memorabilia. The most popular spot is the third floor, where the pool tables and a cigar lounge are located. In good weather, folks head to the rooftop bar.

The Tombs. 1226 36th St. NW. ☎ **202/337-6668.** Cover sometimes on Tues or Sun nights, never more than $5. Mon–Fri 11:30am–1:30am, Sat 11am–1:30am, Sun 10:30am–1:30am. Metro: Foggy Bottom, with a 40- to 45-min. walk.

Housed in a converted 19th-century Federal-style home, the Tombs, which opened in 1962, is a favorite hangout for students and faculty of nearby Georgetown University. (Bill Clinton came here during his college years.) They tend to congregate at the central bar and surrounding tables, while local residents head for "the Sweeps," the room that lies down a few steps and has red leather banquettes.

Directly below the upscale 1789 Restaurant, the Tombs benefits from 1789 chef Riz Lacoste's supervision. The menu offers burgers, sandwiches, and salads, as well as more serious fare.

Tune Inn. 33½ Pennsylvania Ave. SE. ☎ **202/543-2725.** No cover. Sun–Thurs 8am–2am, Fri–Sat 8am–3am. Metro: Capitol South.

Capitol Hill has a number of bars that qualify as "institutions," but the Tune Inn is probably the most popular. Capitol Hill staffers and their bosses, apparently at ease in dive surroundings, have been coming here since it opened in 1955. Or maybe it's the cheap beer and greasy burgers that draw them.

Tunnicliff's Tavern. 222 7th St. SE. ☎ **202/546-3663.** www.tunnicliffs. com. Mon–Fri noon–2am, Sat–Sun 11am–2am. Metro: Eastern Market.

Directly across from Eastern Market, this Capitol Hill institution is named after the original circa 1796 Tunnicliff's Tavern. (This Tunnicliff's opened in 1988.) An outdoor cafe fronts the tavern, which includes a great bar and a partly enclosed dining room. You're likely to see politicos here. Proprietress Lynne Breaux (no relation to the senator) hails from New Orleans and cultivates a Mardi Gras atmosphere that includes live music (no cover) on Saturday night. The menu features some standard New Orleans items, like po'boys, gumbo, and fried oysters, as well as nachos and other bar fare. Families are welcome, with toys and coloring books at the ready.

XandO. 1350 Connecticut Ave. NW. ☎ **202/296-9341.** No cover. Mon–Thurs 6:30am–1am, Fri 6:30am–2am, Sat 7am–2am, Sun 7am–1am. Metro: Dupont Circle, South exit.

Popular from the start, XandO (pronounced "zando") is a welcoming place in the morning for a coffee drink, and even more inviting for a cocktail later in the day. Men: You'll see a lot of cute girls hanging here, drawn perhaps by the make-your-own s'mores and other delicious desserts. XandO also serves sandwiches and soups. The music is loud, the decor a cross between bar and living room. Other XandO locations in DC: 1647 20th St. NW, at Connecticut Avenue NW (☎ **202/332-6364**), and 301 Pennsylvania Ave. SE (☎ **202/546-3345**).

Index

See also Accommodations and Restaurant indexes, below.

FROMMER'S® COMPLETE TRAVEL GUIDES

Alaska
Amsterdam
Arizona
Atlanta
Australia
Austria
Bahamas
Barcelona, Madrid &
  Seville
Beijing
Belgium, Holland &
  Luxembourg
Bermuda
Boston
British Columbia & the
  Canadian Rockies
Budapest & the Best of
  Hungary
California
Canada
Cancún, Cozumel &
  the Yucatán
Cape Cod, Nantucket &
  Martha's Vineyard
Caribbean
Caribbean Cruises & Ports
  of Call
Caribbean Ports of Call
Carolinas & Georgia
Chicago
China
Colorado
Costa Rica
Denmark
Denver, Boulder & Colorado
  Springs
England
Europe

European Cruises & Ports
  of Call
Florida
France
Germany
Greece
Greek Islands
Hawaii
Hong Kong
Honolulu, Waikiki & Oahu
Ireland
Israel
Italy
Jamaica
Japan
Las Vegas
London
Los Angeles
Maryland & Delaware
Maui
Mexico
Montana & Wyoming
Montréal & Québec City
Munich & the Bavarian
  Alps
Nashville & Memphis
Nepal
New England
New Mexico
New Orleans
New York City
New Zealand
Nova Scotia, New Brunswick
  & Prince Edward Island
Oregon
Paris
Philadelphia & the
  Amish Country

Portugal
Prague & the Best of the
  Czech Republic
Provence & the Riviera
Puerto Rico
Rome
San Antonio & Austin
San Diego
San Francisco
Santa Fe, Taos & Albuquerque
Scandinavia
Scotland
Seattle & Portland
Shanghai
Singapore & Malaysia
South Africa
Southeast Asia
South Florida
South Pacific
Spain
Sweden
Switzerland
Thailand
Tokyo
Toronto
Tuscany & Umbria
USA
Utah
Vancouver & Victoria
Vermont, New Hampshire
  & Maine
Vienna & the Danube Valley
Virgin Islands
Virginia
Walt Disney World &
  Orlando
Washington, D.C.
Washington State

FROMMER'S® DOLLAR-A-DAY GUIDES

Australia from $50 a Day
California from $60 a Day
Caribbean from $70 a Day
England from $70 a Day
Europe from $70 a Day

Florida from $70 a Day
Hawaii from $70 a Day
Ireland from $60 a Day
Italy from $70 a Day
London from $85 a Day

New York from $80 a Day
Paris from $80 a Day
San Francisco from $60 a Day
Washington, D.C.,
  from $70 a Day

FROMMER'S® PORTABLE GUIDES

Acapulco, Ixtapa &
  Zihuatanejo
Alaska Cruises & Ports of Call
Bahamas
Baja & Los Cabos
Berlin
California Wine Country
Charleston & Savannah
Chicago
Dublin

Hawaii: The Big Island
Las Vegas
London
Los Angeles
Maine Coast
Maui
Miami
New Orleans
New York City
Paris

Puerto Vallarta, Manzanillo
  & Guadalajara
San Diego
San Francisco
Sydney
Tampa & St. Petersburg
Venice
Washington, D.C.

1333 Q St. 7³⁰

FROMMER'S® NATIONAL PARK GUIDES

Family Vacations in the
   National Parks
Grand Canyon

National Parks of the
   American West
Rocky Mountain

Yellowstone & Grand Teton
Yosemite & Sequoia/
   Kings Canyon
Zion & Bryce Canyon

FROMMER'S® MEMORABLE WALKS

Chicago
London

New York
Paris

San Francisco
Washington, D.C.

FROMMER'S® GREAT OUTDOOR GUIDES

New England
Northern California

Southern California & Baja
Southern New England

Washington & Oregon

FROMMER'S® BORN TO SHOP GUIDES

Born to Shop: France
Born to Shop: Italy

Born to Shop: London
Born to Shop: New York

Born to Shop: Paris

FROMMER'S® IRREVERENT GUIDES

Amsterdam
Boston
Chicago
Las Vegas

London
Los Angeles
Manhattan
New Orleans

Paris
San Francisco
Seattle & Portland
Vancouver

Walt Disney World
Washington, D.C.

FROMMER'S® BEST-LOVED DRIVING TOURS

America
Britain
California

Florida
France
Germany

Ireland
Italy
New England

Scotland
Spain
Western Europe

THE UNOFFICIAL GUIDES®

Bed & Breakfasts in
   California
Bed & Breakfasts in
   New England
Bed & Breakfasts in
   the Northwest
Bed & Breakfasts in
   Southeast
Beyond Disney
Branson, Missouri

California with Kids
Chicago
Cruises
Disneyland
Florida with Kids
Golf Vacations in the
   Eastern U.S.
The Great Smoky &
   Blue Ridge
   Mountains

Inside Disney
Hawaii
Las Vegas
London
Miami & the Keys
Mini Las Vegas
Mini-Mickey
New Orleans
New York City
Paris

San Francisco
Skiing in the West
Southeast with Kids
Walt Disney World
Walt Disney World
   for Grown-ups
Walt Disney World
   for Kids
Washington, D.C.

SPECIAL-INTEREST TITLES

Frommer's Britain's Best Bed & Breakfasts and
   Country Inns
Frommer's Britain's Best Bike Rides
The Civil War Trust's Official Guide
   to the Civil War Discovery Trail
Frommer's Caribbean Hideaways
Frommer's Adventure Guide to Central America
Frommer's Adventure Guide to South America
Frommer's Adventure Guide to Southeast Asia
Frommer's Food Lover's Companion to France
Frommer's Gay & Lesbian Europe
Frommer's Exploring America by RV
Hanging Out in Europe

Israel Past & Present
Mad Monks' Guide to California
Mad Monks' Guide to New York City
Frommer's The Moon
Frommer's New York City with Kids
The New York Times' Unforgettable
   Weekends
Places Rated Almanac
Retirement Places Rated
Frommer's Road Atlas Britain
Frommer's Road Atlas Europe
Frommer's Washington, D.C., with Kids
Frommer's What the Airlines Never Tell You

Gengetu Lu